UNREQUITED

A Gay Memoir

Jonathan Lindstrom

Morcroft-Fields Publishing

Author's Note:

This is a work of memory. Names, including the narrator's, have been changed, and identifying details have been altered to protect privacy. Some dialogue reflects the period's language and casual prejudices. Certain conversations are reconstructed, and some events have been combined or rearranged for clarity and narrative flow. What has not been altered is the truth at the core: the textures of childhood, the confusion of love and friendship, and the search for self in a world that did not always allow it. This book is not a transcript of the past but a reflection of it. The story is told as I lived it, and as it continues to live within me.

For content warnings, see the back pages.

ISBN: 979-8-9952658-1-8 pbk

**Concealment, like a worm i' the bud,
feeds on the damask cheek.**

— William Shakespeare, *Twelfth Night*

Table of Contents

Prologue

We were alone in his car after seeing *A Nightmare on Elm Street*, headlights tunneling through backroads neither of us knew. The drifting made me uneasy. I gripped the armrest, watching the dashboard glow until the words that I had long contemplated jumped out of me.

"We can't be friends anymore."

He turned sharply, "This always happens to me. I lose friends. What did I do?"

Now, I'd have to explain. "It's not about you," I muttered. My hands wouldn't unclench.

"Come on, Lindy. Tell me." The nickname carried a nervous affection.

"It's for the best."

"I'll guess then—Amy? Jenny?"

I shook my head. "It's because of how I feel about you."

He slapped the steering wheel enough to make the horn sputter. "Oh! you're a fag?"

"Not exactly. Just...thinking about you. Missing you too much."

"What is it with me?" His hands tightened and released. "That pervert at the library used to leave me notes when I was eight. The blond hair, the blue eyes. It gets to people."

Silence. The tires hissed through the dark.

"How long have you felt that way?" he asked.

"Since the night you cried about your parents."

He smiled thinly. "Maybe I should wear a mask. Can we treat this like a joke?"

I didn't object.

"You need your hormones checked," he said lightly, then added, still smiling, "Maybe I can beat it out of you."

I looked straight ahead. "Keep this quiet if you can."

I had imagined immediate relief, at least a little. Instead, I just felt lost and exposed.

PART I

Passing through the Netherworld

Growing up, I tried to believe in two things: what was passed down by adults and what I saw with my own eyes. They didn't always match, and sometimes neither were true.

I felt blessed to be born of the manor. My family lived on Clock Lane in the biggest house in the neighborhood. The short road curved around a lush apple tree and flowed right into our driveway, like reaching us was its main purpose. We had a spacious front lawn with abundant broad-leafed trees that provided blooms in spring and shade in summer. Our half-acre plot was conveniently nestled in the heart of Beaumont, Massachusetts — between the railroad tracks and the housing projects.

A few blocks away, Main Street meandered past pristine lawns and historic homes restored to Colonial period perfection, with parks and greenways at every turn. The porches were broad; the cars were shiny, but nobody seemed to mend their fences with scrap wood. The yards were bare, nothing to explore or build with. I remember thinking those people must be no fun.

Clock Lane was the only remaining dirt road in Beaumont, in 1970 and today—left that way through a mix of tight money, stubborn pride, and simple neglect. The road had a fickle personality that changed with the seasons. Each time the town had tar to spare, they'd ladle favors down the Lane's initial slope—a patch, a strip, a borrowed coat to dress the hill in second thoughts. With winter snow, those layers mattered. Without them, the hill would decide who could get out. The road was the lowest point in Beaumont save the railroad underpass at the Center. It would transform into a raging river during heavy rains.

The Lane once housed many ancient souls; most now passed on, their quiet routines slowly being replaced by the noise and energy of younger families. Nanny Peppin had lived at 2 Clock

Lane, but she'd traded houses with her daughter's family—the Blanchards, whose children were Bib and Mary Ellen. At 3 Clock Lane, Bob Radler, an army vet about thirty, lived with his grandmother; his black bicycle parked prominently in the back lot. On either side of us, Old Man Sullivan and Old Lady Elena had no heirs, and their houses had been abandoned for years.

Ours was the last house on the road because Elena's place stopped being on Clock Lane the day a new road was laid in front as a part of the housing authority's modern grid. Out our front windows, we saw more feet than wheels go by. People from the projects streamed by at all hours, cutting across the worn path in front of our lawn like we were a landmark on some unofficial urban trail.

We were also the closest house to the railroad tracks. Within six yards. But, the clatter and the passengers' quick glances had no power over us unless we chose to give it. At least that's what Ma always said. I actually loved when a long freight train passed by at night—the gentle rocking, strobing lights, and steady cachunk-cachunk were quite soothing. The only downside was the occasional piercing horn, which could startle the color right out of your face.

It was clear that we were boxed in by paradox: our lot wide and tree-shaded, the world intruding from both sides. The house felt set apart, yet never alone; private, yet observed. We lived at the edge of an old rural conclave, staring straight into the dense geometry of government planning.

Our house had four bedrooms and a tiny bathroom with just a clawfoot tub—and no shower. My father had "renovated" the house himself, which meant every wall was covered in paneling. The floorboards were uneven and creaked underfoot, and the upstairs heat traveled through shiny metal ducts strapped along the walls instead of hidden inside them.

Although television was broadcast in color, we were only capable of black and white. Once, someone gave Dad a used console television with a good-sized screen, but it never picked up NBC, so we did without that channel for a while. When the tubes finally burned out, the console became a stand for a smaller set that got all six channels.

Curiously, even small things followed the same logic. My baby blanket was pink, and my sister's was blue. An atypical gender mismatch. I always figured my thrifty father bought whatever was on sale on our dates of birth. My brother Denny, who was eight when I came along, remembered it differently and insisted both blankets were bought at that time. Probably a two-for-one deal that made sense before my gender was known.

I was the oldest of the unplanned second cluster. Three much older siblings came before me, and Ma was already weary from raising them. When she discovered she was pregnant again, she ran up and down the stairs, less in celebration than in hope God might reconsider. She told me this years later, when I was a teenager. I felt a hollow shock, as if my very existence had hung by a thread I'd never known about. It's odd to be wanted only after the fact. Surreal. Yet, she was a good mother: tender, kind, and supportive once we arrived.

As is often the case, being in a second cluster means you have tired parents, but you also probably had a few willing, but green surrogate caregivers on hand who might rise to the occasion. My older sister was my additional nurturer during infancy; my brother was my tormentor, K through12. Denny took it upon himself to tighten discipline as Dad became more lenient. He found the energy to narrate my life in real-time, turning minor disappointments into shameful memories and sibling skirmishes into theatrical events. It was two-thirds critical and one-third comical.

He wasn't all bad—his jokes often made me laugh—but his idea of brotherly love came with a tackle and a tickle. As a fan of *The Three Stooges* and *Monty Python's Flying Circus*, Denny preferred slapstick to speech, and spectacle over problem solving. He cast himself as referee, judge, and jury in the endless contests between me and my younger sister, Sarah, reinforcing a lopsided doctrine he made sure I understood: *as a boy, a year older than a girl, you must be better than her at everything by a wide margin or risk being "basically a girl yourself."* I was a sensitive child, a little timid, a little graceful when I wasn't being clumsy. Denny coined nicknames for us—*Ninny* for me and *Sarah Wee* or *Weasel* for her. He used *Ninny* more than *Johnny*. I was determined to prove that nickname wrong. However, despite my efforts, Denny always doubted my intellect and my ability to follow through with anything. Good reports from teachers, he insisted, were just pity-points for the poor little Ninny.

Denny's trademark jab was sharp: "Look, Johnny's about to cry." He'd sneer, "Better get your pink banky." Then, with a smirk, he'd add, "Soft as a grape!" often acting out squashing an invisible grape with a splat. His mantra carried one optional addition: "You watch too much *Mr. Rogers'*."

It stung. Because I really did love my blanket and *Mr. Rogers' Neighborhood*. It was a show that whispered to me that my feelings were real; my questions were safe, and that simply being myself was already enough. The opposite of Denny's message.

The truth was I liked puppets. I played with dolls, but they were men, in compelling adventure/character arcs. I liked drama, but not the kind where people burst into song. I liked sports when

I was playing, not watching them. Especially not adults on TV. My playmates after second grade were all boys. I liked Underdog, not Sweet Polly Purebread.

My parents were a less shrill version of Edith and Archie Bunker from *All in the Family*. My father placed his recliner right in front of the television and ate dinner off a tray calling for salt or another beer from the kitchen. He was the bread winner and king of his castle. In a good mood, he had a slightly goofy, sardonic take on things; when angry, he was intense.

Ma would ask, "How is your dinner, my dear?"

He always answered, "It'll do."

But, when Ma tried a new sweet-and-sour recipe for beef stew, Dad said, "If you make this again, I'll throw it on the floor."

He was quick to threaten a spanking, though rarely carried it out.

His main focus was finding new ways to reduce costs for the sheer satisfaction of it.

Ma radiated good cheer to a fault. Always putting a positive spin on things and encouraging politeness. She was a devoted Christian Scientist and spent most of her free time "Knowing the Truth," reading "the Lesson" or napping.

I cherished the evenings when Ma would tuck me into bed. She would sit next to me, her hands warm and reassuring as she smoothed the blankets. She'd tell me, "You're God's perfect child. Error will never get a hold of you." She'd read the lesson or tell me stories, her voice a soothing melody that lulled me to sleep. Those moments, wrapped in her gentle words and warmth, were where I felt truly loved.

I learned early that love was never simple, and roles were never clear. Even the smallest things—a blanket, a nickname, the rustle of Bible pages—could become signs of how precariously we balanced between ridicule and refuge. I think I chose the pink blanket because it was cotton, sturdy and warm rather than the flimsy blue one with its shiny, net-like fuzz. After all, you mostly just snuggle with it in the dark. You don't sleep with a color; you hug what feels good. I chose the blanket that felt right. A so-called wrong color wasn't going to stop me. And, Denny had no say in that.

2

Bib Blanchard, all of three years old, came tearing back into the yard like he'd just seen a ghost. We and our sisters were using the back-steps-to-nowhere as bunk beds, and he'd headed home to get a pillow. Instead, he came crashing back through the bushes, breathless, eyes wide. "Get your mom!"

I followed him around the corner, and there she was—Nanny—slow-moving, determined, ninety pounds of Finnish iron will, walking down the driveway on the arm of my portly Uncle Stanley. They moved together in a kind of side-to-side waddle, like a two-person creature stitched along one side. If you had ever seen *Creature Double Feature* on Channel 56, you'd know the gait, something between a mummy and a zombie, unstoppable.

Stanley always wore the same vinyl hat with fake fur earflaps that snapped under the chin, though he never snapped them. The flaps just dangled like two deflated water wings. One of his legs was shorter than the other, so his steps had a built-in sway. Nanny leaned on him, tiny but commanding, and somehow, she was the one setting the pace. Both dressed like the 1950s had never ended—thick wool overcoats, dark clothing, sensible galoshes. The kind of sight that could unsettle a suburban kid raised on storybook grandmothers.

Nanny was born in Finland and came to America to work, not to soften. She ran her household like a ship captain. Her voice could slice a room in half. She laughed when she made you cry. Not because she was cruel, but because she thought sensitivity was funny. And, spending Friday nights at her house was non-negotiable. Always American chop suey and *pannukakku,* a cross between pancake and custard chilled to perfection, sweet edges caramelized. The table was always set, the radio low, the atmosphere thick with something. Ma usually did not come along. Love, in Nanny's world, was her way or none at all.

There was history under all of it. When my mother married my father, Nanny didn't exactly welcome her. My father was her *normal* baby, her pride, and the idea of handing him over was not one she entertained gently. When my mother struggled with her willful first-born, Nanny simply took him, as if she was making a fair exchange. My father backed her without hesitation. To him, this was family logic. To my mother, it was heartbreak. Everyone carried this story differently. It was the kind of family truth that lived in the walls, never said aloud.

By the time I came along, the battle lines had cooled into a permanent truce. Nanny and Stanley lived near Twombly Square in their two-family, where they occupied the upper floor and rented the apartment below. Stanley had the kind of social awkwardness we'd now call autism, but at the time he was just "odd," a man who spoke in declarative statements and avoided eye contact as if it were too bright to maintain. Nanny understood him, and he obeyed her.

And so the two of them walked together—slow, steady, unstoppable—toward our house that day. Not as guests, not as invaders, but as forces of nature. Bib had thought something was wrong. I knew better.

That was just my extended family arriving.

3

I was four, nearly five, and about to start school. I was ready—things at home were getting dull. Denny had begun to criticize me for not having friends. His new mantra was *TV's your best friend.*

He had a point. I was an avid viewer—and a budding actor-director.

Our yard and home doubled as a makeshift studio for my imaginary TV show, and for a while, my sister made a decent co-star. *Best Man in the World* was on a mission to uncover why the people of Earth were being secretly relocated underground to an altered replica of the surface. Most early episodes took place in the inter-space—our cluttered dining room, a kind of "backstage" layer between the real Earth and the ceiling below, where the fake sunshine and sky were generated.

Together, Best Man and Police Lady battled enemy agents and shadowy workmen to reach the true surface and now faced their biggest challenge: convincing others the underground even existed.

I tried to enlist the Blanchard children as extras. Mary Ellen, who was three years older than me, insisted on playing Best Baby in the World, which was dumb. Bib wanted to pretend he was Billy Nagen, just another three-year-old from the neighborhood. That was not how to play pretend! I wasn't having it. None of the day's efforts became canon.

Sarah was becoming a temperamental actress as well. More and more, she insisted on directing the plot astray. Her storylines were a bore. They seemed to be just repeating old episode ideas or involved combing hair and a wardrobe change. Like in all our games, she was prone to throwing herself on the floor and crying, quitting, or getting Ma or Denny to intervene.

On the first day of kindergarten, I didn't cry at all. So much for Denny's prediction. Two of the boys cried all day, each needing their own box of tissues. Many of the girls cried off and on; I paid less attention to girls. I befriended a silly, chunky boy who couldn't stop giggling. I appreciated that this boy laughed at my jokes. Little by little, I realized he didn't always make sense. He was one of the Mundts, a family in the project known for being goofy and not very bright.

I made friends with Mickey Nagen first, then Scotty and Chrissy Grable. My friendship with Chrissy lasted the longest. She lived near Joe's Variety, across from the Town Field playground, and I passed her house every day on my way to school.

Chrissy wore glasses, and she was a bit of an intellectual. She was widely read: *The Boxcar Children*, *Encyclopedia Brown*, and *Pippi Longstocking*. We both loved puns and silly word games. She once told me her gray cat's name was Gary "because it's gray spelled sideways." I wasn't sure that was true, but it sounded clever, so I nodded like that made perfect sense.

One warm afternoon, we sat on her porch with a pad of *Madlibs*, playing with words.

Chrissy shielded the page with her arm. "Okay, Johnny, no peeking. First I need a place."

"Cemetery."

She grinned and wrote. "Now a verb."

We kept going, until: "Last one—another adjective."

"Weirdest."

Chrissy started reading silently, grinning. Then, she read it out loud from the top in her best teacher voice:

"Dick and Jane went to the cemetery to explode their lonely balloon, but when they saw the frog crying near the bridge, they decided to hide instead, and everyone said it was a weirdest day."

We laughed so hard we startled Gary, who shot off the porch like a gray blur. I wondered whether the words just fell together by luck, or if God might try to slip in a message.

"Why was the frog crying?" I asked.

"Trouble turning into a prince," she explained. "That didn't sound right at the end though."

"Yeah, the *weirdest* was weird."

"Maybe you just started talking in a different language, Weirdlish."

For a while, I was infatuated with her. I liked her for her smarts, not her looks. People said she was my girlfriend, and I didn't argue. I tried to impress her with newspaper clippings, like the one with my name in print for completing the mile run-for-fun with a respectable time.

When her cousin, Annie, was over, things were very different. They shared a wavelength that I didn't really want to tune into. It was giggly, silly girl energy.

One day, Chrissy and Annie shocked me with a story. They'd gone into the basement of the karate studio next to Joe's Variety after class and saw a boy in his underwear—and another one completely bare. They were laughing as they told it, like it was some hilarious event. But, that wasn't right. Girls weren't supposed to do that. And, they definitely weren't supposed to find it funny. It felt rude, like they were laughing in church. How dare they treat something private so casually? I left in a huff, wounded and indignant.

I realized that the friendship wasn't so perfect after all. Something important was missing.

But, she was all I really had. Ten minutes later I regretted leaving, so I came back—pretending I was just looking for my newspaper clippings.

It was pretty easy to run my show. People were harder.

4

Sledding was easy, so convenient. If you could lug your sled up to the top of the hill, gravity would do the rest. I was a big boy now, in school, able to walk pretty much anywhere as long as I didn't cross a street. That was the rule. I decided to go sledding by myself, so I grabbed the wooden sled with the metal blades and a convenient steering rope. I headed to the slopes, which meant walking straight down the driveway, then veering right after the curve and climbing the first incline. The terrain rose in three steep, rolling waves. From the top of the third, I could pick up real speed and steer all the way home. Four trips up and down the hill, I realized that it was not much fun alone. On a typical weekend day, there would be about a dozen kids climbing up and sliding down, and half the fun is racing or almost colliding with people.

So, I decided I would find someone to sled with, and I knew exactly who I would ask. Mickey Negan was a student at my school, and we had been getting along very well lately. We walked home together sometimes, and once I stopped off at his house. He lived on the East Bank of the projects in the last house before the *normal* houses started.

He lived in the building with the Jefferson Street address. Driving along Jefferson, you'd just think it was a good-sized single-family colonial. You'd never guess it was a part of public housing with four units inside. Each uniform building had in the front, a single grand doorway masking the two inner doors of the center apartments. Two end apartments jutted out in little alcoves with their doors to the side. The town maintenance crew kept the landscaping sensible, trimmed, and tidy. That house on Jefferson looked like the most impressive but was the most modest on that street.

I called for Mickey, but he wasn't coming out. That last time at his place, I hadn't kept my eyes closed when he was changing out of his clothes, wet from digging a snow fort. I wondered if that was the reason.

On the way back, at the house at the edge of the hill, Charlie and a few other kids were playing hockey in the back courtyard.

They said "do not enter, this is our yard."

"What are you talking about? This is public housing." My brother had explained this to me. Four-year-olds can be so tedious—especially when you're five.

"No, it is our property," said the little one scowling. He scared me. Ricky was different with his dark hair and eyes. And, he wasn't pudgy and pasty-white like the rest of us. His mother was Italian while the others were Irish, and I was Swedish/Finnish. But, I was not about to climb up the cement wall into the snowy woods to go around. And, I wasn't going to go near the front of the house and the street. Most of all I was not going to be told what to do by the likes of them. It took some wrestling and squirming around them, and a few very long seconds, but I got through. I wished my sled was right there. It would have made for a very stealthy getaway. Instead, as I headed down the lower hill, they sent a volley of snowballs, a few of them hitting their target. I tried to return the favor, but I was outnumbered, and they had the high ground advantage, so my best strategy was to retreat.

This was just one battle in a much larger war. They sometimes claimed the hill as theirs, which was ridiculous, because people arrived from the far reaches of the project to sled. "We are letting them use it, but not you."

Charlie was friends with Bib Blanchard from up the Lane. Bib was a good-natured little guy, and I never understood how two people so opposite could be best friends. The snowball fights carried on as long as the snow lasted, with Bib trying his best to be neutral. When spring came, we traded snowballs for crab apples. They grew throughout the project, and we had a few trees in our own yard. The largest one stood right at the edge of our property. By then, Sarah was guilty by association. An additional warrior and more ammunition gave me the upper hand. Up the hill they had only a few scrawny trees, picked clean in no time, while we had an endless supply. We filled buckets with crab apples and won battle after battle. Charlie had had enough. He broke the one rule. He started throwing rocks! And, eventually the inevitable happened: one struck me square in the forehead. That required a trip to the Emergency Room and eight stitches.

My father dragged me up to Charlie's house to talk with him and his mother. I was surprised when his mother was not at all apologetic and claimed that I had been throwing rocks as well. This was evil-hearted as, of course, I never did so, but her lies made it worse. She did not witness the events, yet she said she saw me with her own eyes. She did not just make a mistake. I didn't know adults could lie.

Weeks went by without further incident until one day; Bib and Charlie came to the end of our driveway offering lemonade in a little thermos. We were very skeptical, but Bib reassured us. I dipped my finger in the yellow liquid and smelt it. Of course, it was urine. Bib tried to splash it at me. A few drops landed on my shirt. What a terrible betrayal.

That unusual kid, Ricky, showed up only now and then. The first time his words hit me, it felt like a punch.

He'd start with, "What are you doing?" shouted from the road.

"None of your business."

Then came the weapons—*Stupid. Jerk. Girl. Faggot.* Short, sharp. I didn't understand why they stung so much. Sometimes, I'd find him in our yard, echoing my words from last winter: "This is public," he mocked, smirk stretched wide, as if he knew better.

I corrected him, "This is private property. We own our house. A public sidewalk is all around your house connected to the other houses. Open to the public!"

I could tell, from a distance, that Ricky was different with his friends, though. Sharp and quick to laugh. I was fascinated by him. But, none of his good side was directed toward me.

One day, Sarah and I were tossing a Frisbee in the field one tier up the hill. Ricky intercepted it, and I grabbed it back. I ran into my yard, he followed. I went past the garage, into the backyard that was bounded by a fence. Trapped, I looked around and registered the big metal shed, full of junk. I pulled open the door, pulled out the big blue plastic pool, and threw it on the ground. I said, "this is a raft and the grass is the ocean." We both jumped in. At that moment, the tension between us melted. A storm hit and the raft was thrown around. We traveled back past the garage, into the front yard and the open ocean.

And, this was just the pilot episode for a series that lasted the entire summer. I had had many rehearsals of various episodes earlier with my sister. Now, it was time for the real show where plot points were perfected. Ricky was the perfect co-star. Unlike his predecessor, he was not prone to complaining, tantrums, or hogging the limelight. He actually provided the laugh track. He responded to suspense with heightened curiosity. He offered a British or Southern accent, though they sounded the same. At every commercial, he had thoughtful suggestions about what could happen next.

"We're running low on supplies. We cannot live on crab apples and grapes alone. We need meat," He declared.

"You're right the fruit is yucky anyway."

"Commercial!: We could pretend to swim down to the sea floor and dig up real worms and use the apple stems as hooks," he added.

"Perfect, Uncommercial!"

Of course, we experienced pirates, sharks, and hurricanes. There were also guest appearances by Sarah as a mermaid and later as a woman thrown off a million-dollar yacht. Spoiler: she turned out to be a ghost.

On Labor Day, the raft sank. As we tried to stay buoyant on a log, we saw an island in the distance, the vessel became waterlogged, and we were forced to swim for our lives.

There was a happy ending for the shipwrecked heroes, but I felt deep sadness. School would change our daily routine. I felt connected to Ricky more than anyone else. I always had a brief period of infatuation with a new friend, but this was different. My bond with Ricky was ten times the strength of my bond with Chrissy.

In the cold months, Ricky spent time over my house in fits and starts; his arrivals and departures never quite on a schedule. I loved giving a tour of my house to other kids. There was a secret door to the basement in the coat closet, a special way to pass things from the kitchen to the dining room through an open area above the counter, and a bookcase on hinges that revealed a stairway to the attic.

Raftless, we built a fort in my room with blankets and sheets. One version of the fort captured the heating vent in the floor which dropped the temperature in the room and raised the temperature in the tent. We had a fun emergency exit from my room on the second floor. An evergreen plant, a cross between a bush and a tree, was just outside my window. An easy jump and climb made for stylish exits and entries. As snow pants were deemed uncool by Denny and others, I just wore my regular clothes when sledding or building snow forts. Our outdoor activities and our icy ascent to my room left us very damp and cold. I could just change clothes, but Ricky could not. We retreated to the tent fort, and Ricky dried his socks on the vent. Gradually, over several weeks we shed more and more clothing and set up a clothesline in the tent and began calling it our sauna. Eventually we just went naked. I was not ashamed of this at all. I was proud of it. This was something only guys could do together. It represented trust and fraternity. There was something magical about being nude; a raw honesty and simplicity that was comforting.

Ma cleaned house for one family, and Sarah and I usually tagged along. Mrs. Saranopoulos wore her graying hair cropped short and glasses that made her look sharp and exacting. She taught at one of those Cambridge private schools where kids wore blazers with Latin mottos.

Her house sat on the lower slope of Beaumont Hill. It wasn't much bigger than ours, but it carried itself differently: neat clapboards, crisp trim, dormer windows. Inside, everything felt polished and deliberate: fancy curtains softening the light, a graceful stairway, and rumors of old passageways from its Underground Railroad days. Being there felt like stepping back in time and up in class.

My favorite place was the greenhouse, warm and bright, the air scented with a small orange tree. One day I found a flat blue stone tucked into a flowerpot, as smooth as a secret.

"What's this?" I asked.

Mrs. Saranopoulos explained. "A worry stone, Johnny. Sea glass worn down by waves. You rub it, and it takes your worries."

"Does it work?"

She smiled. "Depends how many you've got." She put it in my hand. "You keep it."

Later, on the steps, I showed Ricky.

He turned it over. "Feels nice. Is it really glass?"

We decided to check. Ma walked us to the library.

The children's section had *World Book Encyclopedias* on low shelves. Nothing under Glass or Stones.

"Try W—worry," Ricky said. Still nothing.

Upstairs, the adult library smelled sharper, like fresh paper and ink. I was hunting for a book, but then I spotted something better: a typewriter perched on its table, humming with possibility. I had an exciting idea. Something printed could make our ideas matter. Make our friendship special.

I fed some paper into the carriage and started typing, each clack, a tiny thunderbolt: WORRY STONE CLUB.

Ricky stared. "What are you doing?"

"Making it real. Your name. My name. Secret password. We decide who we let in."

He bent closer, reverent.

But, I wasn't done. I carried the page to the huge Xerox machine near the entrance. I set our paper on the glass, placed the worry stone beneath it, and lowered the lid.

We dropped in a nickel. The machine hummed, flashed, and finally produced warm copies—our certificate in duplicate; the stone stamped at the bottom like a grand seal on a diploma.

Ricky held his copy carefully by the corners. "It looks...official."

"Now we can both have it," I said. "No matter where the stone is, we both have the power."

One day after warming up, drying off, and dressing, Ricky and I played a game of Sorry and Operation on my bed. Getting chilly, we got under the covers. I was so very happy with Ricky, I gave him a big hug and a kiss. I wanted it to be a grown-up kiss which at that time meant it was a kiss like I gave Ma but longer. It was a little awkward. I stopped and began to lean back to my side of the bed when Ricky pulled me in for another bear hug. He squeezed tightly. At that moment, the room felt safe and the world uncomplicated. At the end, I said, "there is nothing wrong with this." He said "I know." There was a solemn moment of silence after that. This occurrence was never repeated or spoken of again.

The urge to connect was there at a young age, right alongside the rules I half-knew but didn't understand. That day planted a question in my heart about what it meant to bond with someone genuinely and whether the wisdom passed down made good sense.

Ironically, weeks later it became clear Ricky was moving. I was heartbroken. He moved to the outer reaches of the project—a quarter mile away. For months it felt like he had gone to another world. No matter how tightly I held the worry stone, being in the empty tent was no fun. It just reminded me of how I felt inside. The project wasn't as vast as I thought, but no one ever gave me a tour. By the time I found him again, I realized he was really no further than Chrissy had always been.

5

In the spring, my brother Denny had a yard sale with two other Big Kids. Sarah and I grabbed our savings and headed into our front yard for a shopping spree. I only bought items from Denny's table out of shyness. Sally bought things from Shawn and Tony. She ended up with new and interesting items, while I had stuff I had played with before. The only thing that changed was the title.

Shawn had a younger sister and four younger brothers. The Flannerys lived a crab apple's throw from our house. Eventually, the three youngest Flannery boys came to the yard sale. They stood together like Russian dolls, each one a slightly larger version of the last. They all had the same long, shaggy blond hair, not styled so much as worn. We talked and shared our ages. One was two years older, another one year older, and the third one year younger. Someone said I was the missing Flannery brother. That sounded neat. Brothers my age would have meant I had friends who would never have to leave.

Large families were the norm in the projects. Irish Catholics averaged seven children, Protestants about four. There were a lot of kids living close by, spread across one hundred apartments. When I was allowed to cross the street, a whole new world opened up. Being friends with the Flannery boys let me enter the world of sports. Casual football and baseball games popped up everywhere, though we mostly played within our group. Bobby Sharpo, the Italian boy across the street, joined us. Matthew Mundt, less goofy than his brother, eventually joined, and surprisingly, so did Madeline Madison, also known as Mad Dog.

I did not like her at all. I had several run-ins with her at school. She was always grabbing my crayons and making stray marks on my papers. One day, after she crumpled my paper, I was about to shove her when Miss Dryer intervened, grabbing me and scolding, "You don't hit girls!" Whenever I was unfairly scolded or felt diminished in the eyes of teachers, I would lay my head in my arms at my desk and go silent for a long time. I suppose there were tears in my eyes, so that counts as crying.

There were haunted houses on either side of our home. Old Lady Elena's house was in rough shape. After the fire, it was left in ruins, with trees growing from within. Kids used to stand in front of her house and sing, "Ol' Lady Elena, are you coming out tonight?" Around the time I was joining the Flannery clan, they tore down Elena's house and cleared most of the forest around it. They dug two deep holes for the foundations of new duplexes. A bunch of us kids went to the edge of one hole to look at the cement footings. Mad Dog suddenly threw sand in my face, and I was blinded. Then, she shoved me down the embankment. No specific reason. Bobby Sharpo led me back to the street and gave me the shirt off his back to wipe my eyes. This meant a lot to me. Mad Dog was insufferable. She was a match for any of the boys once she got one of her wooden clogs in her hands. She never hesitated to hit you in the head or face. She was brutal. I realized that sometimes girls can be underhanded, sneaky, and out and out bullies, and sometimes the toughest boy can be the most kind and loyal one in the crowd.

A Portuguese family moved into the brand-new duplex next door. The vinyl siding still smelled like plastic in the sun. They didn't speak English yet, just waved and pointed, but all summer they went to school for words. The first phrase they brought home was, "Your nose is potatoes," which they found hysterical.

They had a bright red inflatable pool and splashed in it like it was the deep sea. The Flannerys laughed at their tight Speedos, calling them gay. They were accustomed to swimming in long trunks and t-shirts like the water might see too much of them. I wanted to wear a Speedo out in the sunlight, right along with them, but I knew that it was impossible.

Later that summer, I called for the Flannerys. Instead of coming out, they told me to *come on in*. The apartment smelled strange, like hot dogs cooked in a frying pan instead of a pot. We always boiled ours. This smell was stronger, greasy, and smoky, and it hung in the air like it wasn't in a hurry to leave. The kitchen light was dim.

Mrs. Flannery was asleep on the sofa, the TV murmuring to itself.

"Want some tonic?" Patty Flannery asked.

"Yes."

She opened the fridge and looked inside. "All we've got is Tab." One big bottle. A few cans.

She shut the door, crouched, and reached under the kitchen table. She came up with a warm six-pack of Coca-Cola.

"Real Coke," I whispered to myself.

At our house, soda only showed up when you were sick. And, even then, it was usually something off-brand. A request for more soda always got the same response: *You'll just drink it all.* It felt like extreme deprivation.

Danny, the youngest Flannery, was hovering nearby.

"Danny," Patty said, "get ice."

He groaned but went.

She set the cans on the counter. "We'll make it cold enough."

He yanked the overfilled tray from the freezer and used a butter knife to chip some shards. Some slid across the table and landed on the floor. He filled my cup with irregular, sharp shapes, not like the little blocks from our freezer. Jimmy Flannery came downstairs, opened the fridge, grabbed the big bottle of Tab, and drank from it while his eyes darted around to see who might be watching.

Mrs. Flannery said to keep it down, and Patty said, "Ma, time to go upstairs." My Ma took her nap from 4 to 5:30 pm each day, so I was only a little surprised by a daylight snooze.

Patty anticipated my confusion. "She works nights at a nursing home. We share a bed but not at the same time."

We went and took over the couch and played cards.

Later, I asked, "Is your dad going to be home?"

"No, he lives in Boston. Not enough room for him here."

The next time I went inside the Flannery home, it was winter. The apartment felt a little cramped with coats piled up and boots blocking the front door. The heat was turned up high, and the windows were all fogged. It was messy, but it looked like a place for fun.

Jimmy kicked a coat off the couch and spied something from under the coffee table—a doughnut with one bite taken out of it, resting on a *TV Guide*. "There you are."

A taxi pulled up out front. Matt Flannery stepped out like a man on a mission, holding a Filene's bag. Bobby Sharpo trailed behind him watching his feet on the ice.

"He can afford a taxi?" I asked Jimmy as we peeked around the shade.

"Yeah, me and Danny went yesterday. Today's Matt's turn."

They told me that every time their mom got paid, they took a taxi—just the kids—to Filene's Basement and picked out toys.

That sounded unbelievable. I had never been in a taxi, and new toys came only at birthdays and Christmas.

Matt barely said hello. He tossed a Monopoly game onto the living room rug and sliced through the shrink wrap with a pen. The box was pristine—edges crisp, the pieces in neat little bags.

"We gonna play by the rules," Danny asked, "or blow stuff up?"

"I call the dog," Matt said.

Danny slid in sideways. "I get the shoe."

"I'll be the boat," I said, before Jimmy or Bobby could.

We passed the money around and made it through a full roll and a half before everything started crumbling. Danny took the top hat hostage. Matt made his pile of twenties into a launcher and shot the iron toward Baltic Avenue.

Nobody flinched when the board bent a bit under someone's knee.

I looked around. One plastic robot with a missing arm. Some packaging. A beach ball half-deflated in the corner. But, this game was new, and so was the Nerf football they got yesterday, still in the plastic.

At my house, everything was meant to last. Ma reused paper cups at least once. Toys were kept, saved, lined up on shelves, or stored in closets. Even broken toys waited for glue or a screw to bring them back. Most were secondhand from a sibling, rummage sale, or the dump. My room was full of toys. They had new toys that did not last, and no room to keep them anyway.

"What other toys you got?"

"We have some Matchbox cars," said Danny. "Wanna add them to the game?"

"What else?"

"There's not much else."

"How can that be if you get toys every two weeks?'

"Yeah," Jimmy said. "We used them."

That seemed like an odd reason for a toy to be gone.

I didn't know what to think. It was like their life didn't follow the rules I thought everyone followed. It felt like they had more and less at the same time. I was just starting to realize that people used money and weighed the present and future in different ways, and each path had its own consequences.

Danny farted like it was a punchline.

I had my own irritating ways. I behaved like a little know-it-all, correcting other kids' pronunciation: It's breaKfast not breafast!; window screeN not ScreeM!" It's ValentiNe's Day not ValentiMe's." And, I gave uninvited explanations of anything under the sun. I pointed out, with grave authority, "That's not real—it's just actors," which sparked heated arguments when the *Six Million Dollar Man* bent a steel bar or when a wrestler jumped from the ropes onto his opponent. Other kids wanted to believe.

6

I was a controlling little dude. By second grade, I decided we needed to become an organized group and named it the Tiger Club, in contrast to the Lions Club. I set dues, made t-shirts, and claimed a clubhouse by clearing out the twelve-by-twelve shed in my backyard. A sturdy metal shed on concrete, with a carpet and a sofa, gives you a lot of capital.

With the home court advantage, I had some sway, though the Flannery boys still had the votes. They called me "book smart, not street smart," and usually overruled me. If I could win over Matt Flannery early, I had a chance. I lost on barring girls from the club, and Mad Dog was allowed in.

Around then, I'd also made a private rule for myself: no swearing. Most of it sounded gross and irrelevant—bathroom talk. On the other hand, I thought "Oh, God!" was fine. I didn't think kids who swore were bad. I just liked feeling that I was a little better than them, and in control of myself. I even proposed a group rule: *no swearing unless necessary*. No one, it turned out, ever thought their own swears were unnecessary.

I wanted a purpose: money-making schemes, organized activities, drama. They wanted snacks and chaos. We tried everything—puppet shows, door-to-door sales, even a carnival—but cooperation rarely held. For the puppet show, I made paper-mâché heads and borrowed library puppets, then wrote most of the skits myself when the writer's room failed. The premiere took place in a vacant section of the basement in the Flannery's building with Ma in a folding chair and two little girls on a plank balanced on paint cans. The stage was a cardboard lemonade stand with a sheet tacked across the front. Things fell apart: a missing script, a puppet head rolling off, the stand tipping forward.

Ma clapped anyway. "It was wonderful!"

Jimmy Flannery refused to overcharge Ma for concessions as I had planned.

Selling greeting cards went better. We earned points instead of cash, dreaming of sleeping bags and a pop-up tent. Regal Road was our target: the closest rich neighborhood. Lawns perfect, doorbells melodic. Matthew Mundt was overly anxious and said awkward things like "Looks like you'd have trouble going to a store" to an old woman, which nearly made us melt into the porch. Still, we earned enough for one sleeping bag and a flashlight we rotated and constantly lost track of.

The Muscular Dystrophy Carnival was the highest peak we ever tried to climb. I mailed away for official posters. Joe's Variety donated off-brand candy. We set up a ring toss, a marble-guessing game, and food booths. Fewer than ten outsiders came, never for long. Members paid a reduced rate and started rapidly devouring the supply of chip dip, forcing me to ration it. When I stopped Jimmy Flannery, he cried and ran home; his mother stormed into the yard insisting he could eat what he wanted. She valued loyalty more than logistics. In truth, it was more pretend carnival than reality, and I wouldn't admit that to myself. The amount sent to the charity was meager. We tried a simpler business model—raising mice for profit—and ended with an empty cage and escapees scattering across the lawn.

Snake Hill was the only club activity with consistent peace. We'd head over the railroad bridge, cross Serenity Drive, and follow the steep, curving side street to a path through the woods near the crest. Each recon unit returned with new myths: cut-up telephone poles arranged by aliens, ropes across trees, and once, quite an amazing find. Matt Flannery and I found it while trying to build a small hut in a clearing. When I lifted something strange from under the leaves—a piece of plexiglass— a dark hole gaped beneath. I yelled "Run!" and knocked over Matt's carefully built wall. Later, with Bobby Sharpo, we learned it was an underground fort that hadn't been used in years. Rot, mildew, and old *Playboys* told the story. A perfect pit-stop for our travels.

Higher up, where we thought the woods were the deepest, we found a path leading to a sunlit field. To our surprise there was an Olympic-sized pool and a handsome brick building. Inside, everything was child-sized—classrooms, furniture, the bubbler.

"How can this be a grade school?" I asked.

"Why is it in the woods?" Mundt added.

"Look over there," Matt said, pointing to a parking lot through the trees.

The shock wasn't just its surprise appearance, but that someone our age had use of a pool at school, and we didn't.

Those woods made us feel watched and apparently, we were. A photo of us appeared in the *Beaumont Gazette*: four kids spread across the road heading uphill. Caption: "An afternoon of exploration and fun." In the next edition four more pictures with a different tone: a sequence of us walking as a car rounded a bend. "Twisting roads pose real danger to pedestrians," translation: these little idiots are going to get flattened.

The next year, Jay, Bobby's older brother, joined and steered the club toward tough guy activities: football drills, conditioning, preparing to fight rivals. One afternoon on the back-steps-to-nowhere, he dared us all to "show our meat." They all pointed at me to go first. It wasn't undue pressure—it was entirely my kind of thing. I pulled down my waistband. Big laugh. Then quick flashes from the others. Their bodies looked different from mine; I didn't know why or what it might mean. Someone suggested butts next. "No!" Matt barked, ending it.

We tried making a documentary about "the pits of the projects." Disappointingly, most kids said everything was fine. Matt finally offered a usable thought: that the whole town treated the projects like another country. Matt gave the interview of the year—calm, thoughtful, honest—but he later demanded it be erased after Danny Flannery rammed our go-kart during a race and I defended the notion that if we were being tough, combat wasn't cheating. In a fury, he smashed our cart, announced he quit the club, and forced me to tape over his interview. Was this the beginning of the end of my cherished club?

At Beaumont Center, Danny's peeling Tiger Club shirt caught the attention of older boys claiming their own club: the KKK.

"We don't like blacks or fags," one said. "So, we don't like you."

I asked Ma later. "Kitty Kat Klub" she said. "That's what it meant when I was little" and "fags are cigarettes in England." She was wrong, but her confidence was comforting.

Weeks later, a crumpled note appeared in our yard: "*You been warned — KKK.*" Terrifying—and pretty damn cool. The club was invigorated. We set lookouts, patrolled the tracks, held emergency meetings. When excitement started to fade again, I wrote two fake notes myself to revive the tension. It worked. Then, a new one arrived addressed only to me: "The blacks in Boston are coming to get you." I felt sick. Jay eventually admitted writing it. The original note had been sucked up by the mower, leaving nothing authentic left to examine. Our older siblings took handwriting samples, mine deliberately altered, and declared all of us innocent. The club lost its luster thereafter.

That winter, Dad installed a heat stove in the living room and began storing coal in the clubhouse. An old army tent became our temporary replacement hangout and lasted one summer. Eventually the Flannery basement became the center of gravity—less official, less ambitious, less mine.

7

TV raised me in its flickering light, kept me company like a faithful friend, and showed me versions of life that felt both impossible and hauntingly familiar. I watched the *Six Million Dollar Man* and *Wonder Woman*, but it was *The Bionic Woman* and *The Incredible Hulk* that got into my blood. *Bionic Woman* was my favorite for a while. Jaime Sommers was sweet in a way that didn't feel fake, clever in a way that felt fresh and easy. She tried smarts before aggression. She was strong but never angry, and when her body started rejecting her bionics, it was heartbreaking. And, that time Lisa Galloway had plastic surgery to switch places with Jaime, then starts believing she is Jaime because of the love Jaime had in her life that Lisa never had? That stayed with me.

Lisa tried to kill Jaime, and Jaime still hugged her. Still saw the pain in her. I remember how no one in the prison believed Jaime was really Jaime—how identity could be stolen or dismissed so easily, how you could doubt your own identity, and how much it mattered to be seen for who you really were. Jaime's connection to her foster mother, her peaceful rural life between missions; those quiet moments felt warmer than anything I knew in real life. But, then The *Incredible Hulk* nudged ahead, mostly because of that piano theme at the end. That lonely little song that played while David Banner walked down some empty road with his thumb out, nobody ever stopping. Something about that felt true. That you could save the day and still end up alone. That people only saw the monster. It's strange how a green rage beast and a woman with secret robot parts could make you feel like maybe someone out there understood you.

The same identity stuff was already there in real life, just without the neat episodes. Most days felt like a test of whether I counted as one of the boys.

Each of the Flannery brothers took a turn as my best friend, one after the other, in descending order.

Jimmy Flannery came first, mostly by default. With his long blond hair and powder-blue jumpsuit, he vaguely resembled Leif Garrett. He was held back two grades, so now he was in the same grade as me and Matt who was held back once. Of all the Flannerys, he was the one I saw most often, especially during recess. We laid claim to the metal box beside the baseball diamond and declared it our throne. There were boxes like it scattered all over town—rectangular, chest-high, and faintly mysterious. There was one across from Joe's Variety which was great seats for people-watching and being on display. We weren't exactly sure what they were for, but that didn't stop us from treating them like royal perches. Any one of them could become the seat of power, but the one by the ball field was ours at recess.

We surveyed the court and critiqued other students. We gossiped, plotted kickball strategies, and sent an envoy to secure a red rubber ball from Mr. S. before the rest of the class even got to the field. Jimmy was known for his bionic kick. Kickball was really the only sport we could stay competitive in.

For Halloween, I wanted to do something different. I'd been generic Astronaut #102 three years running. Sarah was Princess #211 for just as long. The plastic masks were itchy, the elastic bands snapped too tight across your ears, and the costumes were just a small shirt worn backwards with drawn on features, barely reaching past your hips.

I'm not sure how it started. Maybe it was the wig we found in a Goodwill box. Or the odd little sweater that didn't seem to belong to anyone in particular. I put them on as a joke and got big laughs. That clinched it.

Patty Flannery offered to do my makeup—eyeliner, rouge, natural rose lipstick. Denny didn't object to it. So, I went trick-or-treating as a girl. Jimmy was distant. The go-to insult used by his brothers against him when angry was "girl!" It was just that Jimmy, when he wasn't tense and defensive, expressed emotions intensely. Big giggles or guffaws when amused or a screech or a wale when startled. I don't think he knew what to make of my selection. Dressing up like that was fun. I got a lot of compliments. At the end of the night, a teenager made small talk with me. He never let on whether he knew I was a boy or thought I was a girl. I didn't ask. I wasn't sure which answer would feel stranger.

This occurrence was never repeated or spoken of again.

Maybe as penance for dressing like a girl or just to confuse the universe, I joined after-school sports. I never scored a basket, but I racked up a few assists, mostly by accident. Shooting felt like too bold a move for someone who wasn't entirely sure he belonged on the court. Since team glory clearly wasn't in the cards, I redirected my ambitions to the Presidential Fitness Test. Somehow, I landed above the 85th percentile in all five events achieving the award. Sit-ups and the standing long jump were my specialties. Nothing says masculine redemption like crunches and throwing yourself forward in gym shorts.

I liked competitions with rules. The playground didn't have any.

The swing wasn't moving. Just two chains and a plastic seat, a perch along the main drag. Jimmy had claimed it, hands hooked around the chains; heels wedged into the dirt.

"Get off the fucking swing," one of the older boys said. Jimmy didn't move. He had this way of looking stubborn without ever looking strong.

The tall one with skinny knees stepped up onto the swing's edge. He dropped his weight, knees pressing Jimmy's shoulders. His hands held the chains from above. He bounced, flapping those knees, jarring Jimmy with every drop.

Jimmy grunted, gripping harder. The teens laughed.

I stood off to the side, wishing I could rewind it or offer him a few words in his favor, but I was afraid of them turning the negative energy in my direction.

Mad Dog's sister leaned in, hair to one side, voice sharp: "Why ain't you in Boston with the rest of the fags? Having your little parade?"

For a second, the words just hung there. Then the laughter broke bigger, uglier. Jimmy's face flushed red, raw.

But, finally, after another grind of knees on his shoulders, he slid out and let the seat go. He slouched off. The teens barely even used the swing after. They just wanted control.

I walked with him a few steps, careful not to sound like I pitied him. "They're jerks, Jimmy. You held out longer than most."

He shrugged, lip between his teeth, eyes down. I wished I had something stronger to say, something to make things better.

They tried that with me once. I said "I'll give you the swing if you promise to get off after I eat my ice cream," motioning toward the truck. I got ice cream then I just moved on to something else, believing at least I saved face.

But, a week later, I saw Jimmy pull the same stunt on Rosa. She was the weakest one on the swing set. Refused to give it up to Jimmy. He went up on her shoulders. And forced her off.

It stung, watching him hand the hurt down like it was the only currency he had.

Then, he was gone from Mendall for a while. I'm not really sure why.

He was over at Avington Elementary where they had a special Special Ed program. There was all kinds of drama over there. Then, one day it was decided without much fanfare that he'd come back and be in my class. The teacher arranged our desks head-to-head in a little island of our own. For whatever reason, we started staying inside during recess and after lunch. It just evolved.

One afternoon, Robby Richoux, the class pariah, ended up in the room alone with us. Jimmy and I were near the bottom of the social ladder, with only some of the girls below us, and Robby firmly at the bottom. He was known for bathroom accidents, dark freckles, long curly brown hair, and saying the wrong thing like it was his purpose.

"You two are homos," he said.

"No, we're not," Jimmy replied, uptight as ever. "You are. Why don't you focus on bringing the class another bag of bologna sandwiches that no one will eat?"

"You're more like girls who stay *home*," Robby continued. "You know... and housekeep."

At the time, I thought Robby was just being mean. Just Robby being Robby.

But, now I wonder if, in his clumsy, cruel way, he was the only one saying—out loud and all wrong—what the rest of us had already started to suspect. We were different.

I didn't quite fit with other boys at school, and after a while I stopped trying so hard. Friendships with adults helped make up for my lower standing among peers. Cross-generational friendships had always been the norm. Danny and I often knocked on his neighbor's door just to ask if he had any soda. John Johnson would welcome us in, seat us at his kitchen table, and wait on us like honored guests.

Eventually one of those adults mattered more than the others—to Jimmy and me. Before him, though, we had to learn which grown-ups were worth trusting.

Kids didn't get our questions answered by parents or teachers—not good answers, anyway. Parents gave silly answers, or the kind that ended in "Because I said so."

I asked Ma where babies come from.

She said, "the stork drops you down the chimney."

"But, that leads to the furnace."

"Ask your father."

He said, "Well, we found you at the dump."

Weird.

Teachers gave bleached answers, scrubbed of all useful detail.

"It's biology that you will study in later years."

If you wanted the truth, you went to a Big Kid. They would mess with you at first, but eventually their own pride would kick in, and they'd show off how much they knew. Ryan K, the nicest of the Big Kids, told us: "Babies come from their mothers' tummy. Daddies plant their seed."

Still weird.

The second-best source of info was student teachers. Still young.

One student teacher once asked me why all my friends were SED kids.

"SED?" I repeated.

"Severely Emotionally Disturbed," she explained.

"What does that mean?"

She thought for a moment. "It means they probably won't make it unless something is done."

"Like cancer?"

"No... more like... they're at risk. They might not take care of themselves, might make dangerous choices."

I tried to talk to Jimmy about it.

"Huhn? Alls I know," he said happily, "I get outta class to see the candy ladies."

That's when Mr. Norman came into the picture. He was a student teacher, a substitute, or maybe a counselor-in-training. Some combination thereof. He was the only approachable male role model at Mendell. I told him I was jealous of Jimmy and the candy ladies. He took me out of class and had me do crafts in his office a couple times. We scraped a damp clay sheet to make an ink print template for Christmas cards. He said I was good at it.

When he told us he was leaving the position, he organized a field trip to his house for a dinner. Half of the class went. He lived on Serenity Drive, near Beaumont Center.

The field trips didn't end when Norman left Mendall Elementary. Not for Jimmy and me. If anything, they got better. One afternoon we were at Brigham's in Beaumont Center, standing under the menu board pretending we might actually buy something decent. But, between us, we barely had enough for a single scoop. One of us—I honestly can't remember who—said, "Hey, Mr. Norman lives around here, right?"

The other nodded. "Let's go."

That was the whole plan. No asking for permission. No call ahead. We figured if someone's worth visiting, they're worth surprising.

We walked a couple blocks, found his place, and called for him. When he came to the door, we simply asked "can we come in?"

"So," he said, eyeing us with amused suspicion, "you thought you'd just show up uninvited and that'd be fine?"

"Yeah," we said.

And he laughed. That high, slow-build kind of laugh—like a seal trying to catch his breath and then finally getting a deep one.

"I suppose you'll need a permission slips signed," he said, more to himself than us.

"Do we really?" I asked. "This is friendship, not school."

Our parents didn't object. They didn't even meet him or talk to him by phone, but they trusted him. He worked for the school, and that was enough. Or maybe they would just trust anyone. Eventually, Mr. Norman stopped chasing after permission slips, accepting that the ritual meant more to the system than to the people in it. So, for the next three years, we saw Mr. Norman regularly. Hikes, museum visits, scavenger hunts, root beer floats in his kitchen, sometimes just long talks about the difference between sympathy and empathy. He thought our logic was hilarious, and we thought his life was cool.

Our first outing was a simple hike up Sunset Hill Road a few blocks from Mr. Norman's house. We were headed to conservation land near Habitat; the destination of at least three school field trips a year. It felt surreal walking to a place that had always required a bus.

The day was crisp, and the light came slanting through the trees like visible happiness. We weren't in a rush. Mr. Norman kept pace with us like a fellow human, not a chaperon. At the top of the hill, we spotted a man in his pristine white driveway surrounded by bushels of apples—the edible kind. His mansion was in the middle of an orchard. He was standing next to what looked like a cross between a printing press and a medieval torture device.

Without hesitation, Mr. Norman strolled right up and introduced us. “Hey there, we’ve got a couple of curious minds here. Mind if we watch a little?”

The man grinned and waved us over. He was crushing apples, grinding them down, or pressing the mash to squeeze out juice. He explained the difference between making sauce and cider, how time and air and fermentation could turn something sweet into something with bite. He let us taste the pulp and juice at different stages. The apple cider hadn’t even had time to chill, but it was the best I’d ever tasted.

I remember how Mr. Norman chatted with the stranger. There was no fear, no lesson. Just curiosity, respect, and the simple pleasure of watching something being made from scratch. I didn’t know then that this would be one of my favorite memories. But, I knew enough to keep looking and keep walking. And, believing people could be nice for niceness' sake.

He took us on several fishing trips. Matt came along once. Jimmy and I didn’t handle it well. Mr. Norman said Matt was just getting a little extra attention because he was new, but that didn’t help. Mr. Norman was ours. We got pouty, noisy, maybe even kicked a tackle box. Scared off the fish. It was the only time he ever scolded us.

On the way home, Mr. Norman did a pitch-perfect impression of Jimmy at the water's edge—giggling, squealing, screeching, even arching his back like a wounded cat. It was his way of showing Jimmy what the afternoon had looked like from the outside. Matt and I were howling. Jimmy forced a smile, but you could tell he didn’t love it.

Over time, Jimmy and I started making real money with him—detailing his car, his roommates', even some of the neighbors' cars. In winter, we shoveled driveways. The work was hard, but the tips were generous enough to feel like treasure.

Once, during a party Mr. Norman hosted, Jimmy and I were asked to play bartenders. The wrap-around porch was full of adults and music, and we mixed scotch and soda like it was Kool-Aid. A guest coached us on how to work the room for better tips; another told us not to expect any, since it was a private party. We sneaked a couple of sips when no one was looking. Just enough to feel bold, not enough to get in trouble.

Mr. Norman was always engaged in a scholarly pursuit. He was developing a board game to be sold in museum gift shops. It was based on a game about the afterlife that had been found in Egyptian pyramids. There were tiles, tokens, and sticks, and he let us help test it out. He made us feel like we were in on something important.

Mr. Norman compensated a lot for what was missing in our lives.

Bob Radler was a different kind of friend. He was less a role model, more a cautionary tale. He was in his thirties, lived next door in the rear lot and never went unnoticed. He was silly, plump, and bulb-nosed, four-eyed, toothless, with a voice that carried, and a forehead that made him look permanently surprised. He wore the same outfit every day—a buttoned solid green army shirt, jeans, and black work boots. You'd see him all around town on his bike, and later on his moped, blowing his horn in greeting. The military look wasn't ironic. Bob had joined for a few years, loved America, or at least the idea of it: strength, machines, purpose.

Reading about the Japanese internment, Bob got very worked up.

"Tomorrow I'm heading to City Hall to make sure nothing like that ever happens again!"

"But, Bob," Denny said sternly, "town government doesn't have anything to do with national policy."

"That's where you're wrong. They can pass it up the chain!"

"Yeah, I'm sure they're going to do that for you," Denny muttered.

"They'll listen to me. Radler the Great! Perfect mind, perfect body!" he said, letting out a jagged titter.

Every holiday, Bob delivered. He gave the best presents. At Easter, he hid plastic eggs in our yard with care. Inside were chocolate kisses, shiny coins, or robust plastic animals from a Noah's Ark set that felt like collectibles, not toys. He gave these gifts to me, my sister Sarah, and the Blanchard kids. Fancy stuff. Brand new. It didn't matter that we weren't his kids or even always polite. Bob didn't expect anything back but our smiles. And we gave them, happily.

His yard was cluttered with lumber, gears, wheels, clamps, and broken items he meant to fix but never quite did. Bob was always around to help fix a bike or provide the parts we needed to build a go-kart—he handed over the supplies and dared us to try. In his basement, he had a neat little workshop with a maze of shelves, each lined with small, labeled boxes cut from cereal cartons and other packaging. His spelling was atrocious.

He loved books but could barely read above sixth-grade level. His living room was crammed with textbooks, medical manuals, military history he had bought new. Many were never read. He let me borrow anything I wanted.

I was maybe ten or eleven when I noticed Bob had been saying something that was off. He often chanted "Little girls! Little girls! I love little girls!" I had always thought that was odd, because I decidedly did not.

This time he added "What I'd do to her if I got her alone... I'd wreck her." He laughed. Not softly. It was a giddy, yowling sound. "Six is the sweet spot."

I realized that he was talking about physical attraction. I wasn't that concerned. At the time, I thought: *No little girl would have him. So, nothing could come of it.*

Sometimes adults are interested in children for wholesome reasons. Sometimes they have something more in mind.

8

But, let me not forget the real thread—Ricky. My special friend. Former raft and tent partner. Never again my best friend—was suddenly back in my world again.

The gang had abandoned the all-pavement route to Mendell Elementary, choosing a shortcut—diagonally across the projects, through a hole in the fence, then over the Town Yard office parking lot. It brought us close to Ricky's new apartment, and our paths began to overlap again.

Ricky was unanimously admitted to the Tiger Club just in time for our second round of greeting card sales. Our numbers soared. Turns out, deviating from the script and actually smiling worked. Ricky was a born charmer.

"These boxes have everything but Christmas," he'd announce. "Birthdays, thank-yous, sympathy—you name it. Six designs, five in each, completely random, but if you buy two or three boxes, you'll be covered. I do know that."

He was always welcome, even if he couldn't be with us all the time. Organized sports and a watchful mom kept him busy. But, when he was around, it felt like the club had a little more shine.

By the end of fourth grade, we were looking for places where we could see without being seen. One was the woodchip piles in the Town Yard, faintly smoking from somewhere deep inside, warm, cushiony, and pine-fresh. Our best perch, though, was on top of the maintenance garage attached to the projects' little administration building. The two roof pitches met in a shallow vee that made a natural lounge opportunity, hidden by the overhanging branches of a maple. From there, we could watch anyone walking the tracks or walking along Serenity Drive above, and if we inched up and looked over the peak, we could spy on the Flannerys' front yard where all the Big Kids held court. The building backed directly against the railroad buffer—just scrub brush, broken stone, and junk—which meant no one cared about that land. The other boys relieved themselves off the roof edge like royalty issuing decrees. I pretended I didn't have to go. Truth was, my bladder froze up when given an audience.

We'd lounge up there for hours, leaning back against the warm shingles, looking out over everything. The tracks shimmered in the distance.

One day Ricky peered down at the group of Big Kids. "Is Frank the one with the busted glove?"

He had it along even when no baseball was on the agenda.

"Yeah," Matt said. "He keeps tying it together with shoelaces like it's valuable."

"His Dad gave it to him before he went overseas," I added.

"Frank's solid," Matt said.

"Too solid for that crew," Ricky muttered. "He should hang with us."

We all watched Frank for a second—tossing a baseball into that patched glove, a steady thwap, thwap, thwap.

"Yeah, right. I am sure he's begging to hang out with a bunch of kids," said Matt.

Ricky lay back on the shingles, hands behind his head. "If I had a glove like that, I'd sleep with it under my pillow," he said lightly. Then, softer: "Some stuff is valuable, but isn't worth money."

Matt laughed it off, but I glanced at Ricky. Every now and then he said something that cracked him open a little, and I never knew what to do with that except experience the wonder.

"Frank doesn't care how weird it looks," Matt grumbled.

Ricky stretched out and his shirt rode up, the sun catching the line of his ribs. "You know you're cool when you don't have to explain yourself. You just are." Then, like he could feel himself getting too real, he added, "Also, when you can belch the alphabet."

We laughed.

We sat there in the dappled shade; three boys perched above the world, pretending we already knew how to live in it.

There were four ways to get to Beaumont Center. If you wanted speed, you could take the tracks. If safety was your thing, you could walk straight down Regal Road from Clock Lane and use the foot tunnel. If you were a little more daring, cross the wooden bridge over the tracks, competing with two-way traffic for space—narrow, loud, and thrilling—then follow Serenity Drive. Or, if you had time to waste, go through the woods. The woods were only good if the journey was the point.

It was a bright late morning when I brought it up. "We should go to the Center," I said casually to Ricky and Matt Mundt, who were sitting on the steps on the north side of the Flannerys' building. We had just called for the Flannerys, and their mother let us know they were still sleeping.

Mad Dog heard me from the street like a snake catching vibrations in the dirt. She slithered over with that hard, mischievous look she always wore when she saw opportunity.

"You're just gonna go? Without Jimmy or Danny? Without Matt?" She looked at Matt Mundt like he should be offended on behalf of his namesake. "They didn't say you could go without them."

"They're not up," I said. "They'll probably meet us there later."

Mad Dog crossed her arms. "You're traitors. Hope it's worth it."

"That's dumb; They'll sleep past noon." Ricky muttered. "There's no law against going to the Center."

Matt fidgeted. "Yeah, but... they won't like it. They get mad easy."

"It's time they get more flexible, don't you think?" I said.

That morning, we chose Regal Road. Matthew Mundt kept glancing back toward the Flannerys' direction like he expected them to come charging after us.

"They're not coming," I said. "They'll be cool."

We talked about other things for a while.

Matthew sighed. "My family's been bugging me. It's so good to get away."

"That might be because you have a higher IQ than them," I said.

Matt stopped walking.

"What?"

"I meant it as a compliment," I said quickly. "Like—you're sharp. You're not like the others."

"You're a jerk," he said—and shoved me.

I stumbled back, caught my balance, and shoved him back. He swung. I ducked. We scuffled in the street until Ricky stepped between us.

"Forget it," Matt said, brushing off his shirt. "I'm going home."

I watched him storm off. "He'll bad-mouth us. Make it sound worse than it was."

Ricky shrugged. "Probably." Then he added, "You shouldn't have said that."

I didn't start the fight on purpose, but I didn't mind how it ended. The idea of being alone with Ricky softened any guilt that remained.

We kept going. We walked Regal Road in silence for a bit, then got back to joking. We had nearly an hour at the Center—hitting all the spots: the Lions Club steps, the bench, the CVS back alley where we traded Wacky Pack cards, chewing stale gum, just being free.

Then, we stopped at Finest Supermarket.

I was flipping through the comics rack when I heard a crash. Ricky had been drop-kicked into a tower of Ruffles. Bags of chips exploded around him like popping balloons.

It was Jimmy Flannery. He stood there, wild-eyed. Behind him, Matthew Flannery and Bobby Sharpo flanked him like henchmen.

"Get outta here!" a clerk barked, shoving us out opposite doors.

As we headed into the sunlight, I heard the Flannerys shout after us: "You're dead!"

It wasn't Mundt who lit that fire. It was Mad Dog—spinning what she overheard into a full-blown betrayal. Said we talked about them behind their backs, called them names, said they were worthless. She gave them a story that felt true enough to justify retaliation.

We forged a new way to get back home. They'd obviously be waiting for us at the foot tunnel. So, we went over the tracks behind the gas station and made a wide berth on many streets aiming for the hole in the fence at the other end of the project.

We didn't say much at first, just kept moving.

"You think they really meant it?" he asked.

I shrugged. "They launched you into a Ruffles display. What do you think?"

He laughed, but not because it was funny. "You're right."

"We're not in the wrong," I said. "We didn't break plans with them. We didn't do anything wrong. We just... went."

Ricky nodded once, like he was trying to believe it.

"They don't have to go in when the streetlight goes on. They don't sit around doing nothing when we aren't around!"

We cut behind an old triple-decker where the grass smelled sour and somebody's laundry hung crooked on the line. A dog barked but didn't chase. The sun was too bright.

"It's kind of fun," I said. "You know—being on the run."

Ricky smiled a little but didn't look at me. "Sounds like a tv show."

"Better than sounding like a victim," I said.

Up in his bedroom, we remembered how to talk again—about hopping a train to Boston, a girl that he liked, and how cool it would be to turn into the Incredible Hulk like David Banner.

And the longer we talked, the less the Flannerys mattered. It felt like the two of us had found our footing again. Being outcasts together had some advantages.

If we kept sharing like this, if we kept laughing like this, maybe we'd get there.

I had to leave for New Hampshire for a week of family vacation. We talked about how he could bide his time until I got back, and then we'd figure out the best thing to do.

By "vacation," I mean heading up to our land in Gilmanton, where we had a camp house on a lake and a new house going up. I worked six hours a day helping my father build the foundation. Mostly that meant hauling cement blocks for him to set in place, and filling buckets of sand, water, and dusty cement powder to feed the cement mixer. Not exactly rest and relaxation. But, plenty of time to wish I were somewhere else.

By Wednesday, I rebelled, absconding deep into the woods with Sarah and our dog, Grover. We had a pleasant little picnic in the pines—until we realized we were hopelessly lost. Tired and wanting to go home, we wandered in circles for hours. The lake was on the wrong side. I couldn't tell north from south, or maybe the lake was just more irregular than I'd ever imagined. Sarah stayed calm, saying only, "Know the Truth," which is the fancy Bible way of telling yourself that denial is your friend. I was scared—really scared—for all of us. Why couldn't I just be hanging with Ricky?

Finally, we came to a road. It was the familiar dump road. But, where was Grover? We yelled and yelled for him to come. Then, started walking the two miles home. Passing the entrance to the dump, we heard Grover barking. And, there was Dad by his car with Grover. He had been looking for good finds there. We were glad to have a ride home.

Dad scolded, "If you are going to expect me to help with college, you'll do what I say." It felt like I only counted when I was working.

At the corner, there was a sign that said *free manure*. Dad took careful note.

After three more days of work, we would leave on Sunday, but a different kind of work was in store.

Dad had removed the middle seating of our van to make room for barrels of manure. Sarah and I sat in the back row with manure in front of us and manure behind us in the load area—for the two-hour journey. It wasn't a punishment; it was an economic decision. Not out of dire economic necessity, though. Value and efficiency were ends unto themselves. Ones that reliably outranked our comfort.

Dad began farming in our yard back in Beaumont. Corn and tomatoes did best.

I called for Ricky late Sunday night. He wasn't home. I tried again Monday. Out again. Tuesday, his mom said he was home but *not coming out*. By Wednesday, he finally answered the door.

"I've been busy. Little League," he said flatly.

I squinted at him. "Did the Flannerys come after you?"

He shrugged. "Nah. I gave them the weekend to cool off. Called for them Monday like nothing happened. They were kinda mean at first, but it was fine by the end of the morning."

I nodded. I stopped calling for Ricky.

I was devastated and stubborn. I wanted Ricky to myself and was crushed that he didn't have the same thing in mind. I didn't know what the difficulty getting in touch with him meant. And, I wasn't willing to be the one to extend a hand to the Flannerys because that would feel like defeat.

No one called for me for the rest of the summer. Or the fall. The cold war was persistent.

I tried not to think about it. I talked about it to no one. A new UHF station suddenly emerged from the static, channel 25, and it helped distract me. It felt like a secret room in the TV that only I knew about. After school, I'd watch with Dad's bedroom door half-closed, the volume low enough that I'd have to lean toward the screen. More cartoons, old reruns, programming that felt special to me because no one else knew to look for it.

Every so often a preacher show was on. I heard that people called "homosexuals" were sinful and wouldn't "inherit the kingdom of God." and they could change if they turned toward Him. My secret room had been infiltrated.

Jimmy was in my fifth-grade class, but we never spoke. One day, we all took a standardized reading comprehension test. Jimmy finished first. I finished last.

That night, I called Mr. Norman. His voice crackled over the line, low and calm.

I told him everything—Ricky, the fight, the silence, the test.

After a pause, he said, "Sounds like normal fifth grade politics to me."

"Do you think I'm smarter than Jimmy?" I asked.

There was a soft chuckle. "Well, you're probably smarter in more ways... but not in all ways."

"Then, how come he finished the test so much faster than me?"

He thought for a moment. "Maybe you had different priorities. Maybe you were taking it more seriously."

I didn't say anything right away. I just sat there, holding the phone to my ear, chewing on that.

A week later, I was jolted awake by the long blast of a horn, the wail of sirens, then by cops walking the tracks beneath my window.

Not long after, Denny came into the kitchen, saying one of the Big Kids had been hit by a train. "He would've been alright if he kept his head down." The words startled me, and I was too shaken to ask for clarification on that. I kept my mouth shut. Ask a stupid question, get a stupid label.

It was Ryan M., a boy I hated, but not enough to want dead. In the abstract, we knew trains were dangerous, but this drove it home. Yet, Ryan survived with nothing more than a scar on his forehead. How could that be?

A week later, when I had settled enough to ask a question, Denny explained: "He was passed out when the train came. If he kept his head down, he would've been fine." I pictured him lying between the rails, the train passing over his body, his head lifting enough to brush against the undercarriage.

Months later, I pieced together the real story. Ryan, Denny, and Shawn had gotten drunk up Snake Hill. When Ryan passed out, they carried him down across Serenity and the tracks, laying him against the gravel embankment beneath the rails. He hadn't been hit by a train, he hadn't been run over—only grazed from the side.

I realized then how quickly I jumped to wild, incomplete, and usually negative versions of things—accepting catastrophe before bothering to find out the truth. Believing the worst about myself. Not that I learned my lesson. Admitting what I didn't understand, or what I actually wanted to know, felt more dangerous than living inside my own guesses.

My parents tried to keep me busy, but the sense of being a step behind kept going. I focused on a new job and joined the Boy Scouts. Mrs. Saranopoulos, the lady Ma worked for as a maid, was getting divorced from her husband—the psychiatrist who coined the word *Adyssemonia*, meaning the inability to label your own emotions. She moved to a house on Serenity Drive and needed a yard boy. I worked four hours a week for five bucks an hour, starting with repotting plants and setting up special lights for them in her basement. It didn't feel like a proper job, like a clerk tending to customers, but more like banishment to the basement. I'd seen the grand greenhouse at her old house, fresh and airy, everything alive under the sun. This basement version, cramped and buzzing with fluorescent tubes, felt like a cheap knockoff. Still, I did the work. The money was good, even if the trappings weren't.

Mrs. Saranopoulos had a habit of dispensing advice whenever she handed me my pay.

"Saving money is a way of being kind to yourself later. It isn't love or courage, but it can approximate them for a while." Still, a fresh twenty often led me straight to the Italian Shop for a chicken cutlet sandwich. I needed my love right away.

Around the same time, Dad pushed me to skip Webelos and go straight from Cub Scouts to Boy Scouts, making me the youngest in the troop. I should've been a Webelo. I could've tolerated the odd name and plaid handkerchief if it meant staying with kids my own age. Instead, I was planted in the wrong troop, expected to grow faster than I was ready for.

In Boy Scouts, I was expected to attend a winter camping trip. I bailed, even though my parents had already paid the nonrefundable food fee. At the next meeting, the others made a point of patting their bellies and licking their lips, letting me know they enjoyed the extra rations.

Then came the Christmas wreath fundraiser. I was handed a few dusty leads from the year before and expected to solicit solo. It was stressful, but in the end, I was surprised to have been earning a commission that I could keep. I had more money than ever to buy Christmas gifts.

Denny, to his credit, was a surprisingly thoughtful gift-giver that year. One day he pulled me aside and showed me what he'd gotten Sarah: a shiny new bike.

I was instantly jealous.

On Christmas morning, there were two bikes under the tree, each with a colorful banana seat.

"Sarah got two bikes?" I asked, trying to sound neutral.

"No," Denny said, grinning. "This one's for you. See the bar? It's a boy's bike." The idea that something like that might be for me hadn't even entered my mind.

My frame of mind kept doors closed I never realized were unlocked. I could have tried to talk, testing the ground with the Flannerys and with Ricky, but I wasn't used to reaching toward a hopeful future. I feared that trying for one would only make things worse.

9

Finally, the following March, Matt Flannery showed up at my house. Boredom did what apologies never could. I was in my basement, halfway through setting up a workbench. It wasn't functional and never would be, but I had something to show him anyway.

He told me he'd ended his personal ban on alcohol. And, remembering that I had suggested we give beer a try, he saw me as a potential drinking buddy. A select few in our group were experimenting now. On weekends, those Little Kids told the Big Kids what kind of beer they wanted before the packie run.

"Wanna come over? We got a pool table in my basement now."

Matt and I clicked after that. He quickly became my closest friend. Jimmy had shifted his attention to Ricky and to *General Hospital*, which he now quoted from as often as possible. Someone mentioned something way out in the *boonies*. So, now Jimmy had interject *boonies* or *boondocks* everywhere possible because the word was cool. For someone who hated vocabulary, he cared a lot about words. Matt and I agreed soap operas were for women.

Jimmy and Ricky were like sneakers on a powerline—dangling together, impossible to ignore.

Mrs. Flannery was their chauffeur, always carting them around in her newly acquired station wagon for Happy Meals at McDonald's, for ice cream at Friendly's, or *just for the ride*. I finally got invited to join them on one of their legendary trips to visit Mr. Flannery in Boston.

Matt called shotgun. Jimmy didn't bother to go for the front seat. He and Ricky took the back seat as a rule. Danny and I were in the rear bay.

The drive itself was half the fun. Mrs. Flannery had a little tradition: she'd hit the gas under every overpass, flooring it down and then up through the echo chamber with a devilish grin. We all howled like it was a rollercoaster.

Jimmy unrolled his window. "It's more fun riding around city streets than on back roads in the boondocks." Ricky was engaged with the group that day, trading jokes with Jimmy. I remember the energy more than the words.

Boston was alive in a way our town wasn't—cars honking, sidewalks bustling, buildings that made you overextend your neck. We pulled in front of a laundromat, which I assumed was the meet-up spot. Mr. Flannery was already outside, leaning on the wall. They said he worked there. Denny said he was homeless. I never really sorted that out, but the vibe was clear—he was part of the city, more than the family.

He was eating a banana. When he finished, he casually tossed the peel onto the windshield of the car in front of us. No drama. No explanation.

He and Mrs. Flannery smoked and talked on the sidewalk while we stayed in the car, watching. It wasn't awkward exactly, but it wasn't comfortable either. Danny kept glancing toward his dad, half-smiling like he was hoping for something more—some sign of closeness. Matt and Jimmy acted like it was all normal.

Eventually, Mr. Flannery came over to the car and pulled out a roll of bills like he was dealing cards at a poker game. Each of his sons got two dollars. Each guest got one. "Don't spend it all in one place," he said, smirking. There were few questions, no hugs, no goodbye. He turned and sauntered off; his job done.

I silently wished my father was like that—that he never came home. *More cash, less crap.*

One weekday, with nothing better to do, Matt and I headed over to Twombly Square, where we had heard the bowling alley had just installed three video games. We were some of the first kids to play them. I took to Asteroids, the slow, deliberate kind of game that rewarded patience and spatial awareness, and managed to land the top three high scores by the end of the afternoon. Matt, always more reactive and energetic, gravitated toward Pac-Man and Galaxian, carving out his own glory by getting his initials somewhere in the top five on both.

When I went back the next week, it was like none of it had happened. My Asteroids scores had been blasted, and Matt had climbed higher across all three games. He'd been going every day. I hadn't even known. I burned through my quarters fast and started to worry I'd lose face.

Matt noticed. "You'd do better if you knew how to sit," he said flatly. I didn't know what he meant.

I realized I was perched on the edge of the stool, back arched, knees tight together. Nervous posture. Not a very masculine one, apparently.

One afternoon the next week during a basement pool tournament while Jimmy was sulking over a scratch, Matt leaned back on the wobbly stool by the fuse box and announced:

"Next year's gonna suck."

Everyone looked up.

"Sixth grade. We'll have a different teacher for every class. And mandatory gym showers."

Everyone groaned in unison.

"That's totally gay," Bobby muttered.

Matt kicked a rusted coffee can. “I don’t care what they say. I’m not doing the group shower thing. No way.”

Jimmy nodded before Matt even finished. “Me neither. I’ll be out sick on those days. Every day, if I have to.”

“You can probably wear a bathing suit,” I offered, then added, “Then again, Flannerys keep their shirts on even when swimming.”

“That’s a sun thing,” Matt said. “We burn easy.”

Trying to shift the mood, I said, “On the bright side, we’ll have Home Mechanics.”

“Woodworking?” Matt asked.

“There’s a cooking class too. And we get to eat what we make.”

That got a few approving looks.

“And—” I added, aiming for something bold, “we’ll probably start going out with girls.”

Jimmy looked up, deadpan. “You don’t have to.”

“Well, we’re gonna want to,” I said. “It’s called puberty.”

“Some of us don’t want to be dirty,’” Jimmy added.

None of us knew how weird sixth grade was going to get—but we were already worried.

10

The last day of school was always the best day of the year. The longest stretch of freedom lay ahead—no homework, no tests, no teachers or outsiders watching to see if I measured up. But, with that freedom came an unexpected companion—a secret dread I couldn't shake. It crept in every time I passed a basketball court, a sinking feeling that tied my stomach in knots, whispering the truth I tried not to hear. The layered clothing of winter protected me. Vacations in secluded New Hampshire helped a little, promising fresh air and open space, but even then, the shadow of that court lingered in my mind.

Building walls was one way of keeping things from getting in or out; another was learning how to outmaneuver those who sought to control you. I saw examples of both that summer. It was time to work on the first-floor walls, lifting raw pine planks and setting them against the bare stud frame. We shouldered them one at a time, the resin bleeding onto our arms, the sap sticking to our shirts. Each board came fresh from the mill, slick with sap and water, so heavy it dragged at our arms as we lifted it, and we nailed them tight, sweating with the effort. But, in the weeks that followed, the heat drove the water out; the boards shrank apart, leaving thick spaces that made the walls look like they had been designed to breathe. What we had built to keep the outside world away turned porous almost at once. I didn't know it then, but my own defenses worked the same way—cobbled together with effort, impressive at first glance, but destined to gap and fail over time.

Dad's idea of fun and relaxation involved those time-share lottery giveaways. Free breakfast, a guided tour of some resort we'd never afford, and a decent prize at the end—we scored another 14-inch TV that way. All Dad had to do was sit through the pitch and find a way to say "no thanks," keeping the awkwardness to a minimum. They thought we were hooked by the possibility of a new car, but really we only wanted the consolation prize. And, they thought he wasn't ready to handle the pitch. Watching him, I learned that sometimes the best defense wasn't building walls but nodding along, taking what was handed out, and slipping away without signing anything. Later, the pitches weren't about resorts but about who I was supposed to like. Friends, teachers, relatives—all of them selling the same package: that being a boy meant showing interest in girls, proving it, making it obvious. I had to play along without buying in, accept the eggs and the TV but never the contract.

Sarah and I worked on a couple of TV shows together—the kind you invent to keep from going stir-crazy in a small town. Back in Beaumont, where friends and distractions were everywhere, we'd outgrown that sort of thing. But, up by the lake, four acres of woods, no neighbors our age, nowhere to walk but the dirt road or the empty streets to The Village Store, we turned to each other and the worlds we made up.

The main show was about an engaged couple shipwrecked on an island. Sarah always played the dignified and long-suffering woman, marooned with little more than the clothes on her back. I played both of her love interests: the dependable fiancé who built fires or worked on the lean-to and made dull speeches about staying hopeful—and the thief, a mysterious loner who lived deep in the forest and emerged only when the fiancé was away. The thief had no name, no origin story, and no morals. He existed to tempt her. He'd bring her things he stole—jewels, fruit, stories—and suggest that maybe her loyalty was just another kind of prison. He never stayed long. Just long enough to complicate things.

Sometimes Sarah let her character be swayed, sometimes she sent the thief away in a burst of dignity, and sometimes she denied he'd ever been there at all—but she never broke the world we'd built.

I'm not sure why I found this set-up so intriguing. Maybe the thief was a placeholder for some idea of danger or romance or disruption that wasn't allowed. Maybe it was an attempt to address a conventional story that didn't leave room for the plot the character needed to follow. I liked playing both parts. The one who protected and the one who disrupted. That island game rehearsed my own contradictions: the safe role and the forbidden one, the story everyone recognized and the story I had to keep hidden. It felt oddly satisfying to hold both, even then.

Sarah wanted nothing to do with games that required skill. She preferred the little gambling games—spinners, dice, games of chance. She was more pleasant to be around when she was winning. She considered having good luck to be a personality trait. She also had a few different pastimes she could call her own—the kind where I didn't mind if she outdid me. Musical hand-clap routines, cheer-leading chants—she had her own rhythm. Have at it, girl. Watching her, I decided that when the odds are stacked in your favor, you can afford to treat life like a game of chance. But, when they aren't, luck won't save you—you lean on skill, on effort, on control.

One part of summer back in Beaumont was the endless basketball games, always shirts versus skins. And, it was the skins that undid me. At first it was only a strange itch, sweet and uncanny. I didn't know what was causing it at first. Then, it grew into sudden swells of curiosity, guilt riding on their heels. Seeing the bodies—tanned muscles slick with sweat—stirred me up, pulled at me, compelled me to look, but I knew I wasn't supposed to. Joy and pain tangled together, leaving me stretched thin—until finally, I felt split in two.

I didn't really understand what "fag" or "faggot" meant—only that they were bad. But, I knew what "gay" meant. It meant a thousand things. Anything uncool was gay. A boy who cried too easily—gay. A boy who played clarinet or liked school—gay. A boy who said something kind to a girl, or stared too long at a woman in a magazine—somehow, also gay.

My father had this foolish way of threatening a spanking, "Do you want me to pull your pants down?" I hated when that was overheard. Gay.

I saw a report on the Christian news about a gay pride parade, and I didn't like what I saw on the screen. Gaunt guys with misshapen heads, many in drag. Even the muscular circus strongmen looked foolish to me. These were the people who accepted the difference and held it forward, and to my young eyes, they were ugly. I did not want to join their ranks.

Gay wasn't just a label. It was also a joke. A curse. And a warning.

And all I knew for sure was: I didn't want it anywhere near me.

Matt Flannery came with us up to the lake the weekend of the Gilmanton Labor Day Fair. Sarah and I took pride in showing him the secret spots in the woods—the mossy clearing where frogs clustered, the crooked tree that leaned just enough to climb but never broke, the little rise where you could see the water flash through the pines. Matt couldn't swim, but in the rowboat he was fearless, leaning forward and back as if the rod was part of him. He caught onto trolling quickly, reeling with such concentration that I wondered how someone who couldn't tread water could master fishing so easily. I felt something in that contradiction—envy, maybe, or admiration—that courage could exist right next to limitation.

The fair itself was its own kind of thrill. The air smelled of hay and fried dough, and the whole place hummed with risk. The gambling booths were the real draw: put down a quarter on a number and either walk away with one, two, or three more or nothing at all. Each round was over in a second, but my pulse kicked like it mattered. That small taste of luck and chance with real money at stake thrilled me more than a bald win.

Matt tried the ring toss and, with a throw that curved just right, won himself a jackknife. I felt the pang of paradox—two summers ago I had won one too, but Dad was still keeping it from me, locked away until I was "ready." It was his way of saying I wasn't competent yet, and standing there, watching Matt weigh the knife in his hand, a knife he was allowed to keep, I wondered if competence was ever going to find me.

Back in the projects, we ran into that California kid—someone's cousin in town for the summer. He wore a dress-shirt unbuttoned instead of a T-shirt like the rest of us, his confidence loose and easy, like the summer belonged to him. He talked openly, never weighing his words the way I did. Matt showed him the jackknife just as Sarah and her friend walked by. I saw the look on the cousin's face—half mesmerized, half scheming—and in a blink, the knife was in his pocket. Maybe absentminded, maybe on purpose, but caught all the same.

We called him out, voices sharp with outrage, and he handed it back, smirking as though the whole thing were just a game. But, I knew better.

He said, "I was distracted by those babes."

Later, when we played football, I relished tackling him to the ground. It wasn't just the game—it was justice, payback, and something else too: the rare chance to let my strength speak without words, to make someone who thought himself untouchable feel my weight instead.

What unsettled me wasn't only the jackknife he tried to pocket but the way he looked at my sister— His desire was so evident it seemed to illuminate the air between them. He stared, as openly and as proudly, as an unsheathed blade.

Mine stayed hidden, folded tight—until ironically I wrapped my arms around his bare, smooth waist, drove him down into the grass, and felt the press of his body against mine turning everything I'd buried into a dangerous unfurling.

PART II

Awakenings

11
First Crush

Beaumont wasn't just one beautiful hill—it was two hills with a valley between. There was Beaumont Hill and Haver Hill—not to be confused with, or pronounced like, Haverhill, the city. A running joke made the rounds, always starting with that mispronunciation: H*a*ver Hill, Taker Hill, and between them, Loser Valley.

Six elementary schools fed into Havercrest Middle, where everyone met, collided, and merged—like climbers on a ridge, scrambling for the best foothold. Every kid in town passed through there, bringing new faces, new voices, new kinds of beautiful.

On my first day, Denny said, "Letter grades in middle school. Now we can see how dumb you really are." Ma told me not to listen. "Just do your best, and you'll be fine." I had my heart set on becoming a carpenter.

The school itself was a puzzle. Built in stages, with no master plan, its halls zigged and zagged like puberty itself—confusing, uneven, unpredictable.

Eric was kind of cute, not the most handsome—plenty of boys had stronger jaws, sharper haircuts, broader shoulders. Blond, neat, with little oval glasses and a blue windbreaker zipped up halfway. But, something about him pulled at me right from the start, something deeper than looks. He was careful. Clean. Soft-spoken, but not shy. There was a crispness to him, like freshly folded laundry. He sat up straight. He smelled like Irish Spring. He was unapologetically there to learn—good grades, high goals, college already in sight. Prissy, some would have said. But, to me, he was perfect.

Tuesdays were the worst. I had second lunch mod. Only about fourteen boys were assigned to it. Ten could sit together per table. Kids did not spread out across the room. Of course, we all tried to cram into one table. The overflow landed on an adjacent one. It was like a pathetic game of musical chairs: without music, and catered.

The cafeteria felt hollow. Sound echoed oddly. But, Eric was there.

On one of the first Tuesdays, I managed to slip into the main table before the seats filled up. From the corner of my eye, I saw the Armenian kid with a little mustache, the guy with long, frizzy red hair, and Jimmy Flannery. They had resigned themselves to the other table. No one else would join them. The additional man-out, pulled a chair behind the guys at the main table and ate his lunch in his lap.

Eric spoke freely. Certain. Measured. He said, "Calm down, boys. I'm trying to enjoy my meal." Later, I heard him comment, "I watched a very moving film last night about an autistic child. They may have a lot they want to say but can't get the words out." I felt something fizz in my chest—not nerves, not fear. Something like... soda. Like I'd swallowed it too fast and now it wanted out, but not in a burp way. More like a story that didn't know how to start.

His words stayed with me all day.

Did he say artistic child? What does autistic even mean? I wasn't sure. But, I liked that he thought deeply about things. I liked that he said *meal* instead of *lunch*. I liked the way he paused before speaking, the way he held his fork.

I didn't know if I wanted to be next to him or to be him. Maybe both. I just knew I wanted him to want me there.

I looked across that empty cafeteria and imagined the two of us, sitting at our own table—not because we had nowhere else to go, but because we chose it. Because, we belonged with each other.

Every other variation occurred. Sometimes, I made the main table. Sometimes, I sat alone. Sometimes, the reject table.

"This is Azmat and Andrew," Jimmy said one day, motioning toward the two boys. "I'm around them all day—in the resource room." He said it like it was an obligation. All their academic classes took place in that little half-classroom on the second floor, partitioned off from the rest of the school like a forgotten closet. I saw it as a lazy place; more games, snacks, and napping opportunities.

I was there too, sort of, but only for one period a week—*Learning How to Learn*, the other half of the split classroom. It was an "enrichment" course, supposedly for high-achieving students. But, the wall that divided us was thin and made of fabric coated panels on sliders. I could slip notes to the Flannerys through the gap at the floor. I tried to use it as proof: *See? I am special too.* But, it didn't count much. Being in regular classes was so uncool.

Midyear, our family's income finally dropped low enough that I qualified for a lunch discount ticket. Each morning when we passed the cafeteria, we grabbed the reusable ticket with our initials that were laid out on a tray. I'd pocket it like a badge of belonging. It wasn't the full free lunch the others had, but it was close enough to gesture toward sameness. A soft echo of belonging. I wanted the main table, but I also didn't want to lose status at the reject table.

Nobody spoke much at our table. Azmat mostly ate with his elbows tight to his sides, eyes down. He had several plastic containers with contents I did not recognize. Andrew peeled the crust off his sandwich like he was doing surgery. There was plenty of elbow room.

"You get one of those weird yogurt cups?" Jimmy asked, eyeing my tray.

"Fruit-on-the-bottom," I said. "Tastes like candy."

Azmat looked up. "They ever put one with purple fruit?"

"No," I said. "It's always red or orange. Like they've never heard of blueberries."

At least, we didn't have to yell to hear each other.

Gym class was fine, once you got used to it. Whenever you saw guys in the halls with damp hair, there was a kind of silent solidarity—evidence that we'd all survived the same ritual. Families handed us terms like *peep* and *dink* to describe our manhood. No wonder so many of us hesitated to go public. And, who knew? Azmat had chest hair already, and Andrew's red hair was not reserved for his head.

I'd found an old copy of *Everything You Always Wanted to Know About Sex (But Were Afraid to Ask)* in a box of remainders Dad brought home from the library. The section on homosexuality made me queasy. Those three times I'd played doctor with other boys in fifth grade left me hollow. I didn't want to do the acts the book described—some seemed anatomically impossible anyway—so I concluded I couldn't be gay. I figured attraction to girls would arrive eventually.

And yet, whenever I imagined what it would have been like if Eric and I had gym the same period, I lost my breath and had to think of something else—anything else. I realized I could fall in love with other boys, and now that truth had become amplified. My attachment to Ricky had been a steadier, quieter version of the same kind of pull.

I went on autopilot thinking about it one day when I was walking home alone.

The feeling had occurred in sudden waves before. I was five, and he was ten—maybe eleven. A fourth grader in a school play, barefoot on the stage, a lantern in hand, singing proudly.

"Consider yourself at home...Consider yourself one of the family..."

He was *Oliver*, but really, he was Paul. And somehow, he was light itself—brave enough to stand out.

"It's clear, we're going to get along..." (from Lionel Bart's *Oliver!*)

Afterward, he wasn't famous. Just a boy from the projects with a pleasant smile and fast legs. But, when Ricky waved him into my yard one day, I didn't dare blink, afraid the magic would disappear.

Paul picked up a tuna can, spun a story, turned it into a baseball, a spaceship, a crown. I laughed so loudly. Stood so still.

He left before I asked what I wanted to ask. Or knew how.

That wave came again in fourth grade. That damn fourth-grade musical! Tom Lincoln played *Peter Pan*—tights, spectacle, bravado. I was smitten. And now, with Eric, it was a tsunami.

That year I began using a few beers to help compartmentalize. I could wallow even harder or pivot away for a while.

We wanted cash more than ever, because there were more kids around showing off new stuff. Our methods had changed. Shoplifting and nighttime theft were in vogue. I was involved in a few big heists for good measure, though I never had a clear sense of how wide the crime spree really had been.

Danny and I tried to emulate his brother Matt's recent success—he'd scored a ten-speed somehow. Our version? A sad little pink undersized "Ladybug" bike we mistook for treasure in the dark. We should've just brought it back, but instead we salvaged it for parts.

I was also a lookout for one of the car stereo jobs. I never liked stealing. Even when the rush hit—when someone yanked a stereo clean out of the dash or scored something else valuable—I kept thinking about the owner. What they'd feel, coming back to broken glass and silence.

I knew what it felt like. Our house had been robbed twice—Denny's stereo equipment was the draw. One time, they also chose to grab $3.50 in change from my drawer. It stung. Knowing someone dared to enter our space. And, it was confusing. The Flannery's neighbor, Ryan M, the youngest and meanest of the Big Kids was involved in some kind of way.

Our biggest haul came from an unlocked truck parked at Chrissy's old house. Inside was a heavy steel toolbox full of high quality tools. Danny and I had cased the location. We needed help to complete the mission. We'd been drinking a bit—liquid courage. Since Matt was clearly overserved, he was of no use that night except as extra muscle. He and I lugged the box down the street together until Mrs. Flannery caught us right at the edge of the projects.

"What's that?" she asked, arms crossed.

"Wood for go-karts," Danny mumbled. "We found it in the trash."

"Drop it and come home," she said. I was sleeping over that night. We left the box on its side right under the streetlight. A big steel elephant in plain view.

Five boys. Three beds. One big problem.

That toolbox was sitting right at the halfway mark between the truck and their apartment. We thought that if someone reported it, we would be implicated. Ricky figured the best thing to do was leave it there. It would find its way back to the owners. The rest of us were wigging out. Buzzed and wired, I got a surge of adrenaline and decided to make a move. I climbed out the window onto the roof, spider-walked to the edge, then hung from the gutter and dropped to the ground. I lugged the toolbox through three back yards and snuck it into the Flannery basement.

Getting back up was the hard part. I zipped over to John Johnson's front stairs, climbed onto his railing, leapt up, grabbed the gutter, and muscled my elbows in until I could swing a leg over. I hauled myself up and slid back into the window.

I was the hero of the night.

Our names never made the paper for that—but our damage did.

The next day, we drew lots to divvy up the contents, the way pirates might divide treasure, though ours came in a shiny new toolbox instead of an old chest. My pick was second, leading me to a file set—useful, maybe, but the handle was missing, the metal nubs biting bare into my palm. The real prize was the red Swiss Army Knife, the one with the saw and the scissors that snapped shut with a satisfying click. The knife looked brand new—bright red with a little gold cross on the base, gleaming blade catching the light. If I could bring it to school and leave it on my desk for all to see, I surely would. It's the kind of thing Eric would love.

When it landed in Danny's hand, my stomach dropped.

"That was supposed to be mine," I muttered, trying to keep the edge out of my voice.

Danny grinned, turning it over like a magician's prop. "Guess luck's on my side."

The box itself was hidden off the tracks in a far-away bush, stashed there because it was "too recognizable." Months later they salvaged it, sprayed it over with dull black paint, in an attempt to erase its past.

The whole split was unfair, and I knew it. No weight was given to the extra effort. I'd put in—the heavy lifting, the acrobatics. Everyone shrugged when I mentioned it. I let that go.

In the end, I bought the knife off Danny for twenty dollars. He pocketed the cash with a smirk, and I walked away holding the knife at last, not sure if I'd won a prize or just paid double for something I already deserved. Sometimes that's how I made do—claiming what was forbidden, then paying over and over just to hold onto something others seemed to have ready access to.

Cooking class was supposed to be easy. Fun, even. Eric was in that class, and so was Jimmy, which added pressure. We each had to take a turn cooking something in front of the group under the big tilted mirror—one of those angled contraptions so everyone could see what you were doing from overhead. The mirror's glare highlighted every move, every mistake made. The class was full of chatter, and light laughter, but all I heard was the pounding of my heart thinking about the day I would be scrutinized.

When that fateful day arrived, I picked Pannukakku, Nanny's specialty. Translated as "small family pancake," but it was more like a sweet custard with golden edges and a soft, eggy center. Cold or warm, it always hits the spot. I should've had the foresight to bring a premade batch of hers—served chilled, it might've made up for what was about to unfold.

Things started badly. I cracked an egg too fast and a shard of shell made it into the batter. Eric pointed it out—helpfully or cruelly I wasn't sure—but someone laughed, and then a few others joined in. I felt my ears go red and I shrank to nothing. Amazing how a single eggshell could feel like the whole fragile soufflé of my life had collapsed.

I stirred quicky, trying to recover. The pan was supposed to sizzle when I poured in the batter. It didn't. Just sat there like I'd dumped it on cold linoleum. No hiss, no puff of steam, just dead silence. I knew we wouldn't finish in time for the class to have samples. There was nothing to distract from my failure.

Afterward, I couldn't think of a single thing to say to Eric. I never could. Maybe "thanks" or "good catch." I stayed mute the whole cleanup.

My wood working skills were worse than my cooking. There was a lot of side talk in that class that made me uncomfortable. The home mechanics teacher noticed my shyness. Mr. Hughes had a square head, the kind you'd think only grew on vice-principals and county cops. Thought he was clever. He believed in curing shyness through "immersion." His method? Make me repeatedly yell "YALP!" at full volume in front of the whole class. Some kind of primal confidence therapy. It felt like being thrown in a lake with rocks in your pockets as a swim lesson. So much for my future in carpentry.

Later, I saw Eric in the hall carrying a wooden lamp, lightbulb and all.

I watched Mr Hughes over the next few weeks. He was a braggart and laughed at his jokes more than anyone else did. I began covertly working on the class base piece—a thin rectangle with two rounded corners that we were supposed to turn into a bookend, bookshelf, or lamp base. I carved it into a tombstone.

Carefully, proudly, I burned: MISTER HUGHES R.I.P. It got me my first detention. But, it was worth it—not for Hughes, really. For the carpenter I'd already buried.

Eric was never shy about raising his hand in class. He had a lot to say, and most of it was pretty good. In English, he volunteered—eagerly, almost proudly—to read his paper aloud: My Most Memorable Meal. It was about roast duck and blackberry glaze at a family friend's summer house. He made it sound so delicious, and he sprinkled in touches of humor like it was part of the recipe.

He always seemed to have someone to talk to, whispering confidently to the girl who sat next to him in social studies, cracking a secret joke that made her cover her mouth to stifle a laugh.

Once, when a teacher mispronounced my last name during roll call, Eric corrected her. "It's with an 'r,' actually," he said, like it mattered.

Up until then, I'd half-wondered if I was invisible to him.

One weekend, I was rifling through my father's bureau drawers—as one does—when I found an envelope of old photo negatives. I held them up to the light, flipping through until one stopped me cold.

It looked like Eric.

I stared at it, stunned. The hair was the right shape, the face just a little rounder, but the resemblance was uncanny. Slowly, I realized—it wasn't Eric. It was me. My dark hair, reversed. My features, a little younger.

Eric was a lot like me—but opposite. Same height, same build. He wore glasses; I needed glasses. We both tried to dress well. He pulled it off. Both fledgling intellectuals, one proud, the other ashamed.

What did it mean?

For about six months, the Bee Gees were what we grooved to. The Flannerys had a silver boombox the size of a baby coffin in their basement. To start it played two songs on repeat: *How Deep Is Your Love* and *You Should Be Dancing*. We began parting our hair in the middle with our switchblade combs on the ready in our pockets.

How Deep Is Your Love spun like a slow tide through the buzz in my head, and everything around me—the peeling ceiling, the hum of the boombox, the faint smell of heating oil and plastic—blurred until all I could see was Eric, backlit, golden. A music video directed by longing.

The Bee Gees kept asking *how deep*—as if they needed me to measure it— I didn't have an answer, just images: the curve of his jaw, the clean whiteness of his teeth, the hint of something in his smile that might have meant more, if only I dared to believe it.

A year later, tastes changed completely. Disco was gay.

We had other, more persistent traditions to follow. With Christmas approaching again, it was time for the Flannerys to carry out their family tradition—stealing a tree from the Lions Club. Shawn used to handle it, but this year he was passing the torch to his younger brothers. I, for one, wanted no part of it. Too much of a paradox: the season of giving, kicked off by petty theft.

Our family had its own tradition—pay as little as possible for a tree. Sometimes we dusted off the artificial silver one that electronically rotated. We propped it on a table to make it look taller. Other years we bought an irregular real tree and crossed our fingers. Short and fat is not a good look. One year, my dad scouted our land in New Hampshire and cut down the best tree he could find. It couldn't support a single bulb, just strands of garland and some tinsel clinging to it precariously. Thinking how hard Eric would laugh at our tree made me sad.

Jimmy was determined to find something special for Ricky—something that meant something—so he was willing to travel deep into the boondocks if that's what it took. Among other things, he bought two knitted caps: a green one for himself and a blue one for Ricky.

The Flannery kids picked out their own gifts, played with them for a bit, then handed them over to their mother to wrap. Efficiency and immediate gratification over sentiment.

Members of our family, including Sarah and I, by contrast, took our Christmas shopping very seriously. We tried to figure out what each family member might actually like, scoured the department store flyers, circled sale items, and planned accordingly. Surprise was an important element of Christmas morning.

On New Year's Eve, the Flannery basement was already thick with noise and carbonation by the time I got there. Matt was chugging from a can, then slamming it on the floor with a triumphant, "That's five! Who's behind now?"

"Let's chug number six, race you?" Bobby asked, cracking one open with his teeth.

I tried to catch up. Bad idea. My stomach started to pitch like the sea.

"I gotta—bathroom," I muttered, pushing past kids playing quarters and barely registering the clatter of furniture as I bumped into it.

Somehow, I made it home, slipped past my parents like a spy, did my business, rinsed my mouth, and was back out the door in under ten minutes. I made it as far as the Flannery's basement stairwell—then missed a step. My ankle bent sideways when I tried to catch myself.

"Damn," I barked, falling to the floor.

No one was in the basement anymore. It was eerily silent. Then, Matt appeared at the top of the stairs, silhouetted like an angel or a horror movie monster.

"What happened to you?" he asked.

"Broke my ankle, I think."

Matt came down, helped me up. His arm hooked around me, and we hobbled over to John Johnson's section of the basement—darker, with an old floral couch. His arms felt... solid, warm.

Matt laughed, leaning so I could sit. I didn't let go. I didn't want to. "Dude?" he lost his balance and fell, landing half on top of me. He groaned and rolled off.

"Let's see this injury." He tugged off my shoe, then the sock. "No swelling. You're full of it."

He stood.

"Enjoy the couch, faker," and disappeared upstairs.

I laid there for a few minutes, feeling stupid, abandoned. Did he think I was coming on to him? I wanted Eric in my arms, not Matt. That was for sure. This was confusing.

Then, I heard footsteps again. It was Danny.

"You still down here?"

"I think my ankle's messed up."

He squinted at me. "Let's get you up."

With Danny's help, I got back outside. I kept just my hand on his shoulder for balance. Was not going to have a more full embrace and risk those warped feelings coming up again. Soon something shifted—I had this unexpected burst of energy. Like now that someone believed me, I had something to prove.

I started hopping on one foot. Efficiently. Proudly.

The gang had moved to the center field, over by the Mundts'. I joined them and spotted Matt.

"Hey!" I shouted. "Thanks for ditching me, jackass!"

Matt grinned. "You're faking!"

"You left me!"

"What're you gonna do, pogo me to death?"

Everyone started laughing. Then someone yelled, "Get him!"

It turned into a full-on chase. I bounded toward the big tree near the edge of the field—the one we'd jammed with discarded Christmas trees to make a kooky sort of nest.

I climbed fast, and once inside the thicket of pine and tinsel, the game changed. No one needed to use both feet up there. I could get leverage with each of my three limbs. The re-foliated branches slapped and tangled, leveling the playing field. I held my own in three short skirmishes, evading or besting anyone who climbed up. If only Eric could see me now.

Despite being surrounded, I saw my chance and leapt out, landing hard on my good foot. I hopped toward the tracks and cleared the fence. Alongside the rails, where the wooden ties were being torn up for replacement, there was a long ditch. Perfect. I dropped in and used the ground for balance and support, crutch-walking home like a hero returning from war.

The next morning, Danny stopped by.

"Hey," he said, "your ankle's actually swollen."

I smirked. "Told you."

The alarm went off with a steady scream of angst. Too loud, and sustained past the point of reason. No one feared fire. But, many were distressed, cupping their ears to avoid the hard drone which never seemed to end. Students rose, scraping chairs across linoleum in an unintentional chorus, and filed toward the doors in a slow, disjointed line. We wanted out fast but congested halls prevented more immediate relief. People looked around wondering whether this was a drill or whether someone had played a prank.

"Check everyone's hands for ink," someone suggested to no one in particular.

As the alarm finally ceased, I ended up behind Eric.

Not by design—or not entirely—but once I saw where he was standing, I slowed just enough to fall into the stream behind him. He adjusted his collar, folded his paper with precision, and slipped it into a folder without a wrinkle. Unhurried. Measured.

He stepped down the stairs with care, like every footfall was something to get right.

Outside, the air was mild for January—crisp and dry, the kind that made everything feel thinner, more exposed. Sunshine bounced off the snowbanks, making the world too bright to look at all at once.

Eric's shirt was sky blue. His sleeves were cuffed neatly to the middle of his arms, and the fine blond hair on his forearms shimmered in the light.

I noticed he was tapping his fingers lightly against the seam of his jeans in rhythm with his steps—1, 2, 3, 4. Like Morse code for me to decipher.

I stayed quiet, something hot and sour churning in my stomach. I wanted to say something—I couldn't think of what. I could've caught up to Eric. I didn't. I stayed behind him, step for step.

His rhythm had changed. Now it was 1, 2... pause... 3, 4.

We reached the field and stood in the soft chaos of loosely formed rows. Eric was three feet in front of me. His hands were in his pockets now, his gaze fixed on the treetops beyond the parking lot, like he wasn't really standing there with the rest of us.

For a minute, I let myself believe we were connected. That somehow, across those three feet, he could feel me watching—and didn't mind.

Then the bell rang twice, and the moment, like the drill, was over.

Later that day, I was passing through the cafeteria toward the non-academic wing straining to see if that was Eric over in the corner when Ronny Hanson stopped me, placing both hands on my shoulders.

"You're not supposed to be down here now," he said. "Didn't you tell me you were stuck with Mr. Muir all morning?"

"I just got free."

"Wait, you've got him for homeroom, core reading and writing..."

"And social studies."

"Whoa. I can barely tolerate him for homeroom."

"He's okay."

Ronny Hanson was somewhat funny-looking. Tall but narrow, like his height was mismatched to his frame. He reminded me of Alfalfa from *The Little Rascals*. I thought he might be part Asian. That day he wore a wine-colored shirt with a faint diamond pattern and a small zipper under the neck. He was also in my gym class.

Ronny always had a little comment for me. Usually an observation about my clothes or posture. Then came the questions. Where did I live? What elementary school had I gone to? Whose that you walk to school with? Was Bobby Sharpo really as tough as he looked?

Ronny leaned over during homeroom and whispered, "Do you watch *Saturday Night Live*?"

"Yeah," I said, reflexively. I had heard of it. Denny had been watching it.

He grinned. "Did you see one with Steve Martin? White hair? He does that 'wild and crazy guys' thing—talking in an accent, trying to pick up chicks. You must've seen it."

"Yeah, yeah," I said. "Sounds familiar."

That Saturday, I tried to stay up but fell asleep on the couch during the news. Denny didn't bother waking me, even though he was sitting right next to me.

The next week, Sarah announced she was staying up too, like it was some shared mission. I wasn't having that. She set an alarm; I covertly made sure it wouldn't go off.

I made it through the whole show that night. It wasn't even that funny. But, at least now, when Ronny asked, I wouldn't have to lie with nothing under it. And, I stayed ahead of Sarah.

Then, one day Ronny asked, "What religion are you? I'm Catholic."

He pulled a small item from under his shirt—it looked like a stamp laminated to cardboard, hanging from a string.

"I'm Protestant."

"I wear this," he said, lifting it slightly, "because this saint will let me skip purgatory and go straight to heaven. I wear it all the time, keep it in reach when I take a shower. What kind of Protestant?"

"The usual kind."

"Come on. There's Lutheran, Baptist, Presbyterian. Are you Presbyterian? Were you baptized?"

"No."

His face grew serious. "You need to be baptized. That's the dumbest reason to go to hell."

Chrissy, who used to live near the playground, had moved to another part of Beaumont. I started seeing her in the halls. She looked different now—her hair was cut short, the glasses were gone, replaced by contacts, and she wasn't skinny anymore.

Chrissy called me out of the blue.

"I know you like me," she said. "Your friends told me. I figured we might as well go on a date."

"I used to like you—in first grade. What exactly did they say?"

"They said you still like me. That you're just too shy to talk to me."

"I never told them to say that. They lied."

That was Jimmy and Bobby's handiwork. They had a chuckle about it, but then they were quick to ask, "Why don't you go on a date with her?"

I shrugged.

"I don't know... I liked her when I thought pop rocks were amazing."

They laughed, but I didn't.

It wasn't just about Chrissy. It was about me—the fact that I couldn't like her if I tried.

Liking boys was the worst.

Not liking girls was a close second.

Richard Hanson was girl-crazy. He made it known.

"Who do you want to screw?" he asked one day in the hallway, like it was normal.

I tried to play it cool. "I like to keep my options open. Maybe get to know them first."

He scoffed. "I'd do Cheryl and Hanna. And Kara, but only doggy style."

"So, you're a romantic?" I said.

"So, what girl do you like?"

I paused. "Laura is nice." Eric was better.

It wasn't a lie. Just the safest name I could find.

"I'd screw her with the lights on," Ronny said with a gleam in his eye.

"Won't you go to hell for that?"

"You've got it all wrong. We all sin. You just repent after, and God's good with it." He leaned in a little. "Now—tell me, once and for all, what's your religion?"

"I told you."

"Not specific enough."

"You don't need to know."

"I thought we were friends."

"Too soon to tell... kidding. I just don't want to hear crap about it."

"Would I give you crap?"

"Give me a twenty and I might be in the mood to share."

"Come on!"

I had had enough explaining to kids in the projects about being a Christian Scientist. The arguments always circled back to the same point:

"If your religion says prayer is enough, why'd you go to the doctor?"

There was no answer that satisfied them. Not them, not me.

Ronny went off the deep end. He said I was dodging his questions, lying to him.

He felt insulted. And he made me pay for it. It made no sense whatsoever.

First, he started saying crazy things about me in the cafeteria, in the locker room—loudly, like he wanted everyone to hear. Then it escalated, turned into a chant.

"John Lindstrom gave Ross Most a blow job!"

I didn't know what that was, not really.

He yelled it over and over like he was starting a protest. People laughed. Some joined in.

Ross was just a classmate. I'd talked to him a few times. He had a double-jointed elbow, I had a double-jointed thumb. That was the foundation of our friendship—two odd joints. Now we were linked by something uglier.

This went on for weeks. I avoided Ronny, avoided the echo of my name in the halls.

I couldn't help but wonder if Eric had heard the exclamations. It made my stomach twist. Eric—so composed, so precise—probably hated that kind of vulgarity. *Maybe he thought I was part of it or the kind of boy who deserved that kind of rumor. Maybe he just pitied me. Was he a little intrigued?* I didn't know what was worse: Eric thinking the screed was true, or Eric thinking Johnny was too weak to shut it down. Either way, it built an additional hurdle between us—one I didn't know if I could clear.

Eventually Ronny said he'd stop.

"Just tell me your religion," he said. "That's all I wanted."

I still refused to be told what to do.

"Tell me right now," he said, "or I'll start up again."

I wanted it to end—but not by giving in. "The first word is Christian," I said. "You have to figure out the rest. It isn't Christian Math, not Christian Social Studies, so...?"

He didn't guess. Instead, he chanted using noise where curiosity had failed.

"It's Christian Science, reject!" I snapped. " Now never talk to me again."

For the next week, Ronny was quieter, but not in a peaceful way. He'd walk past without looking at me, shoulders tight like he was holding something in. Once, I caught him whispering to a group by the lockers, their glances snapping toward me like rubber bands. But, he didn't yell again. No more chants. Just a smug smirk some days, like he'd won, and other days, nothing at all. The campaign hadn't ended so much as cooled into silence, the kind that doesn't bring relief—just room for your thoughts to echo.

About two weeks later, Ronny hovered by the lunch table where I sat alone, a chocolate milk in one hand and that same tight-lipped smirk on his face. He didn't sit, just stood there for a second, then said, "I told my sister you were a Seventh-Day Adventist. She said that's cool."

"O-kaay?" I said. I couldn't tell if Ronny was making a joke or if he really thought that's what I'd said. Either way, I didn't correct him. It was easier to let the comment stand.

He gave a half-shrug, "So...you still got that double-jointed thumb?" It wasn't much, but it was something—less a truce than a test balloon, floated to see if I'd swat it down or let it drift. I nodded and bent my thumb back like a party trick. Ronny snorted, then walked off taking that as a win.

I also had a study hall with Eric. And study, I did. He sat one aisle over, two seats up. A safe distance—close enough to see how he leaned forward when he read and how tightly his hand curled around a pencil—far enough to avoid detection. Once the feelings took root, that was it. No more slow build, no more questioning. Just a sudden, irreversible shift. I wanted more.

There was a strange urgency in his presence—an emotional voltage that surged through me like a directive I didn't know how to obey. In his absence, there was a blankness. A dull ache that made everything else seem like filler. I'd catch myself replaying the tiniest memories: the way his mouth moved when he said "obviously," the ripple of his laugh when he got something unexpectedly right. Trivial moments became relics I worshiped in private.

Why him? Why me? Why not him and me?

There was no one to talk to. No vocabulary for it. Not in my house. Not in the neighborhood. Not in school. The encyclopedias—our last-resort source of knowledge—had no entry on the subject. The dictionary definition was curt, clinical, shaming. The puberty section in my book talked about erections, circle jerks, nocturnal emissions. But, nothing about this. Nothing about wanting to just be near someone. Not for sex, not even for a kiss—just to be accepted by him. *A kiss might not be so bad.*

Sometimes I imagined we were already friends. That I could go over to his house after school and we'd sit on his bedroom floor, side by side, passing comics back and forth, talking in low voices—not about school. Not about girls. Just anything else he enjoyed.

One day in study hall, Eric got up to talk to the teacher. I lowered my head and let the daydream cascade out: maybe I'd ask him to tutor me. I'd pay him. Make it sound casual—math, maybe. Or English. I was mid-script in my head when I felt a tap on my shoulder.

I looked up—and there he was. Face to face. Eye to eye. Squatting beside me in the aisle. Close enough to see a tiny freckle under his eye I'd never noticed before. His presence hit like a flare in the dark.

"Do you have the directions for the English assignment?"

What English assignment?

My brain stuttered. This was the moment. *Find the info he seeks. Say something clever. Something that makes him stay. Anything.*

"Sorry, I don't."

He nodded and returned to his seat. I watched him go, heart thundering.

He'd got permission to talk to me. That had to mean something. Didn't it? Couldn't it?

No, stupid. If he felt the same, he'd know how to say so. He'd say something more. He wouldn't just squat and vanish.

What I was feeling was what girls were said to feel when they fell for boys—completely pure passion. I was just a lonely kid, wanting something vague yet vast.

So, I said nothing. And felt everything.

12
Just Friends

I am not sure when it started, but Ricky had a girlfriend in the summer before he entered middle school. And, by all accounts, she was very pretty. While at different schools, he and I both found someone to love. His feelings came to fruition. Mine did not.

His girlfriend had a long blond mane, good teeth, good posture, and was developing early. If she were a horse, she'd be a champion racer. Kisses were exchanged, parents were informed, phone calls were placed on weeknights. Who could blame her? He had a face that could still pass for adorable, but you could already see the handsome in him taking shape.

I had far less angst about loving Ricky than I did about loving Eric. The reaction was more about Ricky than it was about me. He was lovable. He was everyone's preferred friend. Girls liked him. Guys liked him. Teachers liked him. You couldn't even resent him for it. He was just Ricky. Maybe it felt less like a crisis of identity and more like a natural response to something extrinsic and universal. And, the distance between platonic love and something higher involved less of an escalation than a sudden rocket launch from ground zero.

We were on each other's periphery all along, but our one-to-one friendship did not really resume until he advanced to middle school. Overlapping journeys home after school made a real difference. However, his mom was determined to keep her first-born child "on track." College-bound. Well-rounded. Structured. She was a stickler about homework, hygiene, and proper snacks.

Ricky played Little League, Pop Warner football, and swam year-round. I don't know how he had time to sleep.

Still, somehow, he found time for me.

It started to really pour just as we crossed the street by the Lions Club building—the kind of rain that lets loose like a broken dam. Ricky laughed and sprinted ahead, his backpack bouncing, his sneakers slapping wet pavement.

"Come on!" he shouted over his shoulder, already halfway up the sidewalk.

I followed, slipping once, nearly dropping my towel. We reached the inner walkway just as water started to gush from the downspouts, thunder mumbling in the distance.

We both bent over, catching our breath, dripping like stray dogs. Ricky wiped rain from his forehead with the sleeve of his shirt and gave me a crooked smile.

I dried my hair with my towel, then handed it to Ricky. "Who knew we'd have to dry off before we even got in the pool."

This was one of the first times Ricky let me tag along to his swim lessons. He swam laps while I made use of the free swim area—an arrangement that worked for both of us.

"Close one," he said. "You were about to drown on land."

"Speak for yourself. You look like you swam here."

He shook his head like a dog and sprayed me with droplets.

We sat on the cold concrete ledge under the eaves, facing the locked doors of the Lions Club. The train platform was empty except for a crazed squirrel darting between puddles. Below the tracks, the foot tunnel was a dark hole. A shirtless jogger suddenly bounded through, making huge splashes.

"This place always creeps me out a little," I said.

"It's the echo," Ricky replied. "And the fact that the Lions Club has never once let a kid in. I think it's just a secret gym for grumpy old men."

He unzipped the outer pocket of his backpack and pulled out a granola bar, offering half without a word. I took it.

"Your mom really schedules you tight, huh?" I asked, trying to sound chill.

Ricky shrugged. "She says if I have time to stand still, I'll start falling behind."

"You ever want to just stay where you're at?"

"Sometimes," he said, chewing.

"Take the Flannerys. They do whatever they want, and it's like... fun and easy for them. That might bite them in the butt someday."

We were quiet for a moment. The rain softened to a whisper.

"Still," he said, "I envy it sometimes. Like how they can just hang out all day and don't care."

"Yeah," I said. "But, eating frosting for lunch can't be that healthy."

We both laughed.

"I got to make this work," he mumbled. "I only get the in-between times like this to have any fun." He looked around checking for authority, then pulled out a pack of Marlboro's and passed me one.

"The rest is flashcards and Spanish verbs that are supposed to lead to a better future."

Ricky was the only one who took to smoking with any real devotion. I lit up mostly to stay in step with him, to share in the ritual.

I nodded. "Well, for what it's worth, these times are pretty good."

He glanced at me—with a small smile and then softer. "Yeah they are."

A train passed by, making the ka-chunk, ka-chunk sounds, but didn't stop.

We sat there, listening to the water gush from the stone gutter above, the smell of wet cement rising. I noticed how the skin under his eye was smooth; no darkness, just one clean curve of cheek to eyelid. And his shoelaces—each strand was two different colors braided tight together. I thought about how time moved differently when you were waiting with someone instead of alone. It was like time slowed down, and you were happy it did.

Meanwhile, in seventh grade, Richard Germane had been a name long before he was a presence. I'd heard about his fights with Jimmy Flannery, the way he cornered boys over the slightest hint of softness. By the time I had him in class, he'd appointed himself my publicist.

"This is Johnny Lindstrom," he announced one day to an unfamiliar peer. "He's in most of my classes—and he's a total faggot."

After that it was small, regular abrasions. Bowl-job. Blow-job jokes. "Are you soph-th-ticated?" said like a private punchline. Eventually, I tried, "Ask your mother," which only made him worse. Eventually he didn't need words. His stare alone was enough. His attention was the insult.

Ronny Hanson, strange tormentor of the past, sat across from me in art. We worked on our paper-mâché masks at the long table in back, paint-water clouding in jars between us. We'd mixed our own color the week before—mostly red and yellow, a little white, the smallest drop of blue. A loud, stubborn orange. We called it *Vermilion Verve* and painted everything with it. Our two masks looked like variations in the same collection at first. Mine stayed mostly orange, broken by two clean stripes. Ronny covered his with purple and gray, almost burying the color, leaving it mainly on the small irregular protrusion near the chin that looked like a handle.

"Nice handle," I said.

"It's intentional," he said. "Adds mystery."

We traded silly insults. He was careful to avoid eye contact for long. Every time someone walked by, he went quiet and angled away, like we weren't talking at all.

Ms. Deroche stopped behind us. She called mine "strong" and "symmetrical," then moved on without mentioning his. He tried to pretend he didn't care.

During clean-up, I saw the masks side by side. Mine looked loud and deliberate. His looked smaller, half-hidden, the orange barely showing through.

In a later class, I painted a yellow cartoon smile on mine. The teacher was horrified.

Mr. Norman, our long-ago teacher turned friend, had moved into the little house behind the big one with all the roommates. He gave Jimmy Flannery and me a key so we could water his plants when he was out of town. Once, we commandeered the place for an afternoon. The most rebellious we got was smoking on the screen porch—the only time Jimmy and I ever smoked together.

It was cold enough to see our breath. The cigarette tips were the only light between us.

From the front house someone cheered at a television. The porch boards creaked in the wind. "Think he'll still let us hang around once the girlfriend moves in?" Jimmy asked.

"Guess we'll see."

I watched the dark yard awhile, then said, "Do you love him?" I wanted to see how he'd react.

Jimmy froze mid-inhale. "No. That's... weird. Do you?"

"Of course. He's like a father. Or a cool big brother."

He tapped ash into the Coke can without looking at me. "I'm gonna pretend you didn't ask that."

He went inside. The screen door snapped shut, leaving me with the cold and the empty chairs.

Weeks later, Norman showed us the commercial version of his Egyptian game. The one we'd played before had carved sticks and a wooden box with engravings along the sides. This one was a flat board with printed colors and dice.

"That version would cost people eighty dollars," he said. "This one's twenty."

We had gotten used to the sticks. We didn't get used to the downgrade.

The last time we saw Mr. Norman, we went along with him on a date to the movies. His girlfriend picked *Grease;* it was all the rage at the time. At one point I caught myself thinking one of the guys on screen was cute. A moment later he joined his buddies in mooning the crowd. Right there on the big screen. The whole theater laughed. My face went hot, like I'd been caught doing something wrong. Later, during the song about getting chills and losing control, I kept thinking about Ricky—how just standing near him could flip my stomach, how small moments with him carried that same jolt of electricity.

I didn't want the physical part mixed up with what I felt for him. For darn sure, Ricky wouldn't like it either. For a minute I thought about telling Norman what I was going through. He was the only adult who ever treated me seriously. If anyone might've known what to say, it would've been him. But, the words wouldn't come. I kept my eyes on the screen while everyone else laughed.

Whatever it was, I decided to keep it to myself.

Seventh grade science was one long exercise in pretending things made sense. Today's lesson involved a row of four test tubes filled with water—one dyed red, the others clear—and strips of folded paper towel dipped between each of them like makeshift bridges. The red bled upward, crossed the towel, and bled down into the clear water of the second tube, turning it pink.

"So, they're in love now," said Kathryn, from the next lab station.

I half-smiled looking up.

She turned her head toward me. "Which one of you is the girl?"

My stomach dropped.

"Aren't you and Jimmy Flannery gay together?"

"What? No. Where'd you get that?"

"Daniel Vincini said so."

I glanced across the table. Daniel was pretending to adjust the wire rack under his test tubes, his face all pleasant detachment. His brown hair was brushed into place and his light freckles spritzed over his face. Both Jimmy and Daniel had been called *flamers*. But, Daniel made Jimmy seem more like John Wayne.

At a strategic moment I walked over to Daniel, "Why did you say that about me?"

He shrugged. "Heard it from my cousin, Robby. Robby Richoux."

That name hit like a shoe to the chest. Robby hadn't been seen since fourth grade, when he tried to bite a teacher and got sent away somewhere. Daniel was like a smoothed-over version of him—cleaner, softer, but almost as ugly. He was less likely to throw a punch but just as eager to cause trouble.

"Said you and Jimmy ran around together. 'In gay.'"

"In gay?" I repeated. "What does that even mean?"

I hadn't fully realized gay people could be couples. It was usually talked about as an odd behavior. Which is a strange thing to admit because at the same time, I had imagined being together with Eric and Ricky like a couple.

And, with Jimmy of all people? That made it worse. Being called gay was bad enough. Being paired with him was unbearable.

I couldn't focus for the rest of class. Daniel didn't look my way, just kept folding his paper towel bridge with the poise of a wedding planner.

I waited for him after school. He peeled off toward the reservoir path. I followed a few steps behind until we were mostly out of view of the road.

"Hey," I said.

He turned. Smiled weakly. "Oh—hi, Johnny."

"Take it back."

"What?"

I had Daniel by the collar as we reached the end of the reservoir path, half holding him, half walking him backwards. He kept trying to move forward, jaw locked, eyes fixed ahead, making slow, stubborn progress in silence. He slipped free for a second while crossing the street.

"Say it," I said, grabbing him again. "You're the one who's gay. Right?"

He twisted in my grip. "Why would I say that?"

"Just like how you didn't even ask if I was," I said. "You still went around repeating crap."

I pushed him up against a fence post—not hard. Just enough to stop him cold.

Then I heard footsteps behind us, closing in.

"Whoa," someone said, calm and steady. "What's going on?"

I turned. It was an older kid—maybe ninth grade—taller, with serious eyes and a brown corduroy jacket. He looked like the kind of boy who always had a paperback in his back pocket.

"What's going on?" he asked again, walking over like he was joining a hike, not interrupting a near-mugging.

"He said me and Jimmy Flannery were gay together," I said.

The older boy looked at Daniel. "Did you?"

Daniel didn't answer.

"Seriously?" the boy said, stopping beside us.

Daniel muttered, "I just said what I heard from Robby."

"That chronic liar?" the boy said lightly.

The boy sat on the second step of a house with a big porch but a small yard, and touched his chin. I let go of Daniel's shirt. He adjusted it like he'd been hit by a gust of wind, not me.

The older kid—Peter, as I'd learn later—frowned at Daniel.

"You repeated something mean," he said. "Even if you didn't intend it, it had an impact. That part's on you."

Daniel stayed silent, shoulders tight.

Then Peter looked at me. "And you—you escalated it."

"I didn't punch him."

"No," Peter said. "You grabbed him by the collar and marched him halfway across the neighborhood. You're lucky I'm not a cop."

"I was mad."

Peter nodded. "Yeah. But, why that mad? You blow stuff like that off, most people won't take it seriously."

I didn't answer.

Peter turned back to Daniel. "Apologize"

"I said I didn't mean it."

"Try again."

Daniel glanced at me. "I'm sorry. I shouldn't have said it."

Peter looked back at me. "And you—do you really want to scare people into silence? You think that's how things work?"

I kicked a pine cone off the sidewalk. "I just wanted it to stop."

"Fair," he said. "But, there's a difference between stopping a rumor and stirring up more drama."

He stood, brushed off the back of his jeans, and looked at Daniel. "Let's go."

Then, to me: "You're frustrated. And, I think you two should give each other a wide berth for a while."

"Wait," I said. "You're his brother?"

Peter nodded, a small smile crossing his face—like none of this surprised him.

Why didn't I get a beating?

I stood there, watching them walk off, wondering how he'd said exactly what needed saying without sounding like a teacher or a thug. He saw things clearly and made you want to see them that way too.

We'd put together a minibike with stolen lawn mower parts, sold it to Bib for $125 because it barely ran, then bought it back for $100 after Bob fixed it. I put in $80, Danny kicked in twenty. He drove most of the time, with me on the back. I was annoyed at the unfairness, but then it happened—a turn in the road, my arms around his waist, my chest set against his back. The lean firmness of his abs under his T-shirt. It felt very good, like the passing embrace with Matt months earlier when I was drunk. When we came to a stop, I didn't want to let go. Electric, troubling. Both times, it faded after a day.

The minibike started acting up. We sold it back to Bib, though he resisted. Veiled threats were lodged.

Mr. Blanchard and my dad got involved. Smoking his cigar, Mr. Blanchard handed the money back. "Here's every nickel. And if anyone touches a hair on his head, I'll end you."

We walked off satisfied. A week later, Bob fixed it again.

Funny how feelings work. The Flannerys were like brothers to me—no hint of a crush except those two instances, brief and strange. Like the minibike: fast while it lasted, but nothing you could count on to keep running.

Multiple heat sources were an issue, and when the whistle blows? Then, it was for keeps. Attached. Imprinted. Ever-present. It might lay fallow for years, but when the season's right, it bloomed fast—like it never left.

Every now and then, Ricky would do something small that wrecked me for the rest of the day. Call me buddy in passing. Light my cigarette without a word. Pick up a can of orange soda because "I know what you like." He had that rare mix—warm smile, easy charm, and brutal honesty when it mattered. He also had a vulnerable side.

We were crouched inside that odd little building rotting in the woods behind the main library, an old-time train station—the last of our three cigarette stops. The early autumn sun was giving way to the trees, casting long blue shadows. As usual, light chatter had petered into silence without feeling awkward.

After a while, Ricky's tone shifted. "You ever think about what you'd do if you could just...start over? Different family, different town. New name, even."

I shrugged, trying to understand what he was saying.

He continued, "Maybe I'd be someone who doesn't live in an area where everybody knows when you sneeze."

I nodded. "Yeah. Or someone who doesn't feel like he's stuck between being invisible or being a target."

We sat in silence for a minute, smoke wafting upward, the light changing color.

Then, Ricky said, "You ever get those thoughts where... like, you don't want to die exactly, but if a truck swerved out of its lane and hit you, you'd kind of just... be okay with it?"

He didn't look at me when he said it, just kept staring at the door like he was waiting for something to walk through it.

"Yeah," I said eventually. "More like... if someone said, 'Hey, do you want to not exist for a while?' I'd be like, 'Sure, sounds peaceful'.... existing is heavy sometimes."

Ricky drew in a breath, held it, let it go. "And, you can't say it out loud at home, because then they think you're gonna do something. You're not."

"I felt like that during the rift with the Flannerys," I said, though I really meant the part where I lost Ricky too.

We looked at each other then—just briefly—and it was enough. A flicker of understanding passed between us like static.

We sat there a while longer, letting the smoke do the talking.

Ricky stood up then, stretching his arms behind his head. "Welp. Guess I better go pretend I'm an athlete." he muttered, pushing the door open for me, and the screen banged shut behind us.

At the pool, the coach gave Ricky extra free swim time, so we joined a game of water polo. It was easier than basketball—no dribbling, just wrestling for the ball and passing it off. That became our groove: I'd fight for it, then feed Ricky, and he'd score.

When we got close to the net, he'd make me switch roles so I could take the shot myself.

The locker room floor was soaked, so we put a towel on the bench and stood up there to change. It was tight—our shoulders bumping, our arms hitting the ceiling. We ended up prying out the loose panel above us. As people walked by, I felt like we proudly stood on a pedestal. We started laughing hard, trying to wedge that ceiling panel back like we hadn't touched anything.

Days like that buzzed in me for a week.

Ronny Hanson had a whole different vibe. He was quick to share tales of his summer exploits in Texas. He went hunting to win a deer and went to Mexico to lose his virginity. He pantomimed everything: punches thrown, kisses stolen, even intimate acts. He'd play the attacker, then the victim, with full body gestures and perfectly timed sound effects. It was a one-man show for an audience of one.

He looked like Alfalfa and acted like Eddie Haskell—overly polite when a teacher walked by, borderline profane once they turned their back. But, what I liked most was his mind. He treated everything as worthy of analysis and ridicule— including himself. He could break anything down—movies, playground squabbles, teacher politics. He had this endless reserve of facts and theories, always delivered with the flair of someone who knew they were probably full of it and didn't care. That seemed like good friendship material.

"Meet me in Pershing Square," he said one day as class let out. "We'll get some grinders. Real good ones. I'll show you what to get."

"Sounds good," I said, "but, what are grinders?"

He gave me a look like I'd just asked what a pencil was. "You don't know? They're subs—but toasted. It's the toasting that makes it a grinder."

We met by the red newspaper boxes across from the gas station. Ronny showed up ten minutes late, shirt untucked, smelling faintly like bubblegum.

"Ready to have your life changed?"

Ronny stepped up to order with mock authority. "One meatball grinder, extra mozzarella cheese, toasted hard. And a turkey-bacon for my man here. Also hard. Trust me."

When the sandwiches came, Ronny unwrapped his like it was treasure. "Look at that," he said. "Mozzarella melted like lava. You gotta press it with your palm so the juice runs into the bread. That's the secret."

We ate in silence for a few minutes.

He leaned back, wiping his hands. "Where do you think we'll be in ten years?"

"Like... career-wise?"

"No, like having steady women to bang!"

We had exchanged numbers to coordinate plans then quickly fell into the habit of daily phone calls—long, winding conversations that stretched past dinner and into the night. It became routine. Our phone had the last party-line in Beaumont, something Ronny refused to believe until the old lady cut in during one of our calls.

"Are you little boys going to be on all night?" she snapped.

Ronny, without missing a beat, played along like he was the one sharing the line with her. "We pay our bill, ma'am. What's so urgent about your call anyway?"

She sniffed. "Now, that's none of your business. It's not idle gossip and nonsense."

Ronny replied, "Neither is ours. This is a work call—we're planning the future of democracy."

We nearly died laughing.

Ronny called me one night, voice half serious, half amused.

"I'm in trouble with the cops," he said.

"What'd you do?" I asked, already bracing for a tall tale.

"It started as a prank. You know that old lady on Sycamore? She's nuts about her landscaping. She's got woodchips in some beds, pebbles in others—like a checkerboard. Every day, I'd grab a handful of one and toss it in the other. She'd fix it. Next day, I'd do it again. I thought it was funny."

He laughed, then sighed. "Turns out she snapped a few photos of me. Showed the police. They told me I'd have to do community service. Helping her with her chores."

Ronny had that gift—turning everything into a story where he was the sly adventurer.

In a later conversation he updated me, "So, even when my service was done, I kept going back. Helping her. Raking leaves, organizing closet space, crap like that. But, this time she was paying me. And—" he chuckled—"I might've lifted a little booze from her cabinet. Don't worry, she never noticed. She likes me." I couldn't decide whether to shake my head or admire the audacity.

I lacked audacity where I needed it the most.

My connection with Ricky felt thinner once the others were around. We were laying against the shingles, arms resting on the roof peak of the housing authority administration building—Jerry's roof—warm from the day but cooling fast as the sun dropped behind the trees. Ricky lit a cigarette, thumb flicking the wheel in one smooth motion. From up here, we had a perfect angle on the front yard of Matt's building.

Down below, one of the Big Kids pulled a girl onto his lap without asking. She laughed, leaned back into him. Everyone treated it as natural.

"I want a girl in my lap," said Matt.

"Every guy wants that. It's just wired in," Ricky exhaled. He said it smoothly, the way he did when the others were around.

"How's it hanging, homos? You guys hear?" Danny called as he climbed the gate and hauled himself up. "We made the paper again."

"Crime log?" Ricky asked.

Matt shook his head. "That poster the Big Kids put up."

"The one with the pig in a police hat?" I asked.

"Yeah. 'Wanted: Dead or Alive—Beaumont Cop.' Reward was a six-pack."

"The article was half dumb, half cool." Danny brushed grit off his palms. "Oh—and I know why Keith Kline's been MIA. He's dating Mary Ellen. They are up in his room all day, everyday."

"But, she's four years younger—?" I said.

"And a bitch," Matt muttered.

We fell into a quiet moment. The last of the sun flared orange off the windows across the tracks. A song on a radio somewhere played too low to make out.

Matt leaned in like we were planning a football play. "Girls like show. You gotta make 'em feel important. Flatter them."

"You don't know what girls like," Ricky said.

"I think you really gotta like their personality," I offered.

They talked right over that.

Danny leaned forward. "I'd run out of stuff to say in twenty minutes. Why stay in so much?"

Matt laughed. "To do stuff that doesn't require talking."

"They want tenderness," Ricky said, almost seriously.

Matt barked a laugh. "Yeah, okay."

Ricky smiled to himself. "Girls want different things than boys."

Quite by accident, we discovered some strange glitch in the phone system—if you started dialing with the rotary, caught it before the full recoil, then dialed again OR hung up and quickly picked up again, it sometimes dumped you into this surreal in-between space, like a telephone limbo. And, we weren't alone. Other teens had found it too.

One night a girl named Gail from Jefferson Street who I knew only vaguely, was on. We talked a bit. When I told her my name, she said, "Johnny, the fag?"

I hung up so fast the receiver nearly broke the cradle. I told myself it didn't matter—she was just some random girl. But, it did matter. The words sank in my stomach like sand. I hated how easily one person could make you feel weak. And, I hated how familiar that feeling was.

Sarah kept using the line to talk to strangers. She befriended a sixth grader from a nearby town and even got her number. I got on with her once—Tracey was her name—and she said she liked my voice. That flattery went a long way. Before long, we were "going out" via phone. It gave me something juicy to brag about with Ricky and Ronny—something to make me seem more normal. Maybe it could awaken something in me?

After a few weeks, Sarah arranged a visit. Tracey was coming to meet me in person. I panicked. On the way home from school, I told Ricky I wasn't ready to meet her and asked if I could go to the pool with him instead. Usually, he'd invite me, but this time I invited myself, but he left without me. Later, he said it was to push me to meet her.

I stalled in the projects, walking loops around the buildings like a trapped animal. Eventually, I crossed paths with Sarah and Tracey. I made a clumsy excuse—something about needing to help my boss—but I could see the disappointment in Tracey's face. She later said I looked cute though, which softened the blow. She broke it off a few weeks later. It wasn't a dramatic ending. We both knew it wasn't working. That it was just a trial run all along.

Looking back, I think I wanted the idea of a girlfriend more than the girl herself. I wanted proof I could be liked that way, even if I didn't really feel it in return. That stood in contrast to my earlier statement about real feelings being important. And, that gap—between what I felt and what I performed—was starting to stretch so wide, I couldn't see the other side.

Jimmy, it appeared, was taking a different path.

Ricky and I were walking the train tracks in the dark, footfalls noisy on the newly packed gravel. Ricky's voice became softer, trying to sound calm.

"Hey... I've got something to tell you."

"Okay."

"I had a problem with Jimmy."

"Oh?"

"Well... He messes with me when I sleep over. Gets into my boxers. Acts like I'm his girlfriend or something."

I stopped walking.

"What do you say to him?"

"Nothing. I just pretend I have to pee, get up, and he backs off. One time I wore jeans to bed so he couldn't get in. He unzipped them."

"Jesus. Maybe you should tell Matt."

We walked a few more steps in silence.

"I read somewhere," I said, trying to fill the air, "that sometimes guys experiment when they're teens. Like, they get horny, they get curious. Circle jerk kind of stuff."

"Yeah," Ricky said. "But, that's when they're awake. Still wrong. But, when someone's asleep?!" He kicked a rock into the woods. "That's evil. I think he's sick."

I didn't know what to say. I just walked beside him, keeping pace.

Eventually I said, "This means... nothing bad about you."

He said, "I know."

I couldn't stop thinking about what Ricky said.

It rattled something loose in me, something I couldn't pin down.

Because, I'd had feelings in the dark, too. I wanted Ricky to just... Choose me. Yet, somehow, what Jimmy did and what I felt got all twisted up in my head.

I knew I wasn't evil. But, I also knew I wasn't normal.

I felt sorry for Ricky. Part of me felt sorry for Jimmy. Part of me hated him. And, part of me felt sorry for myself, for even being in the same category. It dawned on me. Maybe I had been sparring with Jimmy for Ricky's attention for a very long time without realizing it.

All I knew for sure was I didn't want Ricky to stop asking me to the pool. Didn't want Ricky to stop trusting me with things. And, didn't want to look at myself the way that girl on the phone had, just for saying my name.

A few days later, a flood of memories rushed in as I lay in bed, trying to sleep. My mind skipped like a scratched record, circling back to moments I hadn't thought about in years—confusing situations with men that I'd brushed off, but that were starting to arrange themselves into something troubling.

The first was Bob.

That afternoon, Sarah and I had wandered over like we sometimes did. Bob didn't mind. He was always home, always willing to entertain. We ended up in his bedroom, which was dim and smelled like old blankets. He was under the covers, watching cartoons on the small color TV at the foot of the bed. Sarah and I sat cross-legged near the edge.

Then it happened—suddenly.

Something behind us. A shape. Suspended in the air just long enough to register before he yanked the covers back over it. I didn't understand what I was seeing at first. It felt like catching a glimpse of something out of place in a dream. Sarah saw it too and burst out laughing.

"I'm telling Mary Ellen!"

Bob's voice snapped. "Don't tell anyone."

We didn't.

This occurrence was never repeated or spoken of again.

Still, it stuck. It hovered in my memory like static electricity, impossible to forget, hard to process. I wasn't scared, exactly. It hadn't felt violent. It had felt... odd. Suspended between normal and not. At the time, it was just a surreal gravity defying quandary.

The thing is, I liked Bob. A lot of us did. He gave out candy routinely, gifts on holidays, taught us how to make go-karts from scrap wood, told wild stories. He was kind. He paid attention. I don't know if he ever hurt anyone. I hope he didn't. But, I've carried that moment with me, wondering what it meant. Bob made childhood both better and stranger.

Then, there was the underground fort—the second one we found up Snake Hill. This one was legit. Built into the side of the hill with new lumber, a ceiling high enough to stand under, and living plants woven into the roof and front wall to hide it. We were cooking hot dogs there, when I noticed a bush that didn't look quite right.

A second later, Matt walked back from taking a dump and pointed. There was a young man in the bush, sitting cross-legged, watching us. He stood up slowly, like he didn't want to startle anyone.

"Any of you want to earn five dollars?" he said.

"Sure," someone answered. "Doing what?"

"I'll give you a hand job."

We were too dumb to get it. Thought he meant manual labor.

Matt understood. "No. Run!"

We scattered in every direction.

We told the Big Kids about it days later.

"Why didn't you tell us right when it happened? We could have buried that guy."

We thought it was a one-time thing. A fluke. But, it wasn't.

A few weeks later, it happened again. Different man. Older. Same offer. He was climbing up the embankment on the north side of the tracks as we walked home from Twombly Square.

"Hey, want to earn five dollars?" he shouted.

We didn't wait this time. We just yelled "No!" in unison and booked it down the rails. This time, we didn't wait to hear the rest. We already knew.

I kept turning all this over in my mind. Not just the incidents, but how they made me feel. There was fear, sure—but more than that, confusion. And, a kind of guilt or shame that I didn't understand.

Was I bad too?

Did wanting Ricky put me in the same category as someone in a bush offering five bucks?

I hated that thought. Hated it so much I felt sick.

I lied in bed trying to separate it all out like laundry—this is a good feeling, this is a bad one. This is just friendship, this is something tainted. But, the piles always got mixed up again. I wanted there to be a line—thick and bright and clear—that divided good from bad, real from fake, love from abuse. But, there wasn't. Everything bled together. What I felt for Ricky wasn't about physical gratification. Yet, I changed clothes next to him, showered next to him, like it was nothing. And it made me feel... good. Not turned on. Just important. Just open. Like I was allowed to candidly exist.

But, when you're a boy and you feel that way about another boy, nobody tells you what to call it. They just tell you what not to be.

Homo.

Queer.

A faggot.

That's the vocabulary I had—and none of it matched what I felt. None of it accounted for enjoying a close friendship or longing for affection.

I had no word for love and no word for self-hate.

So, I just lay in the dark, going over it.

Snow came early that year—and so did an invitation from Ronny.

"Want to come over after school sometime?" he asked.

I told the Flannerys and the others not to wait for me that afternoon. Instead, I headed home with Ronny, up past the giant reservoir as flakes drifted down around us.

In the distance, someone called out.

It was Brian Monty—a pudgy pest with a voice too loud and facial features that oddly reminded me of Bob. Ronny didn't call back or slow down. If anything, he sped up, motioning for me to keep pace.

Brian started running toward us.

"Run," Ronny hissed.

But I didn't.

I stopped. Turned around. Walked down the hill in route home.

It was clear—Ronny didn't want to be seen with me. He was ashamed. Hiding me.

He apologized the next day, but it took a week before he convinced me to try again.

The house was immaculate. No clutter anywhere.

"Mom's full-time job is keeping the household in order," Ronny explained. "She manages the cleaners and such."

His mother was a friendly fast talking Mexican woman with a sweet accent. "Juanito, welcome to our home," she said with a warm smile. "Ronny, show him around and make him feel comfortable."

"Let's start in the basement. This is my domain," he said. "My room's a bit small, so I mostly hang out down here."

The basement was finished, with decorative plaster etchings laid into walls and framed finger paintings hanging. A fireplace at one end, a small bedroom at the other, and in between, three sofas arranged around a large TV.

"Is that a color TV?" I asked.

"Yep. And we have HBO on all our sets." He added, picking up a booklet, " I can plan what I watch. Small "n" nudity there will be tits, capital "N" nudity, there is sex, may see bush."

He led me through the other rooms—utility space, laundry area, and a small workshop with nice tools. The rudimentary bathroom right there in the basement impressed me for some reason. He grabbed two dome-shaped air fresheners off a shelf. “Smell this—pine. I like it better than floral. But, here’s floral. Which do you like better?”

I humored him. He wanted my input on everything.

Upstairs, the tour continued: kitchen with a microwave, TV room where his dad camped out, a living room and formal dining room with chirping parakeets, and a breakfast nook. He grabbed a jar off the baker’s rack.

“This is cereal my mom mixes for my dad—granola, three kinds of nuts, those nugget things...”

“I thought it was birdseed.”

He laughed. “Wanna try some? It’s dry but good with milk.”

I did. It was very satisfying.

Everything looked clean and new and perfect. I was impressed and jealous and sort of intimidated, but also happy just being allowed there.

“Let’s retire to my chambers,” he said grandly.

His bedroom was upstairs—half the size of mine. Just a bed, a bureau, and a nightstand. He opened the top drawer and pulled out two empty nip bottles of vodka, holding each to his lips and tilting his head back, treating it like precious nectar.

“I got these at the country club. Sometimes I drink with my sister’s friends there.”

Hard liquor. That felt... advanced. Adult. Exciting—but dangerous.

He told me to sit on the bed and wait. Then, from a corner, he brought out a two-foot plastic hobo wearing tattered clothes. He wiped the mouth with rubbing alcohol and a tissue.

"I practice making out," he said.

He acted out an entire date. Welcoming the girl to his room. Complimenting her. Sharing an heirloom. Touching hands. Locking eyes. Then, kissing the hobo.

"Your turn," he said, wiping down the mouth. "Use tongue."

I hesitated. Then mimicked him—awkwardly, self-consciously. It was silly. And oddly informative.

"Okay," Ronny said, tossing the hobo back in the corner. "One more. But, this time, no hobo."

"What do you mean?"

"Get used to looking into another human's eyes. I mean we do it for real. The whole scenario. So, you know what it actually feels like. Not me. The *idea* of someone. We just run through it like we did with the hobo, but without the prop. You'll see—it's way better practice."

He sat back down on the edge of the bed.

"So, you welcome her in, right? You've done that part. You show her something meaningful—" He picked up his watch from the nightstand. "Like this. A memento. Something that says you trust her." He held it between us for a moment, then set it down.

"And then you talk. Get close. Make eye contact."

He turned toward me. His knee was almost touching mine.

"Like this?" I asked, uncertain.

"Yeah. And, then you wait for the right moment. You can feel it building. The tension."

There was silence. His eyes held mine.

"And then—"

He leaned in.

I flinched back hard, head jerking away, nearly falling off the bed.

Ronny burst out laughing—loud, theatrical, slapping his knee. "Oh my god! You seriously thought—" He could barely get the words out between laughs. "You thought I was gonna kiss you?!"

My face was on fire. "No, I just—"

"Dude! Your *face*!" He kept laughing, doubled over now. "That's *hilarious*! I was just showing you the lean-in. That's the whole point—you read the room, you make the move. I wasn't actually gonna—oh man, that's too good."

"Shut up," I muttered, trying to laugh along but feeling humiliated.

"No, seriously, that was perfect though. That flinch? That's exactly what happens if you misread it. See? Now you know what *not* to do when a girl leans in." He wiped his eyes, still chuckling. "God, you really thought I'd kiss you. Like I'm some kind of queer."

"I knew you were joking," I said, but my voice came out wrong.

I wished I had a script for what to say to Ricky, one that told me exactly how to say it.

My whole history with Ricky involved ebbs and flows. I wanted a steady flow, and I think he started to notice. Invites to tag along to swim lessons were sporadic. Sometimes I got the nod, sometimes it was Danny Flannery instead. Danny didn't swim—just watched, arms folded, like he was waiting for someone to call his bluff. The one time all three of us went together, it felt like a trial I didn't know how to close.

The pool itself was loud and glossy, echoing with shrieks and whistles, bodies moving in every direction like a shaken snow globe. Ricky did laps. Danny sat in the bleachers, throwing wet paper towels at the lifeguard stand when no one was looking. I drifted in the free swim area, too self-conscious to play water polo but too stubborn to leave. I wanted Ricky's attention—his time—but the harder I tried to orbit closer, the more I felt like space debris, circling but never quite docking.

Afterward, we spilled out onto the sidewalk, steam still in my nose from the overheated locker room.

"So, why even come, if you don't swim?" I asked Danny.

"The free heat," he said. "And somebody's gotta yell 'Stick it where the sun don't shine' when Coach is under water."

I smirked. "You just sit there like Walter Matthau after one too many."

"That's called style," Danny said. "Anyway, I was making sure Lover-Boy didn't embarrass himself with Tatum O'Neal over there in lane three."

"She's nice. She's not Tatum O'Neal," Ricky said, flicking water from his ear.

"She could be," Danny snipped back. "All she needs is a glove—but she'd tell you to take a hike before you even got to first base."

"...and she'd pitch you a fast one right in the ribs." I added, trying to get in on it. "Looked like she was checking me out."

Danny let out a slow, stupid laugh—"Haw, haw, haw"—the kind of sound people make when they're imitating someone with half a brain. "Checking you out, in a 'Why's that kid drowning in the shallow end?' kind of way."

Ricky barked a laugh and nudged him with his elbow. That stung more than the comment. I thought he should have, at least, stayed neutral.

Their rhythm became too quick and too mean for me to match. They kept up a volley of insults about who'd make a better movie star, darting ahead of me.

I picked up my pace. It didn't help.

Then, without warning, the invitations stopped. No explanation. Just silence where our routine used to be.

Within the group, I still saw Ricky, but it was over focused on performative chaos: dogpiles, insults, wrestling matches, heavy metal jam sessions that blurred the line between bonding and brutality. It was mildly captivating but hollow.

I started trying to initiate small plans, grasping for any version of connection I could invent. Most attempts fell flat.

But, one did click—fittingly, the day after they chased me through the neighborhood like a hunted animal. As usual, some kind of disagreement ended with someone yelling "Get Johnny!" and transformed into a half dozen kids in loose formation, pursuing me across yards and fences like a scene out of *Lord of the Flies*. They boxed me in at my house. I had seconds to react. A ladder leaned against the wall—Dad left it there after running out of paint for that side of the house.

I climbed fast, adrenaline sharpening every movement. Towards the top of the ladder, I realized the angle was wrong—the roof too high, eave in the way. If I tried to haul myself up, I'd get dragged down or fall backward. They were halfway up. My eyes scanned the roof, then the tree four feet away, the one just outside my bedroom window. It was locked, so entering the house wasn't an option, but a surprise move could work. I came down a few rungs, pivoted, leaped toward the tree. My fingers dug into the rough bark as the trunk swayed against my weight like a rubber straw. It righted itself. I scrambled down, darted by the kids still on the ground, and vanished to the front of the house, victorious.

The next day, still sore and proud, I invited Ricky back to reenact the scene. I wanted to relive it, show him how I'd outsmarted the numbers. I wanted to impress him. But, this time, I miscalculated. I climbed one wrung higher on the ladder than before. I leapt in the same way. Caught the trunk. Held tight. The tree swayed in the other direction.

Then, the trunk snapped.

It was fast and slow at once. The pop of the breaking wood, the rush of air, the thunk of my body hitting the ground. For a few seconds I saw stars—or maybe nothing at all. When I opened my eyes, everything was warped. Ma called an ambulance. I'd broken my collarbone and had compressed vertebrae.

But, the real injury—the one I didn't talk about—was the irony. Because loving Ricky was exactly like that jump. A reckless leap toward something that seemed strong enough to hold me. A calculation fueled by hope and desperation, with no plan for the landing.

He was the tree. Beautiful. Reliable until he wasn't. And, when I held on too tightly, he couldn't hold the weight.

13
Sabotage

The hospital room smelled like industrial-strength soap. My bed was positioned next to the window, offering a view only of a ventilation unit, vibrating unsteadily. I had a brace around my collarbone, a bruise blooming across my ribs, and a headache like I'd swallowed a sledgehammer. It was the first week of eighth grade, and I was going to be out for a while.

Danny and Matt Mundt shuffled in, fresh from the bus.

"Hey, you still alive?" Danny said. "You look like crap."

"Better than I feel," I croaked.

Matt glanced at the IV tube. "Did it hurt?"

"Only the landing."

They both laughed. Danny dropped into the visitor chair, the old cushion deflating beneath him. Matt, restless, paced the room, accidentally bumping the IV pole twice before finally standing near the foot of my bed.

"We heard from Ricky," Danny said. "Told us what happened. Said you flew like a flying squirrel, except you forgot the gliding part."

"He called yesterday," I said. "Said he'd come by later in the week—with a six-pack of Orange Crush. Fancy."

They both nodded but gave each other a look. Nobody thought he'd show. He didn't.

About twenty minutes later, the door creaked open again. Matt Flannery ducked in first, followed by Bobby Clemson—Peachy—his blonde fuzz catching the light like a dandelion. He grinned widely, his snaggle-tooth giving him the look of a cartoon chipmunk who'd been in one too many bar fights.

"Yo," Matt Flannery said. "You look like someone dropped you from a helicopter."

"They kind of did," I said.

Peachy leaned against the windowsill. "I ran into a screen door once. Didn't get a hospital room, though. Just a bloody nose and a lesson."

Danny raised an eyebrow. "You guys walk here?"

"Course," Peachy said. "You don't think I got this built and beautiful sittin' on no buses, do you?"

I looked at him, memory flashing. He'd zoomed across the Town Field that day, with his brother's football jersey contorting in the wind.

"That shirt really swims on him," said Matt.

He came at us at a reckless speed like Evel Knievel's odd little cousin, jammed his front brakes, flipped the bike vertical, and dismounted like a gymnast. The bike continued end over end off to the side; he landed and threw his arms in the air, like he'd just landed a vault.

"You live with that other kid," I said, tucking my gown underneath me. "The one with the feathered hair."

"Timmy Salinger, my upstairs neighbor," he said proudly. "He's the pretty one. I'm the personality."

"I thought he was your twin. Same house. Same height and hair color. Paternal of course."

Matt Mundt squinted at him. "Wait, are you Peach Fuzz?"

Peachy nodded solemnly. "Only to my friends and sworn enemies."

"I'm thinking of getting a whiffle," said Mundt.

Peachy tapped his own head. "You can get a whiffle, but don't get confused—I'm still the prototype."

They joked about hospital food and bet on Matt Mundt's walk home—Peachy said it would take an hour, Matt Flannery said thirty-five minutes.

"Screw you, I'll wait an hour for the bus," Mundt declared.

As they left, Peachy gave me a Vulcan hand signal and said, "Heal up, Johnny Rocket. I expect a full aerial reenactment next week. Safety net optional." What a fun addition to our crew.

It was half past seven when Ronny showed up, still in time for visiting hours, barely. He slipped through the doorway carrying a dripping Styrofoam cup from Friendly's.

"Strawberry Fribble," he said, holding it out like an offering. "Told my mom I'd drop it off and be out in twenty."

"What, she didn't want to come in and see me in my gown?"

He set the milkshake on the tray and poked in the straw.

"Nice. Thanks. I had four visitors earlier, and all they brought was tall tales."

Ronny shrugged and pulled the visitor chair up to the bed. "Any, uh, awkward procedures yet?" he asked. "Catheters? Nurse walks in just as you're—"

"No comment."

"How'd the sponge bath go?"

I blinked at him. "Fine."

He leaned forward, as if he knew this was the good part. "Go on."

"Well, the nurse came in with warm water and all that. Wiped down my arms, chest, and legs. Then, she kind of handed me the sponge and said, 'You can do between your legs yourself.' Then left."

Ronny looked personally offended. "What, she bailed?"

"Yeah."

He lowered his voice, serious now. "Okay. So I saw this movie, right? Like an old porno. But, the guy's in a hospital bed, and the nurse stays for the whole thing. It's about being helpless. That's the angle."

I raised an eyebrow. "You're saying I should act more helpless?"

He nodded, all in. "Exactly. You want the full bed bath, you gotta look like you can't do it yourself. Like... your arms don't bend right. Or you don't know where your legs are."

"That's insane."

"No—it's strategy," he said, voice hushed, like we were planning a breakout. "You wait till she's there with the sponge. You hesitate. Say something like, 'Sorry, I just... I'm still kinda disoriented,' and maybe let your hand shake a little. Not too much. Just enough. She'll feel bad. She'll finish the job."

I stared at him.

He nodded again. "Trust me. They train for that. Good hygiene is part of their code. It's about dignity," he said. "You shouldn't be left to do it like a sad raccoon in a sink."

I laughed, shaking my head. He didn't laugh with me. Maybe he meant it.

He stayed until the nurse poked her head in and gave him the five-minute warning. As he stood up to leave, he added, "Seriously. Just try the shaking hand thing. Works in the movie."

He waved and slipped out the door. I finished the last of the Fribble and watched the hallway go quiet. And, I couldn't help wondering—just for a second—what would happen if I did try the handshake.

It took me years to see how much the world of boys ran on petty power plays: tiny leverage moves, small challenges, little pacts that felt like bonds.

Weeks later, still on the mend but mobile, I took the 72 bus to Harvard Square with Matt Flannery. I dropped my only dime into the fare box, the coin clinking like a warning bell. Matt dropped his in too and gave me a lopsided grin.

"I'll cover your fare back, I will," he said sarcastically.

"Don't play around."

"Geez, I said I would. Relax."

The bus wheezed up Mass Ave, past places we couldn't afford. It was cloudy and warm. When we stepped off, the air smelled like cinnamon and something sour from the storm drain.

We walked through Harvard Yard, pretending to belong. A man with a beard and a tweed jacket crossed in front of us, carrying a cello case. Matt muttered, "These people take the wrong things seriously."

The Yard made me feel smarter just by walking on the bricks. Matt, on the other hand, kept announcing fake facts aloud as if he were a tour guide.

"That statue? This guy is famous for adding little pieces of colored paper to toothpicks used for cocktail sandwiches."

At The Garage, we wandered up the twisting ramps and narrow walkways, checking out the tiny, cluttered shops that filled old parking bays. Comic books, incense, bumper stickers, chessboards made of crushed glass. I turned over a cheap metal ring shaped like a tiger's head in my hand. Matt bought a pretzel and ate it slowly, tearing off chunks and letting the salt sprinkle like confetti.

"You want a piece?" he asked, holding it out.

"Yeah."

He pulled it back. "Oops."

I let it slide once. He offered again. Then, I tried to grab a chunk, and he twisted away, laughing.

"Come on, I paid for this. With my own money," he said, emphasizing the last words.

Clearly, he thought he could treat me this way because I was at his mercy for the bus fare home.

It escalated. I swatted at the pretzel; he shoved me. I pushed back, then hit his chest and ran.

I knew the Square well enough to vanish. He chased me out of The Garage, past a street musician doing a wheezy harmonica version of *Don't Stop til You Get Enough*. I ran down the sidewalk, took a sharp left past the Coop, then spotted an alley between two brownstones. I ducked in.

Dead end. Chain-link fence on one side, a high wooden fence on the other. I climbed. I swung my leg and vaulted over. Pebbles clacked against the fence just as I dropped to the other side and landed on my knees, scraped but triumphant.

I stepped out onto the next street, brushed the dirt from my pants, and ran a hand through my hair, trying to look presentable. I crossed toward the Brattle Red Line station, entering with purpose, then changed direction at the last moment as if I'd just exited a train. At the agent window, the guy barely looked up. "Here," he said, sliding me a paper transfer slip.

I took the next outbound bus home, licking my wounds and nursing my pride.

He'd tried to control me with the power of cash. The pretzel, the dime, the casual disrespect—it wasn't about snacks or cents. It was about leverage. But, I turned it. Not by winning a fight, but by thinking and running just far enough ahead to remind him: I could leave the game anytime. And, maybe, just maybe, he needed me in it more than I needed him.

The next afternoon, Ronny invited me over to his house again. It was almost as strange and exhilarating as the first time.

Inside, the house was calm but felt bustling with life. Family photos crowded the hallway wall, and knick-knacks balanced on every surface, each with a story waiting to be told.

As we passed through the kitchen he said, "Come over to the sink. I wanna baptize you."

"Nah. I'm good. And, that's not holy water."

"It couldn't hurt."

He said it like he was offering salvation, like he wanted to be the one who fixed things, even if he didn't know how.

We trailed our book bags to the basement den, sinking onto a sofa and setting up two trays as makeshift desks. And, started going over the social studies questions.

"We need to fill ten pages answering six questions. That's a lot of BS," Ronny said. "We should divide 'em up—each take three."

"And hand in identical papers?" I asked.

"No, get creative. paraphrase, reorder. Teacher barely reads it anyway."

"Look here—we'll be needing three references for the BS, in addition to the textbook."

"Let's just figure out who does what," he said, turning on the TV.

I flipped through the packet. "Not Colonialism. I don't want to write about a bunch of white guys thinking God gave them land."

"Might makes right," Ronny said. "You take the Pensacola Siege. Spain against Britain. Too personal."

There was a pause. He flipped to a page in his book but didn't read it.

"You ever meet Joaquin?" he asked, matter-of-factly.

"Who?"

"Joaquin. My friend. I see him a couple of times a week. Helps with stress."

I blinked. "Never been acquainted."

He smirked. "Helps me get my money's worth, y'know? Before I go to a whore. I whack off. Otherwise, it's thirty bucks for thirty seconds. You gotta clear the pipes first."

I chuckled—confused, embarrassed, and curious about how relaxed he was about the whole thing. I hadn't even managed to say the word out loud without my voice cracking. Total taboo in my neighborhood. Ricky said it was gay—his logic being that any male hand touching a male part was gay by definition.

But, apparently, girls could go for it.

I had never met Joaquin, but I was a distant advocate in theory. Dr. Ruth had explained it on the radio, and she had a PhD.

Like swearing off swearing, I felt a little bump in my self-esteem for maintaining control.

Before I could say anything else, his mother called from upstairs: "Juanito, you're staying for dinner. I already added extra carrots."

At the table, I kept my elbows off and my eyes down. Ronny's sisters filed in—one older, two younger—and made little whirlwinds of noise that his mother calmed with nothing more than a glance. His dad wasn't there, which helped. The older sister—Jessica, I think—asked me polite questions about school, then launched into a story like we'd known each other a while.

"We had Father Tierney over last week," she said, putting a napkin on her lap. "And I swear, the whole time, he wouldn't even look at the photo of Father Fry we keep on the end table. It was like a showdown. Eventually, he laid it down on its face."

Ronny snorted. "That's 'cause he and Fry are rivals. Who gives the best mass? You would think priests can't be petty, but they care about popularity like anyone else."

His mother gave him a look that was more amused than stern. "Don't give Juanito the wrong impression. Priests are closer to God."

When the food came, I grabbed my fork, but Ronny leaned over and tilted it in my hand.

"You're holding it like it's a handlebar," he said. "Don't shovel. You eat like a Neanderthal."

I felt my face heat up. I adjusted the grip and avoided eye contact with the others, which made it weird, because that left me constantly facing Ronny.

His mother watched us with a kind of solemn understanding. Her voice was sweet and her questions kind. She asked a few more questions about school but never pressed. Every time someone interrupted or talked over someone else, she smoothed it over like ironing a sheet.

On the following Thursday evening, I made my way to the Twombly Square library, which occupies the end section of the same low brick structure as the fire station. Sometimes you were startled by an engine roar while you were at the card catalog. My purpose that night was to meet Ronny to exchange notes and use the library's Xerox machine. Ronny had obtained several highly graded responses from a previous year's project, sourced through the sibling of a classmate.

I had just stepped past the Town Field, when I heard Peachy's voice echoing from behind me. I turned. Matt Flannery, Peachy,

Timmy Salinger, and, the new kid, Will Patrick were already coming my way. Our group was absorbing fringe characters from Twombly neighborhoods.

"Where you going, school boy?' asked Matt.

Timmy fell in beside me. He was shirtless under a black leather vest, tan from summer, and too good-looking to really fit in with the rest of us, although he occasionally graced us with his presence.

"I didn't know this town had a night school," Timmy said.

"It's called homework, people," I said.

"Well, your home is in the other direction," said Matt.

"I do all my homework at school instead of class work," said Peachy.

"Smart," I said. "I have a spy ring pulling together test answers. It's our weekly meeting at the fire station up ahead."

Inside the library, I made a beeline for the Xerox machine, loaded in a dime, and flattened my notebook pages one by one. Will flipped through old issues of Highlights, while Matt poked fun at the fire safety posters: "Stop, Drop, and roll a doobie on the fire escape."

Then the door opened again—and Ronny walked in, wearing a crisp green polo accompanied by a shorter kid with wire-rimmed glasses and long, but neat brown hair.

"Bruce Freegate," Ronny said, pointing, and then realizing the others were with me, he continued, voice quivering. "He is in McRay's fifth-period class. He lives on the other side of the Res from me."

Bruce gave a stiff nod and a half-smile, suggesting he was used to being evaluated. He stood tall, though he was short. Then, we all left the library.

Matt leaned over to Will. "Look, Hanson brought backup. Another one of the Hill People."

Timmy smirked. "Trust fund babies?"

Will jumped in, pointing at Ronny. "I seen him in gym. Walks on his toes, like he's dodging puddles. He gets way into square dancing, too—like claps and everything."

Ronny's face flushed. "No one ever told me I was supposed to walk differently."

Bruce took a step forward, inserting himself between Ronny and Will with a quick look that said enough. "Different strokes for different folks. Okay?"

Will raised an eyebrow but didn't push it.

Matt turned to Bruce. "Nice glasses, four eyes."

Bruce shrugged. "Thanks. They help me spot people who still think that's an insult."

It landed well enough to shut Matt up for the moment.

Peachy, watching the whole thing, leaned sideways and whispered to Timmy, "Do people from up the hill always talk down?"

Timmy snorted.

"Why are you friends with this kid?" asked Will as I traded papers with Ronny.

I mumbled something about grades and hoped they'd move on.

As we walked away from the library in different directions, the tension had fizzled to a low simmer. But, distance gave Ronny confidence.

Ronny called out, "Must be exhausting carrying around that much attitude with that small a brain."

Matt turned, grinning. "Look who's talking—tippy toes himself."

Matt, Will, and Timmy tossed a few more lazy insults—something about inbreeding and band practice. Will threw a half-empty cola can in their direction, missing by twenty feet and nailing a parking meter instead.

"That's what happens to you socs when you come into our neighborhood," Peachy yelled after them with theatrical bravado. "Greasers rule!"

"Calm down, Ponyboy," I said.

Watching Ronny get humbled—roughly but deservedly—was satisfying. But, what stayed with me even more was how Peachy, Timmy, and Bruce each lit something inside me. It was like trying to tune into three radio stations at once, every signal pulling me with its own rhythm. I wanted to tag along with each of them, to figure out what they were all about. They were witty and spontaneous, but it wasn't just that. In their jokes and jabs ran a current of humor tangled with calculated risk, and a kind of power I'd never felt I could touch. By then, it was harder to insist this was all just about friendship.

For the first time, I let myself wonder if what I felt wasn't just camaraderie but something sharper, more fragile, and more important. Maybe Eric and Ricky weren't flukes, like I had thought. And, was someone out there like me—someone who might feel the same toward me?

The thought was thrilling, and it scared me. I could play it safe: keep building friendships with these guys who fascinated me and manage the rest quietly, pushed to the margins. Or, I could let the feelings move closer to the center, out in the open, come hell or high water. One path was safe but muted. The other was risky and carried the possibility of being fully alive. That tension spun inside me, asking questions I wasn't sure I wanted answered.

That next week took a dark turn. The news spread fast. By morning, everyone knew: some of the Big Kids had been driving back from a party, the car full of people and bad decisions. Ryan M., just sixteen, was intoxicated behind the wheel. Ryan K., who was basically the Little Kid's favorite big brother, riding shotgun. Aaron, the quiet older brother of Sarah's friend, and Frank— solid and worthy of our crew—were in the back.

There was a terrible wreck. Aaron and Frank didn't make it. Eighteen years was as old as they'd ever be.

And, once I knew Frank had died, the memory rose up on its own— the busted leather glove pulled tight with mismatched shoelaces. Frank tossing the baseball like he had all the time in the world.

The wake was in the church hall, with lines curling out into the parking lot. *Free Bird* played on a loop: "If I leave here tomorrow, will you remember me?"

People stood around in coats too heavy for the weather, the smell of cologne and cigarette smoke wafting. Inside, there was that low murmur, the sound of people trying to be solemn but still making small talk. You could see the same face over and over again—red eyes, polite nods, the look of someone unsure if they should cry or find the door.

The next day at school, in college-bound science, Mr. M—lean, mustache, corduroy blazer—pulled a folded newspaper from his briefcase. He read the headline aloud to the class, then the article, as if it were part of the lesson plan.

"This," he said, shaking the paper for emphasis, "is what happens when you drink. Blitzed out of their minds. Don't be stupid like these kids."

No consideration, no sense that anyone in the room had ever seen one of those boys, let alone grown up alongside them. Just a flat voice and a moral tacked on at the end, as if the only thing worth noting was the beer cans in the wreck.

After school, I told the Flannerys about the teacher while we stood in their courtyard, the air damp and cold. Matt's jaw tightening. Danny's face—he looked at me like I'd said something worse than the teacher.

"You never stick up for us," he said, stepping in close.

"What?" I asked.

"You hear somebody talking like that, you're supposed to say something," Danny said, his eyes fixed on mine. "You don't just let it slide."

"Was I supposed to stand up and say 'I object?'"

"We're people, not bad examples," said Matt.

I wanted to say more. I didn't know how—that it had all happened too fast, that I didn't want to draw the class's attention to me. But, the words didn't come. Danny turned away first, muttering something I couldn't catch, and Jimmy and Matt followed him inside.

I stayed in the courtyard a moment longer, staring at the foggy kitchen window, wishing I'd said something in that classroom and wondering if it would have made any difference at all.

Peachy straightened from the neighbor's stoop, where he'd been half-hidden in the shadows.

"Man, they got worked up," he said, nodding toward the door.

"You heard?"

"Teacher says something stupid, you freeze. They want you to swing a chair through the window."

I huffed out a laugh I didn't fully feel. "Guess I'm not much of a chair-swinger."

We stood there for a moment, watching our breath in the cold air. Then, Peachy gave my shoulder a quick tap with his fist.

"For what it's worth," he said, "those guys wouldn't have given a damn what some science teacher said. They only cared what we thought—and that every girl in the town cried over 'em."

"Yeah," I said. "I still wish I'd told the teacher: I know these people. He doesn't."

The next week, Matt informed us, "Ma's on the rag over what happened." Not five minutes later, as if summoned, Mrs. Flannery suddenly entered our basement nook. It went quiet—Ricky and Bobby still holding their beers, not lifting them, not setting them down, like something worse might happen if they moved. Matt had his six-pack parked beside his chair, sweating onto the concrete. Nothing in his hand, thankfully. She stopped short, took it all in, and snapped, "Jeeps Cripes, put that down. We don't do that. We're good Christian people."

She grabbed a work-out towel and started scrubbing an impossibly dirty end table, shoving junk into tighter piles, straightening what didn't need straightening. "This place is a pigsty," she said, breath sharp, hands flying. "I'm not having it."

She didn't look at Matt's beer. Not once. My face felt hot, my stomach tight, like I was about to be sick or faint. No one said car or road or dead. Mrs. Flannery kept wiping in furious little circles. Then, she left without another word. That was the only time I saw her in the basement, before or since.

Beyond that, we did not talk about the accident, tried not to think about it. And, at the time, this strategy seemed to work.

Ronny was absent from school, so that left me and Bruce meeting without him for the first time. We were sitting side by side on the edge of the steps behind the school, papers rustling in the fall wind, our outlines spread out like a failed mutiny. Bruce kept scanning Ronny's "contribution" as if it were some ancient parchment.

"He literally just rewrote what you said about indentured servitude and what I wrote about rum production," Bruce muttered.

"Only dumber," I said, squinting at Ronny's paragraph. *Molasses were like the ketchup of the triangular trade*?

Bruce closed his eyes. "He's not even helping. He's just trading off our work with weak paraphrasing and keeping everything for himself."

We sat in silence for a minute, watching a lunch lady dig violently in a trash can like she had thrown away her paycheck.

Then, Bruce said, "Wait a minute. What if we're engaging in the Triangular Trade?"

I laughed. "So we're like... molasses and tobacco?"

"I call tobacco," Bruce said immediately.

I smirked. "Fine, I'm molasses. Aren't you forgetting, I can turn it into rum?"

Bruce roared. "And Ronny's the slave ship. He sails between us, picks up our labor, and unloads it for personal gain."

"Or maybe he's the merchant in Europe, counting profits and never breaking a sweat," I added.

"Either way," Bruce said, "he's not in the fields."

We leaned back against the cold metal railing, smug and newly allied. There was something thrilling about uncovering the scam together, like we'd just exposed a spy. And, now that we'd named it—turned it into a historical reenactment—I felt giddy and motivated at the same time.

"We can't let him get away with it. Let's make him do the rest for us." I said.

"I say we dump some bad cargo on him," He said. "Rotten paragraph. Just believable enough that he'll pass it in."

"—-and stupid enough to lose him points!"

Bruce tilted his head, delighted. "Historical sabotage."

"I could feel it starting again—the buzz just beneath my ribs, the light-headed charge of being next to someone who got it. Bruce's irreverent smirk —the way he always managed to turn an insult into insight—made me feel like we were collaborators in something more than a school project. Maybe this was what I needed all along: the momentum flowing from a common enemy, a reason to have inside jokes, and someone whose laughter made me feel whole. There was the sense that something in me was waking up and turning toward the light, but still under the soil, not ready to show itself. I hated it. I loved it. I wanted it to stop and to keep going.

Ronny's parents were away, and he was staying at Brian Monty's house. Monty's yard was darkening, the air crisp with that clean October chill, smelling of dirt and smoke and something spicy. The porch light hadn't been turned on yet, but you could hear the static of a TV from somewhere inside.

Bruce knocked hard.

No answer.

He knocked again. Still nothing.

I glanced up at the window. "He's in there."

Bruce stepped back and called, "Ronny! Come on. We know you're there. We just want to talk."

The front door creaked open a few inches, and Brian's sister slid halfway into view. She was in sweat pants and a pink cardigan, holding a phone on a long cord in one hand while keeping the other on the door frame.

"You two," she said flatly. "It's a school night."

"We're not here to hang out," Bruce said. "It's about the project."

She exhaled, long and slow. "Then you can yell about it in school tomorrow. Not on my porch."

"We just need five minutes," I said. "He's not answering. And, we're not letting this slide."

"He sucked us in!" Bruce added.

She narrowed her eyes. "I won't be spoken to that way. Such vulgar language."

Bruce stiffened. "That's not vulgar."

I stepped forward. "He's not doing his part. He's copying from us."

Monty's sister shook her head and called over her shoulder. "Ronny! You've got two honor students out here ready to riot!"

There was a pause.

Then, the door opened wider, and Ronny stepped out in socks. He looked like he'd just been woken from a nap he was pretending not to have taken.

He didn't look at us right away. Just stood there, arms folded, the porch light finally blinking on above him.

"I've been working," he said, defensively. "I used your notes, sure, but we agreed to share stuff. We're all getting the same grade."

"That's not sharing," Bruce said. "That's freeloading."

"You didn't say I couldn't use your stuff."

"You are supposed to write up answers too," I said.

The wind picked up a little, rattling the dry hedge along the walkway. Ronny rubbed his arms and looked down at his socks on the cold concrete.

"So what do you want?"

"We want you to finish the rest of the questions," Bruce said. "The ones we haven't done yet. All of them. Your work."

Ronny frowned. "What about the children's leisure one? That stupid primary source packet with the diaries?"

"We'll give you that one," I said. "But, the rest? All you."

He hesitated. Looked past us like he was hoping Brian would appear and rescue him. Then finally: "Fine."

Monty's sister leaned against the door frame and said, "This is the most foolish fight I've ever heard. What happened to just doing your own work?"

Bruce turned to her. "Economic expansionism."

She sighed. "Lame."

As we walked up the hill, the sidewalk slick with leaves, I felt lighter and tenser at the same time. Bruce didn't say anything until we reached the corner.

"We're giving him a messed-up answer, right?"

"Obviously."

He nodded. "Let's write it at my place. It's not far."

We walked the rest of the way in comfortable silence, our breath just barely visible in the cold. Bruce's house smelled like onions and something sweet baking. We dropped our bags in the hallway and stepped into the kitchen, where his mom stood stirring a pot of rice on the stove.

"Did you two sort out your revolution?" she asked.

"Treaty signed," Bruce said.

"No casualties," I added.

She smiled—soft around the eyes, wearing a sweatshirt that said *North Conway is for Lovers.*

"You'll eat here?" she asked, already knowing the answer.

"Yeah," I said. "If there's enough."

"There's always enough," she said.

Dinner was ground beef, rice with soy sauce, canned peas, and slices of buttered toast. The kind of meal that tasted like nothing fancy and everything right. Bruce's little brother, Nate, sat across from us, and their mother moved in and out of the kitchen. Everything was friendly and relaxed.

Nate said, "Feels like winter already. You think it'll snow before Halloween?"

Bruce smiled. "If it does, I'm going as an Eskimo. Plenty of pockets for candy."

"That's practical," I said.

"At least it beats teenagers who don't wear a costume, and just show up with a pillow case begging for candy," Nate added.

"So, when are you officially too old to trick-or-treat?" I asked.

Bruce raised his eyebrows. "Never, if you're short and wear a mask."

"Always sneaky," I said. "I like the way you think."

Bruce laughed, loud enough to make me feel warm inside.

After dinner, Bruce and I cleared the plates and washed up. His mom left us with the drying towels and a warning not to stay up too late.

"Big day tomorrow," she said, ruffling Bruce's hair as she passed. "You'll overthrow a government or something."

Back in Bruce's room, we sprawled on the carpet with our notebooks open and a shared goal: to take down Ronny via well-placed nonsense. Time to beat him at his own game.

"Okay," Bruce said, cracking his knuckles. "Colonial leisure time. We want it to sound just real enough that he won't question it."

"Weak but plausible," I said.

We were giggling like idiots. It felt like we were seven again, making up planets or secret codes—but smarter. Sharper. The laughter had teeth now.

"Hold on," Bruce said, getting up. He opened the cabinet above his closet, pulled down a ceramic snowman, and twisted off the hat like a lid.

Inside was a bottle of rum.

I stared. "Seriously?"

"My mom used to bake with it. She forgot about it."

He poured a splash into two plastic cups. We tapped them together, drank, and coughed.

"Good lord," I said. "That tastes like paint."

"It tastes like freedom," Bruce said, eyes watering.

The rum hit slow and mean. I didn't feel drunk, exactly—just loosened. Like my insides had gone warm and the space between me and Bruce had compressed to something molecular. His face looked different in his desk lamp glow. Kinder. Sharper. Like it had been cleaned and restored.

We finished the fake write-up, our masterpiece of made-up colonial trivia:

"According to 18th-century family diaries, children of the time occupied themselves with such pastimes as 'Thread and Pail,' a coordination game involving buckets and wool yarn, and 'Parsnip Racing,' wherein root vegetables were balanced on sticks and rolled down muddy lanes. Other diversions included Whackstick, barn-hurdling, chimney mimicry, and competitive hoe sharpening. These games were believed to promote moral rigor and a strong work ethic."

We wrote "Ronaldo H." in big dumb print and sealed it in an envelope labeled: "PRIMARY RESPONSE #3."

We went for a snack and stopped by Nate's room. He was already out cold, the cat rising and falling on his chest with each breath like a sleepy heart monitor. Bruce tucked the covers in tighter and clicked off the light. The warm wholesomeness of the evening made the mischief feel like spice.

Back in his room, Bruce stretched and smiled. "We're going to hell."

"We're going to finish eighth grade first."

He laughed—open, easy, no shield at all. Then we both lay back on the floor, staring at the ceiling.

The rum buzz was fading, but the other feeling wasn't. I could feel it gathering again—a warm tide in the chest, tugging gentle and deep. There was joy in it. The wish for him to be satisfied, full, complete. The hope that I might matter in his life. And, beneath all of it, the feeling that he really did approve of me. But, could I be cherished the same way?

I turned to look at him, but his eyes were already closed, smiling still.

For now, there was this: a full stomach, a stupid prank, a soft cat breathing on a younger brother's chest, and the boy who made me feel like everything I said was worth hearing.

I was heartbeats away from another Eric tsunami, already bracing for impact.

After school later that week, Jimmy exhaled, talking over the commercial. "You know Luke and Laura are on the run?"

We'd all started watching General Hospital.

"From the mob," Ricky said. "I think. And, the cops."

"They're a couple now. No more Scotty. She chose Luke," said Jimmy.

"Didn't he... you know... rape her?" I asked, keeping my voice steady. I wasn't sure I was doing the right thing.

Ricky flicked his eyes at me, quick and unreadable, then stared at the carpet. Jimmy's gaze stayed fixed on the TV, but his smirk thinned for a second before coming back.

"Yeah," said Mad Dog, picking at her teeth, "but then she fell in love with him. So it doesn't count."

Patty leaned into the doorway, arms folded. "You all know why that's unrealistic and wrong?"

Danny frowned. "They're gonna get married," adding his attempt at defense.

Patty shook her head. "If someone does something to you when you don't want it, that's a big deal."

Jimmy shrugged without looking at her. "Well, it works that way on TV. He's the good guy now."

Patty shot him a look. "They just let it go because the actor turned out to be popular."

"That's messed up," I said.

Matt said, "Anyway, he's got cool hair."

Everyone nodded. The hair comment shut it down, at least on the surface. I still didn't know what you were supposed to do when you knew about something real. I hoped that little chat was enough to keep certain lines from being crossed again. It bothered me that the show could rename harm into romance, and we could deflect it with hair.

We got C+'s on the colonial project. Ronny somehow pulled a B-minus—a reward for keeping more of the high-fluting language and knowing how to smile and nod while turning in absolute fiction. The teacher hadn't noticed the chicanery.

Bruce and I didn't talk about it. I kept waiting for something to spark—another secret plan, another fist bump, another night of rum and closeness. But, it didn't come. And without the cover of pranks and obscure history, I didn't know how to reach him.

I needed a setup. A side quest. A veil.

The next project was on the Civil War. Before I realized what was happening, we were a trio again: Bruce, Ronny, and me—like nothing had ever happened.

Only this time, nothing was ready the day it was due.

I went along with Ronny's idea: skip school, finish it in downtown Boston. "The McDonald's on Park Street," he said. "We'll knock it out in less than three hours, then maybe walk through the Commons. Check out the swan boats."

It sounded illicit and meaningful. Like we were breaking a rule that might clarify something.

That morning, I walked to school with the Flannery brothers like always. But, when they turned left toward homeroom, I peeled off. Slipped out the side door.

Later, I found out Matt Flannery had seen me through the big cafeteria windows—watched me vanish off school grounds, never having shared my plans.

So much for stealth.

The Park Street McDonald's became base camp for an unexpected tour of duty. We opened the Trapper Keeper on a table near the back, and set up our folders. Ronny ordered hash browns. Bruce got a Coke, grinning at the cashier in that easy way he had. I sat still, soaking up the hum of fluorescent lights and the low, oily buzz of the fryers. We organized our papers a bit and did some reading.

But then everything changed.

The plan to finish the project gave way to "taking a break." We handed our binder over to the counter staff—so we wouldn't have to carry it—and headed out to "clear our heads." We wandered through the Combat Zone. Where neon signs buzzed over strip clubs and movie theaters, and the air was thick with old beer and something even more sour. Glimpses into adult novelty shops felt like looking into a space alien's workshop.

Two girls passed. Bruce smirked at Ronny. "Bet she's wearing a thong."

They laughed. I kept my eyes on the cracks in the sidewalk, wishing one would open up and take me.

We ended up along the river or was it the harbor? We saw a stray headlight and so many glass bottles. They got stuck in that weird, feral rhythm of boys with time and no boundaries. Bruce and Ronny threw rocks at the glass and glass at the rocks. Repeatedly. They shouted just to hear the echo.

I stopped talking.

Bruce didn't question that.

Neither did Ronny.

I was furious that we had cut school to get the work done, and all they wanted to do was play. And, I didn't like what they were playing at. I was jealous that Ronny was growing closer to Bruce instead of me over something I didn't care about. An area I had no desire to compete in. It all felt like a pointless waste of time. Not a good way to prove ourselves.

They talked about sports. About which NBA players could kill a man with their bare hands. Bruce laughed at something Ronny said and lobbed a wine bottle toward a cat behind a dumpster. I watched it arc through the air—long enough to wish I could stop it, too late to do anything. The cat was startled out of its skin.

Then, the older boys showed up.

High-school-aged thugs. Shoulders hunched, faces stubbled, half-shadowed, stomping loudly in their boots. One person commented on my hair. Another asked if we had cash.

We didn't run—we just moved. Fast enough to seem motivated, not afraid. We ducked into a crusty little convenience store, and the man behind the counter—long gray hair, nervous tic—stepped between us and the others. He said he would call the police.

"You boys need to wait this out," he said, not smiling.

They left.

We didn't say thank you. We just backed out, quieter than when we came.

By the time we got back to McDonald's, the shift had changed. New workers. New menu. Our binder was unaccounted for.

Bruce started laughing nervously, saying someone probably tossed them in a dumpster. I didn't laugh.

After five long minutes, they found our Trapper Keeper tucked somewhere underneath a register. A grease stain on the corner. A fry in the spine.

Not a single page completed.

Bruce said, "We could still knock out something on the train."

I didn't answer.

At Harvard Square, they wanted to check out the newsstand.

"I'm just gonna take the bus home from here," I said.

"What?" Ronny looked confused. Bruce was already halfway across the street.

I walked away without another word.

That night, the phone rang.

It was Ronny.

"You just left," he said. "I know you were mad."

I said nothing.

"Sorry, we got off track. Didn't mean to stop talking to you. It's just... You don't really say what you're thinking. Bruce—he's different. He just... makes things known."

"I don't—what?"

"You and me, we're close," he said. "You're the one I can be myself with. He's just more fun when we're out."

I let his words sink in. They stung, but only on the surface, like cold water on the skin.

The hurt that mattered was somewhere deeper, and Ronny couldn't see it from where he was standing. He thought it was about the project, or about being left out of the fun, but it wasn't. The silence was heavier than that—an unspoken story, a longing I couldn't admit, a jealousy I didn't want him to know about. The pauses carried more than words could, even if to him they sounded like nothing at all.

"Okay," I said, "I've still got that assignment."

"Right."

"See you tomorrow," I said, and hung up.

The line went dead. I sat there holding the phone, staring at nothing, feeling the kind of silence you only notice when the person you want to hear from isn't the one calling.

Ronny was suddenly really into weed. Not just casually—he was into it, like it had cracked open some part of him that had been waiting to come loose. He talked about it like a secret religion, as if each joint gave him access to a private hallway in his brain that most people didn't know existed.

I gave it a shot. A few sleepovers, a few slow passes of a roach between two fingers. I didn't hate it—but I didn't love it either. It made me feel like my thoughts and perceptions had been scrambled and put on a slide projector backwards. I'd forget what I was talking about mid-sentence, laugh at something that wasn't that funny, then get gripped by the idea that I had maybe said something unforgivable, even though only I seemed to notice.

But, those late-night excursions to the reservoir were fun.

We snuck out way past midnight, cutting across the field like fugitives. Ronny carried a towel in one hand and a pilfered flashlight in the other, whispering about undertow myths and killer pipes that could suck you down and pin you like laundry against the grates. I didn't know if it was true, but I knew one thing: we always swam in the known safe spot, over the gate and off the dividing wall, where the water was still. That didn't stop my heart from banging like a drum in my chest the first time I jumped.

Ronny said he and Bruce had been doing the same kinds of thing with him—only their version came with a detour: the renovated house across the wood patch at the bend in his street. They'd go there high and smash windows one by one with whatever loose gravel they could find. Ronny said they once did their whole routine in their boxers for no reason at all. "Just something that happens when you're high."

Then, it started closer to home. Some of the guys from the project gang got into casual property damage, the way some kids get into baseball cards. New condos were going up at One Clock Lane, all framed out in fresh two-by-fours, no roof yet. One night, I heard a group had climbed up to the second floor and just started kicking the walls in. Kicking like they were mad at the wood. A petty play for dominance?

The next evening, we were on our way to the Police Athletic League that took place in the station's basement. The Flannerys, Will Patrick, and Peachy scooted across the property at One Clock

Lane to reach the tracks when the workers from the site came running out, yelling and pointing. “You think that’s funny?” one of them shouted.

We froze. They knew it was kids. Maybe they didn’t know which ones. Maybe they didn’t care.

We scattered like marbles dropped on a floor, sprinting down the rails or into the woods. Somehow we made it, hopping ties and ducking through the brush. All of us, except Will.

Will was on crutches, from a fracture he got trying to jump a ditch the week before.

The workers caught up and surrounded him. The rest of us stopped and hovered from a distance, stuck between the instinct to run and the shame of leaving him behind.

They didn’t touch him. Just blocked him in and barked questions. “You think it’s a joke to destroy people’s work?”

Will shook his head. “Wasn’t me.”

“Your buddies then?”

They looked up at us, the rest of us frozen like deer. One guy motioned with his hand, aggressive, more furious. “You want to pay for that?”

We inched closer, a little braver in a pack. “We’re just going to PAL,” Peachy said. “Nobody did anything.”

And maybe that was true. Maybe none of us did. Maybe it was a different group altogether. But, I remembered the broken beams and thought: Someone did. And, someone thought it was worth it.

It didn’t make sense.

Even stealing, as low as it was, had some logic. You wanted something. You took it. I couldn’t stomach it, but I understood it. But, this wanting to break something just because it stood; this was something else.

What was erupting in the male psyche that made pointless destruction feel good?

Why did Bruce like it?

Why did Ronny laugh when he talked about smashing windows?

Maybe it was about power. Or having none. Or trying to prove something to a world that didn't seem to care about you unless you made a loud impact.

Or maybe it was just about being fourteen and full of biochemicals and messages about masculinity.

After a lengthy standoff, Danny suddenly said, "What are you going to do, harm the handicapped?" He let it hang, sharp and absurd.

That broke the tension.

The men exchanged a glance, and the taller of the two stepped forward, veins bulging in his neck. "Keep screwing around, and you'll eat wood. I catch any of you punks near that site again, I'm dragging you by the ankle to your parents. Or the goddamn morgue." Then they stepped back.

Will limped forward, and we headed off for Foosball and ping-pong.

I kept thinking of the twisted two-by-fours, the empty house, the broken glass. That was the end of the Bruce episode. I had wanted to play house with him—some version of comfort, closeness, working for a cause—but he preferred the thrill of smashing it down. I lost something. I felt it. A crack in trust, a dimming of hope. Thank God the wave hadn't risen higher with him—because the further you rise, the harder you fall.

I liked irreverence. I didn't like when it cascaded into cruelty, when the rush mattered more than the fallout. And, I hated it most when it erased people—like they'd never been there at all.

Part of me knew I'd just learned something important. I just didn't know what to do with it yet. Whatever boys were reaching for, I could already feel myself reaching for something else.

14
Competing Hearts

When we moved up to high school, we all started trimming the "-ys" off our names, like it was the price of admission to adulthood. Peachy became Peach—still fruity, but at least without the extra syllable. We stopped calling the older guys, Big Kids. Ron and I went to Beaumont High. Eric, a Beaumont Hill kid all along, hear tell stayed on the hill and went to the private school there. The project crew caught the bus to the Regional Vocational Technical High School, a place known for cigarette smoke and hallway deals. That school seemed to chew people up for fun, eventually spitting many of them back to regular public schools after enough detentions piled up.

Rick and his mother shelved the college dream. The sting was real—grades slipping just far enough to close certain doors, the unspoken verdict that the college-bound classes hadn't been worth the strain. But there was also relief in stepping off the treadmill: no more nights wrestling with material that felt like a foreign language even more so than Spanish class, no more measuring yourself against the kids who seemed born knowing the answers. In its place came a looser, more practical kind of thinking. He would train to become a carpenter, or maybe something else in the trades. Options that felt less like defeat and more like breathing room.

My own standing shifted: the "fairy" whispers faded, replaced by "nerd" as testosterone finally made its move—voice lower, body changing, just enough edge to make the old taunts sound dated. And, my intellectual pursuits became more prominent. Getting good grades was my priority. I considered joining the chess club and going to a Star Trek convention, but did neither. Ron started getting his hair permed which gave him some increased razzing, but he looked a whole lot better. For a time he was focused on getting his tongue clipped. Actual surgery to be better able to pleasure the ladies. I guess we were both chasing upgrades—mine measured in hypotheticals, his in hair chemicals and oral surgery.

In junior high, everyone wore the same gym uniform. By high school you had to bring your own workout clothes. I didn't own any printed t-shirts that weren't ragged, and my newer tees were just plain white. At Bradlees, I asked my dad to buy me a blue shirt with an eagle logo splashed across the chest—something with personality. He shook his head and held up a three-pack of solid blue shirts.

"See this? Just over double the price of the one you picked, but you get three. Get these or nothing."

I chose nothing.

Meanwhile, boys like Eric and Ron had a steady supply of Izod alligator polos. I started collecting my own, one by one, from Filene's, but by the time I caught up, Ron had already moved on from alligators to Ralph Lauren polo players. My yard-boy wages couldn't keep pace. And, then there was the cruelest part: a muscular blond sophomore dating Ron's seventh-grade sister. He could stroll into class in a plain white t-shirt and let his body supply all the status he would ever need.

Beaumont High School wasn't just a school; it was a campus—sprawling like a small college. A third of my walk each morning passed the athletic fields, manicured and endless, their lines so crisp they looked designed by Ancient Egyptians. The field house loomed beside them, all polish and echo: indoor track, basketball court, a hidden stadium that unfolded like a magician's trick on game nights. Even the pool glittered Olympic-blue, as if a slice of the tropics had been poured indoors.

Inside, the place felt just as grand. Corridors stretched long and orderly, each wing devoted to its own discipline. Labs gleamed with glassware and gas nozzles I'd only seen in encyclopedias. Even the cafeteria felt less like a lunchroom than a modest restaurant, chrome bright, with a school store tucked beside it as though learning required equipment.

Everywhere you turned, the school seemed ready to shape you into something—grease under your nails in the auto shop, greasepaint under the hot lights of a real theater. There were no "study halls," only "free periods," idleness rebranded as opportunity. You could wander to benches around Peat Moss Pond or slip into the hushed two-tiered library, or stand in the atrium at the center of everything—a glassed-in courtyard where sunlight was curated like an exhibit. It felt like the school was displaying its idea of perfection and inviting you to imagine you belonged in it. Beaumont High had everything—everything except an admission of what it meant: working-class rebellion and upper-middle ambition sharing the same halls, pretending not to notice each other.

I became a member of the Columbia Record and Tape Club, thumbing through the glossy fold-out catalogs, treasure maps with catch. A penny for ten tapes? How could that go wrong? With disco finally dispensed with, the project gang leaned into grittier fare—Cheap Trick, Foreigner, The Knack. Cassettes stacked on top of the stereo, plastic cases clicking together.

We'd sit around with the music blaring, arguing about lyrics, though the arguments were more about ourselves than the words. For a while, *My Sharona* owned us. That riff—dun-dun-dah, dun-dun-dah—buzzed like electricity in your ribs, and we'd shout the stuttered "M-m-m-my Sharona!" until the rafters shook. Then it was Cheap Trick's *I Want You to Want Me*, ricocheting off Matt's basement walls while he drummed the armrest with pencils. Ricky and Peach bickered about The Knack's *She's So Selfish*, each trying to sound more worldly, while I insisted if it was on the radio it couldn't possibly be about sex acts. They leaned into the bravado, decoding lyrics into innuendo, proving they knew what the songs "really" meant.

I leaned back and let the sound crash over me, but my mind was elsewhere. The guys leaned into Pink Floyd, pounding their fists and shouting along with the part about not needing school and teachers leaving kids alone, like it was gospel. I let them chant, but in my head I was hearing a different kind of chorus. Beneath the noise, a softer thread tugged at me—music I secretly ordered from Columbia or taped off the radio late at night and replayed when no one could hear. Air Supply's *All Out of Love*, like a diary entry I wasn't supposed to write. Christopher Cross's *Sailing*, smooth and wistful. Kenny Loggins' *This Is It*, REO Speedwagon's *Time for Me to Fly*. Songs you could hum under your breath walking home alone, each one a bandage for an ache you didn't talk about. Their music raged at the world; mine tried to make sense of being lonely in it. That was my secret soundtrack, tucked away like a note worn soft in a back pocket. I forced a smile, but inside I was already humming *All Out of Love*, just for myself.

Overnights at Ronny's house became a regular thing that year. His mother was wonderfully warm in a way that made me feel adopted. "Juanito, we have everything you like in stock," she'd announce as I came through the door, as if I were a VIP customer and not just her son's friend. And, she did: Weaver's Chicken Rondolettes, Ellio's Pizza, the good soda. On big weekends, Ron tried to get me excited about HBO boxing events—Marvin Hagler,

Roberto Durán—fighters whose significance I couldn't quite grasp. I barely followed the matches, but his enthusiasm, the snacks, the running commentary—that part I loved.

Getting high together carried its own strangeness. We would end up in the basement flipping through his father's European exotic magazines—some of them confusing in ways I didn't understand. "Hermaphrodites are real?" Ron caught where I was focusing and teased me, "I can't believe where your eyes are going," laughing like he saw through my lies.

During the basement remodel, before the new carpet in the den and the modernized bathroom were finished, we slept on the dining room rug—it was thick, almost like a padded wrestling mat. One night, Ron rolled over and lay across me like I was just another mattress, warm and familiar. After a minute, he just rolled over and fell asleep. I lay awake longer, the weight of that small closeness settling bizarrely.

In spring, Freshman track was a big deal. Everyone was joining the team. Last year, Coach had taken Beaumont High freshman all the way to the State meet and came home with a trophy. He was also known for providing free pizza on the regular.

Coach knew somebody at the *Beaumont Gazette*, so every week our warm-up lines and awkward poses would show up in the paper. That brought in the off-season football and baseball guys who wanted their names and faces in print.

On top of that, my oldest brother's name still sat in the school record books, holding the mile and two-mile for the past ten years. Those were big track shoes that I wasn't going to fill.

Karl—cute, skinny, dirty blond, was running distant events like me. He was a Beaumont Hill resident, an honors student, a band geek with a haircut you didn't see on anyone else: long and bushy, except for these cropped bangs that made him look both sharp and messy at the same time. His quiet confidence made something in me hum.

During practice, it became clear that Karl was working harder than anyone. Coach surprised all of us by making him captain. We figured it would go to a football star, but no—Coach pulled the modest kid with the odd haircut to the front of the line. Karl stood there, stiff, then raised his arms like it was nothing, leading us through arm circles.

One Monday afternoon, less than two weeks away from our first meet, I staggered light-headed from intervals, and there he was, suddenly standing on a locker-room bench.

"You're not taking this seriously enough," Karl said loudly, voice cutting through the steam and sweat.

We all froze.

"You think just showing up gets you into shape? That getting your pictures taken makes you a star. Coach expects more. I expect more. We have a reputation to uphold."

Murmurs. Somebody muttered, "Okay, Hitler."

Karl didn't flinch. "Fine. But, don't cry when we get blown out of the water."

It was the same day Reagan got shot. A surreal afternoon all around. For me, it set butterflies loose I couldn't catch.

I started watching him closer—on the track, in the halls, on the way home whenever I could. He mostly talked with the other honors students. He was a bit aloof or just... occupied.

Later, more captains were named—one from football, one from baseball. I figured that was that. So when Coach announced me as the final captain, I just sat there dumb.

"On your feet," Coach instructed.

I stood, cheeks hot. Karl gave me a small nod—approval, maybe, or just acknowledgment. The promotion meant I'd be Karl's partner for stretches. We'd hold each other's feet for sit-ups, lend your back for leg extensions. The whole thing felt choreographed by someone bent on torment.

The meets started, and the pattern for the mile was set: Karl first or second, me always third, the other team's best guy breaking between us. I had the best view of Karl's races—the arms pumping, the lean at the tape. Close, and yet unreachable.

Conversation was impossible.

One day I tried. "Good sprint."

Karl glanced at me, already pulling his sweatpants on. "Thanks." Then he drifted back to his friends.

Here we go again. Fascination and frustration—two sides of the same coin I kept flipping every week. Fairly quickly, Karl carried his own soundtrack in my head—*Keep on Loving You* drifting up whenever I glimpsed him in the distance, the melody tinting him with a kind of glow. And, when the song found me suddenly on the radio, my heart lifted and ached at once, as if the world knew my secret and was humming it back.

The only thing worse than these periods of intense attraction were those times when there was none.

Ron was as girl-crazy as ever, always convinced he could read girls' secret signals. He swore that the girl sitting in front of him in English deliberately tossed her hair over his desk top so he could run his fingers through it. So he did. Daily. The fact that he somehow got away with it—never once caught—amazed me. He treated it like proof of destiny rather than creepiness and dumb luck.

Ancient History, though, didn't go so well. One of his crushes leaned over like Cleopatra, whispering embarrassing questions and instructions, and Ron followed like a soldier taking orders.

"What's that you have in your lap, a boner?"

"It's just a fold in my pants sticking up."

"Come on, tell us how it's hanging."

Then the crush's friend echoed, "How's it hanging, Ron?""

She and her friend huddled, giggling, then dared him to lean back and ask the jock at the end of the row, "How's it hanging?" And worse—tell him how his was hanging.

Ron obeyed. The words left his mouth, and the jock's fist landed square in his face before he had time to regret it. The girls howled with laughter, nearly falling out of their seats. Ron sat red-faced, blinking, as if the punch had woken him from hypnosis.

The teacher—Mr. Cole, with his booming voice and endless supply of jokes—didn't miss a beat. He slammed his pointer against the desk with a crack like a gunshot. "Gentlemen! This is Ancient History class, not gladiatorial combat!" His eyes twinkled even as his jaw tightened. Then he shook his broken pointer like a scolding finger. "You may save your contests of manhood for the Colosseum—or the locker room—but not my classroom."

Eventually, he had to replace that poor pointer with a thick wooden dowel from Plywood Ranch, which only made his dramatic thwacks louder.

"You saw that whole disaster, huh?" Ron said that night.

"I saw it," I admitted. "Hard to miss."

Ron groaned, then chuckled. "Man, I can't believe I actually said it. 'Mines hanging low' Like some idiot puppet with Shannon pulling the strings. And, then—bam. McQueen's fist. My ear's still buzzing."

"She set you up," I said.

"Yeah, but no one else would've actually done it. Only me. Because Shannon bats her eyelashes and suddenly I'm Mister Obedient. I hate myself for it, but at the same time... she's got this laugh, you know? Like you'd do anything just to hear it. Even take a punch. That's gotta mean something to her."

"So, you actually think this was just an embarrassing chapter in a larger story that will have a happy ending?"

"Of course. And, by happy ending, we mean a hand job."

Ron always had people he could unload on. He didn't have to sit alone with it. If he made a dumb gesture, he could tell Monty, me, or Bruce, or even his sister, who half-mocked him but still listened. And, gave killer advice. If he got laughed at by a crush, it turned into a story—something to laugh about later. His screw ups seemed to melt into the air the minute he spoke them out loud.

I didn't have that. I couldn't sit down with Matt or Sarah and say, "I think I wanted to kiss Karl," or, "I can't stop thinking about him." That wasn't an option, not in Beaumont. Not anywhere I knew of. So, I kept it inside—every mistake, every rush of attraction, every confusing thought—stored up like secrets in an overstuffed locked box. If any of it were public, there would certainly be consequences.

Jenny Sutter, a junior, who ran sprints was the sister of our shot put-er, Tom. She crossed paths with us a lot, ponytail bobbing, smile locked onto me.

She caught me after a race once. "You always finish third," she teased.

"Thanks," I said.

"No, I mean it's good. Reliable points for the team. Some of these guys—" she swung her chin toward the group laying on the pole vault mat—"they don't place, they don't even finish the workout."

I shrugged, but inside I glowed.

"Anyway, you're kind of cute when you're sweaty."

I froze. Karl was ten feet away, stretching against the fence. He didn't look over.

"Oh, your shoe's untied," she warned.

"Is this where I look at my tied shoe, and then you say 'made you look'?"

"Now, that would be childish. It really is untied, and the other is loose. Oh, I'll just do it!"

She did just that, right there on the track in front of whoever cared to look.

And, then during one Saturday practice, Jenny asked softly. "What are you doing after?"

"I work. Need to rake in the bucks."

"Where?"

"It's just landscaping for a lady over by the police station."

"I will visit you. I want to watch you while you work."

Jenny was pleasant looking and pretty funny.

But, even then, I could feel Karl near, the weight of him pulling at me. Jenny's offer spiraled in paradox—she offered what I couldn't even dream of asking from him.

After a pause, I said yes. Because it's easier to take the sure thing than to keep chasing the specter of probably-not.

She showed up that afternoon, just like she'd said—on the sidewalk where I was planting boxwood in a row behind the junipers I already planted. I had a spade in one hand and mud caked on my sneakers. She stood there in hemmed shorts, arms folded, grinning like she'd bought a ticket in the bleachers, and she'd been upgraded to the front row.

"Very manly," she said.

"Yeah. Nothing sexier than dirt under your nails."

She laughed and sat on the low stone wall, close enough that I could smell her shampoo. I pretended to be absorbed in tamping soil, but really I was watching her watch me.

"I work too. You know? I babysit," she bragged. You can visit me there, or just come to my house. You'll like it there."

"Really? Will there be snacks?"

"Sure. And, I can cook for you."

Suddenly, I noticed someone watching us and signaling with her hand.

"Who's that at the corner, is she with you?" I asked.

"Oh her? That's my neighbor, a foreign exchange student."

"Is she your back-up?"

"Yes, I brought her along in case you attack me."

"Whose side will she be on?" I asked.

"She's not going to help you attack me, I'm pretty sure. Let me go check with her for a second," She said.

"Actually, I have to work in the back after these two plants are finished."

"I'll be back fast, and I won't stay long."

I planted the last two Boxwoods. When I looked up again, the wall was empty, so was the corner. Jenny was gone.

I had to go onto the next task on my list.

I went down the garden path into the rough patch, searching for stones to line the drainage ditch. It was a tedious job, but every time I unearthed one that was the right size and shape, it felt like a prize. They sat cool and solid in my hands.

"Hello!" Jenny startled me. One moment it was just me, bucket in hand, the next she was there—ponytail swaying, grin like she'd hit her target.

She'd circled around the municipal buildings, slipped down along the railroad tracks back towards me, and cut into the yard from behind.

"Guess who found you?" she said, eyes bright, grinning like she'd cracked some code.

"I thought you left," I told her, though I couldn't stop my own smile.

"I did. But, then I thought—what if you're hiding treasures back here? A secret hideout? A forbidden lover? At the very least, a stash of candy bars."

"No candy bars. Just stones." I lifted my bucket as proof.

She laughed. "That's it? I track you down like Nancy Drew and you're just... picking up rocks?"

"That's exactly it."

"Why?"

I set one in the bucket so she could hear the clink. "Drainage ditch. The lady wants it filled before monsoon season."

Jenny glanced toward the rail bed, where thousands of gray rocks stretched under the steel lines. "Why not just take those? A whole mountain of them right there. Seems a lot easier."

That was not allowed. I'd been told flat out: not from railroad property, not even one stone. I told her so, and she shook her head like she couldn't quite understand why I'd follow something that stupid.

For a second, the dilemma hit me—pursue the easy or the right? Hunting these scattered stones among the trees was like searching for a boy who might actually fit: slow, uncertain, full of effort, and patience. The rail gravel was different—stones seemingly available in easy abundance like girls, sanctioned by everyone else but not for me. I could have scooped them up in minutes, but it wouldn't have been me. But, could it be?

Jenny stepped back, bent down, plucked a stray chunk of gravel, and dropped it in my bucket with a clink that echoed against the others. "Guess that's one more."

Her smile widened, reckless and inviting. And, I liked—God, I liked—that she'd come back. That she'd circled around just to stand in the bushes and be silly with me.

For a moment I let the thought of Karl drift off like smoke. Jenny's attention landed heavy and bright, and it was joy—pure and simple—to feel chosen, to feel pursued without even half trying.

Many good things seemed to be clicking into place, as though the Lane itself had fallen under a spell. Owen Masters arrived on Clock Lane like a man on a mission. With his famous Realtor wife selling million-dollar homes up on Beaumont Hill, perhaps he felt compelled to prove himself equally grand—a developer of merit in his own right. He carried himself like a savior descending into a neighborhood in decline, the benevolent baron coming to lift us up.

He tore down the old Sullivan house next door—sagging roof, weary clapboards—and in its place began raising something new, squared and crisp, like a dollhouse scaled to real life. He spread fresh gravel down Clock Lane, right across our driveway too. He passed out gallons of paint to homeowners like tokens from a generous king, each color sealed with the promise of modernity.

Even when his men crushed our garden at the common edge, Owen was quick to provide recompense: a mountain of rich, black loam, dark as enchanted soil. From that heap, Dad rebuilt the garden directly in front of our house—twice the size, twice the fertility, rows so neat they might have been drawn with actual farm equipment. It was as if ruin and renewal had been conjured in the same breath, as if Owen's arrival had brought both the destruction and the gift.

Jenny's house sat at the base of Haver Hill, right where the road tilted upward into the steep climb that broke cross-country runners on their first try. The course was notorious: up that hill, twice around the reservoir, and back down with your legs shaking like wet noodles. Brutal if you weren't ready.

Her house was the opposite of brutal. Comfortable, clean, lived-in but updated. The kind of house where the wall paper was refreshed every three years and the carpet was soft underfoot.

Jenny practically bounced through the doorway, tugging me along. "So this is the living room. I spend no time in here. Mom picked out the couch last year—it's way too stiff, but she swears it's 'classy.' Oh, and don't sit in Dad's chair. He says it molds to his body, which is gross."

She swung us toward the kitchen. "And here—this is where I bake brownies for when I babysit, which makes kids like me way better than their parents do." She grinned, daring me to question what that meant.

Her mother who was older than expected poked her head in, smiling her warm patient smile, like a hip grandma. "You two hungry?"

Jenny waved her off. "Later, Mom. I'm giving the tour."

We ducked into a little alcove off the living room, a TV room with a door that conveniently could be closed. She shut it. "Best part of the house. Private movie theater." She flopped on the couch. "Don't spill the popcorn."

I sat next to her, pretending to watch the show flickering on the screen. When she leaned in, I didn't stop her. Our first kiss, quick and certain. French. My second thought was I better start taking the lead.

The door slammed open. Tom bounded in, smirking. "What are you doing?"

"Watching TV," Jenny snapped, as if the volume of her voice could erase what he might have seen. We sat like statues until he left.

Her chatter carried us through the awkwardness. "So, my older brother's in college. He's got one friend, this guy who's—well, let's just say the floor sags when he walks on it. They're harmless. Mostly upstairs with pizza."

Jenny fiddled with the wired remote, flipping through channels too fast to watch.

"So cool you have a remote control." I popped out. "We can just stay relaxing on the sofa."

"I know. And, I can jump rope with it during the commercials."

We laughed.

"You know what's weird?" Jenny said suddenly, her grin fading. "My last boyfriend. First kiss, right here in this room two years ago." She flicked the remote, eyes on the TV though she wasn't really watching. "And, a year later I'm sitting here, same spot. I hear an ambulance go by. Sirens screaming."

She twisted a strand of hair around her finger. "Didn't think much of it—'til five minutes later I see my boyfriend flying down the hill on his bike. Racing like he could outrun death. His brother had fallen off their roof. Landed on the fence. Impaled."

The word hung there, flat and sharp.

"They tried, but he didn't make it." She exhaled, slow. "I'll never forget how fast he rode. Like if he just went hard enough, he could keep his brother alive."

My mouth went dry, like I'd swallowed chalk dust. All I could picture was the sirens, the hill, the fence—and her boyfriend bent low over the handlebars, not braking, letting only the limits of physics contain his speed. Suddenly, I didn't feel like I was watching Jenny's story, I felt like I'd been dropped inside it.

Finally, I asked, "Were you close with his brother too?"

She shook her head. "Not really. He was older. Always outside. Playing sports. Climbing trees. I barely knew him."

"What happened after? With you and the boyfriend, I mean."

Jenny's eyes flicked to me, then back to the screen. "We lasted for a while, but he wasn't the same. Couldn't be. He was always somewhere else. He was always focused on that day, and eventually he stopped calling."

I nodded, though it felt too small, too polite: "That's... intense."

She gave me a half-smile, almost rescuing me. "You're allowed to say it's the worst story you've ever heard on a first date."

Her dad passed by the door once, younger and more rough around the edges than I predicted having met their mom. Jenny muttered, "Head janitor at like three different places. He thinks that means he's basically the mayor of maintenance."

Later, the doorbell rang. Jenny whispered, "Oh, that's my friend, the foreign student neighbor. She's from Holland. Real prim."

I tried small talk —about running, the weather, anything neutral. She nodded politely, her accent light, her gaze darting like she was taking inventory. When she left, Jenny tugged me aside, still half-grinning.

"She says you were staring at her the whole time."

"I wasn't."

Jenny laughed. "I know. But, it's kind of funny, right? She thinks every boy is either after her or judging her."

Jenny was very happy about something. If anyone was staring, it was her, at me. Her eyes were shining like she'd just discovered another special secret. The kiss, the teasing, the house itself—it all added up to something dizzying. For a moment, I let myself believe I fit right there, at the base of the hill, in her world.

The gun cracked, and the pack spilled forward in a rush. Sneakers slapped the asphalt, four quick strides and we settled into the lane. Karl surged ahead, long legs chewing the curve, Lexington Kevin and I tucked close behind. The rest of the field strung out after us, already fading.

By the end of the first lap, the three of us had locked into formation: Karl in front, Kevin shadowing his right shoulder, me just off his hip. We circled the same backdrop again and again—the scoreboard, the low bleachers, the cluster of parents and kids milling along the fence. Each time I passed the start line it felt like déjà vu, as though nothing moved but our lungs and legs.

Jenny was there, of course. Even when her team wasn't racing, she came to my meet with her mother to see Tom throw shot put and to see me, and she never missed a chance to cheer. Her voice carried over the din, calling my name, telling me to push, to claim second, to take the lead. The sound of it thrilled me, but part of me shrank from it too.

Because Karl was only five strides ahead—close enough that I could feel the rhythm of his pace beating in my chest. To pass him would mean daring something reckless, and I feared the sight of his scowl more than my own burning lungs. I didn't want him to see me as a rival, or worse, a threat to his record.

Their shoulders brushed once, the rhythm of their steps hammering out a challenge. I stayed right behind, my lungs searing, legs still finding a rhythm but holding, just barely. The pack behind us was gone, strung out like laundry on a line. It was down to the three of us.

We rounded the curve: scoreboard, bleachers, fence, Jenny. Her voice rose above the rest, calling my name, begging me to push. I wanted to answer her, to be the boy she saw me as. But, ahead was Karl, still fighting, still proud, his back as magnetic as it was unreachable.

Kevin surged, and Karl broke with him, both of them lifting into something fierce. I tried to go too, legs churning, breath clawing, but they pulled away—first five strides, then eight. Karl grimaced, fighting to hold the line, but Kevin's form was clean, relentless. Kevin slipped free, arms pumping, stride opening.

Karl strained, face twisted, but he couldn't reel him back. Kevin's strength was the straightaway, eight strides clear, and the race was his. Karl crossed next, pride battered but intact. And, me—third. Solid, steady, no collapse, but no glory either.

Jenny clapped loudest for me anyway, as if she hadn't noticed who'd actually won. She smiled like the finish belonged to me. And, for a flicker, I let myself believe it.

But, my eyes strayed forward to Karl, bent at the waist, hands on knees, sweat dripping off his chin. Even in defeat, he was the one I measured myself against. I stood there on the track, caught between them—the joy of being cherished by her, and the ache of still wanting to be approved by him.

On the track, it was about who could hold the lead through the last lap. Among my friends, it was a different race: who was edging ahead in physical intimacy, who was stalled at the starting line. Ricky had had an on-and-off girlfriend for years, and that alone put him in front. I was the second one "to land one," which gave me standing, though shaky. The rest— the Matts and Danny—were still warming the bench, but that never stopped them from playing coaches.

"So, who's actually made it past first?" Danny asked, narrowing his eyes like a prosecutor.

Ricky shrugged, slow to answer, like he wished the question would pass him by. "Third," he admitted at last.

"Third?" Matt's jaw dropped. "You serious?"

Ricky nodded, deadpan. Not bragging. "Just happened."

I tried not to look like I was calculating. "Well," I said, "I'm in the first inning. Solid first base. Nothing wrong with that."

Matt snorted. "First base? That's barely in the game."

"Funny," I said, "coming from guys who haven't even picked up a bat."

Danny scowled. "We're holding out for quality."

"Right," I smiled. "Meanwhile Ricky's on third, I'm on first, and you two are still in the dugout... polishing your helmets."

Ricky burst out laughing, nearly choking on his Cheetos. Even Matt cracked a smile, though he tried to hide it.

Sometimes, I thought maybe I was straight after all. First base felt wonderful—God, I could have stayed there the whole game. Second was interesting, third tolerable. Plus, I was always entertained by the glossy girls in Playboy—perfect smiles, hair like golden waterfalls, soft curves—but when I opened Hustler or Penthouse, the bluntness made me queasy, like being shown the inside of the engine when you only wanted to admire the finish. What did that mean?

I went into a trance as I jogged a few laps alone. I was remembering that time up New Hampshire, my father brought home a stack of second-hand magazines from the dump, and buried in them was a single Playgirl. I smuggled it behind a shed in the salvage yard, then carried it deep into the woods. There I stripped naked, laid back in the sun, and let the pages shine over me like stained glass. Later, I hid it under the overturned base of a grill. The heat scorched the ink and the dampness fused the pages together until the images bled away to ghosts, but I still poured over it long past the point of sense.

I felt unfinished like our "new" house—four years old and nowhere near completion. It was tailored with windows my father scavenged from auctions and the dump over the years. Ten of them, each of them a rectangle, but each a different size and proportion. The place looked crooked, restless, but alive. It was embarrassing, sure, but part of me loved that it didn't match. Each room held its own mystique. Then, one day he tore them all out, replaced them with store-bought standards, neat and uniform. He filled the odd gaps with stacked two-by-fours until every edge lined up. The house looked proper at last. Normal. Almost Finished.

Jenny was like those new windows—clean, acceptable, admired by everyone. Being with her made me look more finished, more normal. I liked her—God, I did—and when she smiled at me, I wanted to believe she was a perfect fit. Some part of me still remembered the mismatched panes, the odd angles that let in light differently, strangely, beautifully. And, I wasn't sure whether I was being built up or boarded over.

Being wanted and wanting someone turned out to be different things.

By May, Jenny and I had settled into a rhythm. She passed three notes for every one I managed. There was a predictability to it—locker drops before homeroom, a hand-off by the stairwell after third period, another folded square slipped into my palm after lunch. I half-dreaded, half-anticipated each one, the way a person feels about a test they're not sure they studied for.

Her notes read like diary entries—long, looping, full of everyday details. Mine were shorter, but I tried hard to keep pace. She made me want to.

Jenny's Note #1 (stuffed into the crack of my locker, folded into a perfect triangle):

Johnny—

Today feels endless already. First Mom forgot milk, so it was dry cereal and forbidden coffee. Then in English, Mr. Birk called on me even though my hand wasn't raised. I got it right though! Do you think teachers keep a list of kids they want to torture?

Also: if you could live anywhere besides Beaumont, where would it be? And what's your favorite song right now?

mmm... (remember, that means I love you).

—love, Jenny

John's Note (written hurriedly in geometry, neater than usual):

Jenny—

I think teachers just go after whoever looks like they want to be somewhere else.

If I lived somewhere else? Portsmouth maybe. I like the water there. It feels open, like anything could happen. Song: My Sharona.

—Love John

PS— I want to try being "John" and leave "Johnny" behind.

She came by my desk later that day, tapping her finger on the paper before slipping it back into her notebook. "See? You're learning. A whole paragraph." She winked. "And too bad, you'll always be Johnny to me."

Jenny's Note #2 (three pages worth crammed onto lined paper, delivered with a smirk at the stairwell):

Johnny—(yes, Johnny!)

If you stop being Johnny, who saves all the stories you already lived? Who remembers the backyard raft and the fort? You can't just graduate out of your own name. Math was torture today. My chalk squeaked so loud the class laughed.

Also, guess what! Tommy says Karl has the best stride on the team, but I don't believe it. I told him, I think you do. You just hold back because you don't want to make Karl mad. Am I right?

Questions:

Favorite smell?

Do you like my hair shorter or longer?

Would you come over Saturday even if Tommy and Mom are both home?

mmm...

—love, Jenny

When I saw her at lunch, I asked, "Why would talk to Tom about me? And, say I am holding back because of Karl?"

Jenny only grinned, like she'd lobbed a pebble into the pond to see how big the ripples would get.

"Is it true?"

"Maybe a little. But, why are you broadcasting it?"

"Because it's true. And, because you can do better than third place."

That afternoon at practice, "Lindstrom!" Coach yodeled in front of everyone. "Quit holding back—you've got more in you than you're showing."

The words landed like a slap. My stomach tightened. I hadn't told him that. I had only told one person.

Then I glanced at the bleachers. Jenny was there, beaming and waving like she'd just done me a favor. She'd gone to the coach, told him I wasn't giving my full effort. Behind my back. Was she specific about Karl? That was the one and only peep I let out about Karl to anyone.

I wanted to be grateful—she believed in me, wanted me to prove myself. But, the truth was, I hadn't asked for her help, and now every eye on the track saw me as the kid who'd been called out for loafing.

We lined up for a test mile. The pack held tight for two laps: Karl steady and fluid, me shadowing him. Jenny's voice cut through the air: "Come on, Johnny! Take the lead!"

On the back stretch I surged, heart hammering. For one delirious stretch Karl was behind me, his stride falling into my wake. I'd done it—I was ahead.

But, the third lap dragged, and the weight of it all was too much. Jenny's eyes on me, expecting more. Karl's presence, steady, inevitable. The coach watching to see if I lived up to what Jenny had promised.

By the final bend, Karl swept past, long stride eating the distance. He crossed the line first, me second, everyone else a distant blur. Jenny clapped like she hadn't noticed.

Karl jogged back. "Good kick," he said, and there was just enough steel in his voice that I didn't know how to take it.

I jogged a cool down lap, lungs raw, throat burning, world spinning. Part of me was proud I'd dared to pass him. But, another part burned with shame: that I fell on my face.

Karl's pass wasn't just about racing—it was about authority, about not letting me step too far into his territory. Did he ever think of letting me win a practice run? Would he respect me more for beating him or for staying out of his way? I was moving in two directions at once.

I was never sure which loss cut deeper: Jenny handing my secret to the coach, or Karl proving, again, that I couldn't keep what I'd tried to take.

After practice she was waiting for me by the bleachers, arms crossed but smiling like she'd done something helpful.

"You're mad," she said before I even opened my mouth.

"You told Coach I was holding back," I said. "Why would you do that?"

She tilted her head. "Because someone's gotta give you a little nudge."

"That wasn't your call."

Her smile faltered. "I didn't mean to embarrass you. I just wanted him to notice what I notice—that you can beat Karl if you let yourself." She touched my arm. "Don't you get it? I believe in you. I want everyone else to, too."

I shook my head, half-angry, half grateful that I wasn't entirely alone in my struggles. "You don't understand. ... it's not that simple."

The Wakefield meet was supposed to be routine, but it had a different energy. Karl and I were jogging the warm-up loop when one of their guys—a tall miler with a wide smile—slid in beside Karl like they'd known each other for years.

"Good turnout today," the boy said easily, his voice smooth. "You guys running the mile?"

"Yeah. How about you?" Karl asked.

"Yeah, I stick to distance. Sprints are for guys who want to look fast without thinking. Not my thing." He chuckled, light and confident. "In long distance, though—there's strategy."

Karl nodded. "Knowing when to push ahead."

"And hey, your people get to cheer you on four times." he said and then in a lowered voice, "I heard there are Ivy League scouts out there in the crowd."

Karl shook his head. "If only. They're not that serious about track—especially freshman."

Wakefield nodded, lobbed another question, and soon their words passed back and forth so naturally I might as well not have existed. At one point they laughed together—Karl laughing with a boy he'd just met, an opponent—and it made my chest feel hollow.

I wondered how he did it. How a stranger could just glide into Karl's attention, no effort, no risk. If I tried suddenly pouring on the friendliness, it would feel like I was revealing too much.

Later, when I went through the locker room to the toilet, I caught fragments of the Wakefield boy's voice again—this time lower, sharper. He and another teammate snickered near the showers.

"... Psychology," the miler said. "You act friendly, maybe he softens. Doesn't know whether you're competitor or comrade. Half the game, man. Just getting into his head."

I couldn't tell if he meant it or if he was just covering, so he wouldn't look soft in front of his own team. I didn't know. I only knew I hated how easily he'd charmed Karl. I wanted to erase it.

Jenny walked beside me on the way back.

"Something's off with that team," I muttered.

"You may be right. See that kid? The one adjusting his socks? He's done that five times in two minutes. That's either superstition or he just really likes the fabric."

Karl stretched out flat on the grass, one leg curled, the other extended. I hovered nearby, waiting. Jenny stepped in, then leaned over Karl so her shadow fell across his face protecting him from the bright sunlight.

She just smiled, then looked at me, like she was saying: see, it's not so hard to take care of him.

I cleared my throat. "Karl. That Wakefield guy? I overheard him. Said being friendly was just...messing with you."

Karl sat up slowly, sweat dripping, eyes narrowing. It turned into the longest conversation we ever had.

"Where'd you hear that?"

"Locker room. Him and his buddy."

"Wonder if I should say something."

"Just be clear on people's real intentions," I said, though my own voice shook a little.

Karl nodded once, got to his feet, and marched over. "Hey. You faking friendly for some reason?"

The boy blinked, looked at me then back at him, then smirked. "Man, relax. I never said that, it was just a joke."

I don't know whether those pre-race happenings changed anything. Maybe Wakefield just had better runners. But, that day, Karl was beaten by two of their milers—his only third-place finish all season. I didn't place at all.

It struck me, for a second, that maybe Wakefield and I were both putting on shows—him pretending friendliness, me pretending indifference—just different costumes in little plays of our own making.

I told myself I'd done the right thing, being Karl's eyes and ears, giving him something to fight against. Underneath, I knew it was the only safe way I could approximate closeness: not through warmth, not through acts of inquiry or caring, but by handing him the external driving force of a common enemy. That might push us together. My concern could be easily disguised as team loyalty if need be. If I'd tried to bond any other way, I risked two things at once: falling flat, killing the fragile hope of a future between us—which was my oxygen—and exposing myself as a freak, which would have felt like stepping in front of a firing squad.

We hosted the state meet that spring. The Beaumont Gazette had quoted our coach the week before: "This isn't going to be a cakewalk like last year." He wasn't wrong. It was a fruitcake crawl—dense, lumpy, and left a strange aftertaste.

We were spread thin—half the team had drifted away over the season, and those of us left were asked to cover gaps we had no business filling. Karl and I each ran three events: the half mile, the mile, and the relay. By the end we felt like worn-out chess pieces moved in circles with no hope of capturing the king. Ron ended up in the quarter mile, an event he'd never trained for. God bless him, he lumbered down the home stretch, arms windmilling, finishing a good fifteen seconds behind the field. But, at least it was more memorable than the mediocre performance we had in the mile. There's nothing interesting about being one of eight kids clustered in the middle of the pack, with no hopes of winning, just straining to shave a few seconds off their best times. The five-minute barrier still taunting us like some cruel mirage. But, Ron's experience—that made a better story. His disaster had character. It took first place in the comedy of errors.

In second place, Tom Sutter uncorked a shot put so wildly off-angle it ricocheted toward the refreshment table. For a second it looked like the world's slowest missile had been launched and a row of parents jolted back with their sodas sloshing. Coach said nothing, just pinched the bridge of his nose like he was trying to reset the sequence.

When it came to Karl, nothing felt funny.

Before the last heat, he stretched out on the pavement, and I lingered, trying to think of something to say. I shaded his eyes with my shadow.

"Any plans for the summer?" I asked.

"Nothing specific. How 'bout you?"

I mumbled something about boxwoods and mulch, words that felt as thin as the air between us. What I wanted to say was, *Do you want to practice together this summer?* But, it stuck in my throat.

In the relay, I passed him the baton and he carried it clean, strong. But, afterward, it struck me that this was our whole story: me handing him something, him running on ahead, and me trailing off, never able to catch up by design.

The season ended with him out of reach, and me left holding nothing but air.

PART III

Acts in Compromise

15
High Fidelity

It's hard to grieve what you never really had. The hurt comes in warped. The familiar empty spaces are still there—only bigger now, the thin traces of hope erased and replaced with more vacancy. You get used to the gaps—the silences, the maybes, the almosts. You learn to tolerate the distance and the waiting. And, when the object of your affection is finally gone, the love survives on that familiar emptiness for a while until you realize you aren't missing the person anymore, but just the shape of the air they left behind.

That summer, I tried to be faithful—to Jenny, to the script, to the idea of who I was supposed to become. And, expected to collect on the investment.

We went to Zayre one Friday, then to *Friday the 13th: Part II* with her new best friend, Kathy. Jenny bought a pack of Play-Doh on a whim, and in the dark theater she shaped crude little "adult toys" and slipped them into my hand with a wicked grin. By the time Jason hacked his way through the cast, Jenny and I had pushed to third base—our own absurd subplot unfolding between popcorn buckets.

I thought it was time to parade Jenny in front of my friends, though it didn't go smoothly. She made an offering of doodled caricature. Crossed eyes was her trademark comic touch. Matt exploded when he saw his. He spoke with rising fury, and then stormed off. I didn't understand until later—that he carried a faint eye injury from a childhood accident, falling out of a car. I had never noticed. Jenny's casual detail landed right on an old wound. I stood there stunned, realizing how little I understood about even the faces I saw every day.

Another night, Jenny and I visited Ron's basement den. After some pot, a game of truth or dare surfaced quickly, with dares sending couples into the adjoining bedroom. At Ron's request, Jenny showed me her breasts in the open light. Previously everything had occurred under the cover of clothing or darkness. She refused to reveal herself below the waist due to a childhood operation; for that I was grateful. After kissing Ron, Jenny dared Ron and me to make out, we both refused, sharing an unspoken taboo against crossing that kind of line. The whole thing dissolved into nervous laughter.

Then, came my so-called home run, in my bedroom. Not bad, but something was missing. I realized I was more caught up in the kissing than anything else. One kiss was so absorbing I lost track of the rest of myself and deviated from the script. Jenny whispered, "Don't just sit there," and something in me snapped. I was doing this for her—not for me—and she dared to criticize? Two minutes more and I stopped cold, blurting out that I was afraid she'd get pregnant.

Jenny understood her role and the dynamic between boys. The next day, when we were fooling with a tape recorder, on her turn to speak, she suddenly said "Johnny makes me wet" and later blurted out: "Can I say Johnny fucks good?" I couldn't tell if she was helpfully providing positive feedback and proof, implicitly encouraging more, or just offering a reckless joke. Regardless, the recorded words carried weight.

Then, came another complication, a troubling erotic dream. My subconscious was pressing against my agenda. Maybe it was residue from that foolish soft-core porn Ron made me watch on pay-TV—hetero, but clumsy, and so dumb it was almost a parody.

My head was filled with bodies moving, bare butts in the air. The magic of dreams had replaced the bimbo nurse and two doctors with three co-captains. I was with Mr. Baseball and Mr. Football—guys I'd never felt warmly about, suddenly in the middle of something I didn't really want, not fully. My dream wasn't even about Karl. Thankfully, I suppose.

I woke queasy, like I'd betrayed someone without meaning to. That morning I called Jenny, hoping her voice would rinse away my fifth, clear the slate with something sweeter.

There was some shakiness in my efforts to be faithful to the bit. My penchant for absurd humor could derail me at times.

One Saturday towards the end of June alcohol didn't just loosen me; it set me off like a rocket. After a six-pack in the Flannerys' basement, with pent up track-star energy, I shot out the door like I was in an event for the Olympics nobody asked me to join. Down the Lane, up the little hill, over the wooden bridge, and then down to the business end of Serenity Drive, I sprinted toward Twombly Square.

Right then, everything looked so sharp and clear. Running by at night felt like moving fast forward through a carnival of color. I actually looked at things: the beauty salon glowing with hair dryers like alien pods, the foreign auto repair shop with letters that seemed like a code to crack, the vet's office faint barking from within and right in the middle, the John Birch Society headquarters—stuck there like a crank uncle at Thanksgiving.

At Twombly, I slowed to a brisk walk in front of the Railway Corner Grill just as Peach, his sister, and brother came out. I gave a casual, "Hey," like I just happened to be strolling by. His brother started to open their car door. A block down, I picked up speed again and at the fire station, sprinted back towards the projects via

Twombly Road. After the diagonal trek across the fields, I rested on the steps on the side of the Flannery's building.

Just as Danny sat down next to me a few minutes later, the same car pulled up—no sister this time. Out came Peach, and the second his eyes landed on me, he nearly toppled over.

"Wait. Weren't you just at Twombly?" he asked with a faux level of drama.

I'd already been back long enough to catch my breath. They must've stopped at home to drop off his sister.

"Nope," I said, to see where this would lead.

Who drove you back?"

"No one."

"He's been here all night." said Danny with authority.

Peach staggered closer, eyes huge. He clutched my arm like he was checking for flesh and bone. "You—you've got a twin! Admit it! You've been hiding a twin brother this whole time!"

I shrugged, biting back a grin.

He pulled me up, wild-eyed. "Don't play games with me, Johnny! This is black magic. Teleportation. Time travel. What the hell is going on?"

Danny muttered, "You're high. Pretty much explains it."

But, Peach wasn't done. He circled me like I was a UFO crash site, muttering about impossibilities, demanding answers, grabbing my shoulder every few seconds to test if I'd vanish. He was lit up—grinning, flushed, half-drunk, half-high, and in my personal space.

And, it did something to me. His excitement, his awe, his grip on my arm that lingered, it all sparked hotter than before. What had been a slow simmer for months boiled up much higher, disguised under his comic frenzy. He laughed, petted my arm, and begged me to explain the riddle.

I finally smiled and said, "Maybe I just ran."

He blinked, searching my face, then laughed again—a laugh full of awe and disbelief—and pulled me closer. "No way. Not possible."

And I let him believe whatever he wanted, because the truth—the real truth of what was sparking between us—was too complex.

All I knew was: the joke was on him, but the fever was upon me.

The next morning, I woke up hungover and in a completely different frame of mind—still smarting about Karl, confused by Peach, but I doubled down on my earlier plan to make things work with Jenny. I hopped on my bike and rode to meet her at the Commons. I made a private bargain: *if I could clear the hill at the end of the Lane without stopping, it meant I loved Jenny. If not, I was doomed.* I did it with ease that day and had renewed confidence.

I hadn't been over by the Center in weeks, and in the meantime the town had refurbished and moved that little train station ticket booth that used to rot behind the library. Now it sat right in the Commons, painted bright yellow, its roof pointed like a wizard's hat. Restored to its original condition, it felt like a space capsule that had plopped down overnight.

Jenny was already on the porch of the "spaceship," waving as if she'd just landed.

I smiled. "Was this here yesterday?"

"Welcome to Starbase Commons," she announced. "Population: me."

"Did the Martians drop it off, special delivery?"

"Don't be jealous," she said. "They chose me as ambassador."

"And, what's your first act as ambassador?"

"Mostly sitting here until someone buys me a Coke."

We settled into a long, drifting conversation—the kind Jenny was good at pulling me into. She wanted to talk about *Friday Night at the Movies*, the network's latest offering, *Ode to Billy Joe*. I didn't think so at the time, but maybe she was on to me or trying to test my reaction?

"I used to hear that song in the Flannerys' station wagon," I told her. "Every time it came on, we shut up. Wanted to know why Billy Joe jumped off the Tallahatchie Bridge. We thought we just never caught the whole song. But, it turns out the song never explains it."

Jenny shrugged. "Well, now you know. He was messed up about that girl."

"Not just that," I said carefully. "The movie made it seem like... something happened with that old man. I didn't get it. Why that ugly guy, and not the nice young girl? It made no sense." I left the sharper edge of my curiosity unsaid. If Billy Joe was involved with a handsome young man that might have cleared it up for me, but that wasn't what happened.

Jenny wrinkled her nose. "It was just Hollywood being gross. I don't think about it."

The father and brother mentioned Billy Joe's death the way you'd mention rain and I couldn't shake how cruel it was to erase someone that easily. Jenny said that's just how men are.

The conversation sagged under its own weight, so I tried to push it lighter. "At least Jack Tripper on *Three's Company* doesn't mind when people think he's gay. He even has fun with it."

Jenny laughed, rolling her eyes. "Yeah, but his reward is the two chicks he can live with, and that's just TV. Real life's a whole different thing."

Jenny nudged me with her shoulder. "Anyway, I've got babysitting Tuesday night. You should come over. We can hang out after the kids are in bed." She gave me a sly smile. "Don't worry. I'll have condoms."

I kept feeling like I owed her something I hadn't agreed to give.

"You better have tranquilizers for the kids."

"Warm milk should be enough." She grinned. "And if not, I'll just make you read them stories until they conk out."

Owen Masters' renewal efforts took a darker turn when the fence went up. It wasn't just any fence—it was tall, raw wood, planted further out from the side of his new house than anyone expected, running all the way back to the tracks.

"The thing cleaved the yards like a fort, cutting off the Indians." Denny observed.

Owen said the property came with a path to the railroad, that he was merely reclaiming what was his. That Bob had been mistaken all along. In the process, Bob's stacked wood, his second-hand lawn furniture, and that odd back-stretch contraption of his ended up crowded into other areas of his yard. It felt like Owen was taking something that was due him by default, something that had always been Bob's. And, on top of that, he was asking Bob to just go along with it quietly.

Bob wasn't having it, though. After weeks of asking, he tore out a section of fence and reinstalled his chairs and tables like a little frontier outpost, staking his claim. For a time it stood, a stubborn camp planted on the disputed land.

But, Owen hired men to come hammer the boards back, tossing Bob's things over as if they were worthless. A lawn chair bent. A table leg split. And, when Bob stepped forward to hold his ground, Owen fell theatrically to the earth, crying assault. The police came at once, siding with the man who had staked the claim and built the wall. Bob was led off in cuffs from land that had been his as long as anyone remembered, while Owen's fence remained. To me, it just seemed like money gave people the right to do whatever they wanted. It felt unfair in the simplest way: One person's wish was treated as natural; the other's reluctance as something that didn't count.

Jenny had an overnight babysitting job across the street from her house. I slipped over after the kids were asleep, and we poured a little something from a bottle we found in the cabinet. The first sip burned; the second felt like a door unlocking. Condoms were impossible to get, so Jenny teased about a substitute activity, whispering like she wanted to be sure her family could not hear. Out loud, I just laughed, trying to keep it light, but inside I felt the walls move—reckless, exciting, dangerous in a way I can't describe.

"Imagine if their parents came home early."

" I'd just say you were here to deliver a package."

"Yeah, where's my uniform?"

"You don't really need one—at all."

I smirked, staring at the flickering candle she'd lit as a prop. Outwardly, I matched her tone, leaning into the comedy of it. Inwardly, I felt the rush of how precarious it all was—like holding a lit match too close to paper.

We laughed, but the laughter turned into silence that pressed down around us. That's when she leaned over and kissed me, quicker and more certain than I expected. Her hand slid across my knee, lingering—half a question, half an announcement. By the time the night was over, she'd stolen third base, and that landed differently than I thought it would. I didn't get the nuances of baseball.

Walking home, the night air cold against my face, I tried to square what I showed her—the laughs, the casual bravado—with what I carried inside: a strange mixture of triumph, confusion, and a nagging edge of guilt I couldn't shake. She'd gotten the proof of my body, a sign of my love?; I'd gotten a twist I couldn't explain.

That summer, a couple of makeshift bike trails popped up—one behind the Town Yard office, with carefully constructed wooden jumps and high, narrow berms artfully sculpted at the many curves. The other, deeper along the woods between the train tracks and Regal Road, was way more elaborate and intense. Someone with access to a shovel and a grudge against their femurs had built an honest-to-God launch ramp at the start, a sheer drop starting near the old wooden bridge on Clock Street. It was less a trail-head and more a dare.

I spray-painted my bike frame metallic black and swapped my banana seat for a torn leather saddle I found. I couldn't get it tight no matter what I tried—it rocked back and forth like a see-saw. Made me feel like I was riding a loose tooth.

The course builders took it seriously. We didn't. We were tourists in their adrenaline temple.

One day, I met Peach, Danny, Matt, and Ricky at the Regal trail-head. Ricky, the most serious among us, put on his fingerless gloves and careened down the drop-off. The rest of us were starting to lower our bikes down from the bridge and follow a less steep path.

I was halfway down when a territorial beef reignited behind me. Some older kid we didn't know was giving Peach the side-eye after Peach made one of his wisecracks. It wasn't even that rude—

just a "Nice training wheels, bro." But, the kid was maybe seventeen, thick-necked, and bored enough to take the bait.

"You got a problem?" the kid said, stopping his bike sideways in front of Peach.

Peach dropped his kickstand with theatrical care. The other guy dismounted and squared up, fists raised like a boxer.

Peach dismounted, walked up to the guy imitating his stance. He tilted his head, and said, "Screw this."

Before anyone could process what was happening, Peach dove. Like, full-body lunged into the kid. Didn't swing, didn't shout—just bear-hugged him and hurled them both off the edge where the drop-off began. We heard the crash through the brush before we could even move.

We scrambled down the switchback path—me in front, Matt and Danny behind.

At the bottom, Peach was sprawled in a bush, scraped up with one eye already puffing purple. The other kid was limping around, muttering curses and brushing dirt off his jeans.

Peach wasn't moving. Ricky turned the bend completing one round of the course looking ahead in astonishment.

I knelt beside Peach. "You better be breathing."

Nothing. Just leaves and dirt and the buzz of a bee somewhere nearby.

I leaned closer, listening.

Then he suddenly opened his eyes. "Johnny, always stay gold." he said in a purposefully weak voice.

I was a little shocked for a second. "You faker!"

Matt snorted. "You were really worried, John. You thought he was dead."

Ricky grinned. "You think you know CPR?"

Danny chimed in, "You can still give him mouth to mouth if you want."

I flipped them all off and looked back at Peach. "You have a bit of a shiner."

Peach got up limping. "You should see the other guy."

Friday night, Dad and I drove up to New Hampshire to work on the house. He'd added a whole second floor like an afterthought, and now it was finally time to finish the roof. I was lugging shingles up the stairs, out the window to the scaffolding, and onto the roof where he tacked them into place. By dusk, with my arms rubbery from work, I pocketed quarters and walked to the phone booth outside The Village Store.

" ... mmmm." she insisted.

"Likewise, I'm sure."

"I don't like when you're gone. Feels... emptier. Sometimes I wonder if you have a girl in every state."

"No competition up here," I said. "Just me, shingles, and Dad."

"You'd better not let anyone replace me," she said.

"Not unless they can babysit and provide other services at the same time."

She said "I am writing you a long letter. Will you write one to me?'

"No chance," I said, and then after a pause, quieter: "Actually, I have enough down-time to write a novel. Be careful what you wish for."

When I got back to town, Jenny's mother dropped us at Walden Pond. "Be back at four. No drowning, now."

The three of us—Jenny, Tom, and me—trudged through the sandy lot and out toward the beach. The pond spread wide and serene. The treeline curved like an amphitheater around us, green tiers watching in silence.

Jenny kicked off her sandals immediately, wiggling her toes in the sand. "This is basically paradise. But, Emerson, Thoreau—whoever— should've put in a snack bar."

Tom snorted, hauling his towel over his shoulder. "Watch your language. It's summer."

We staked out a patch of sand, Jenny spreading her towel like she was claiming territory. Tom ran straight for the water.

The air was thick with pine and lakeweed warmed by the sun, and threaded with faint laughter from families further down the beach.

We waded in slowly. The water gripped our ankles cool, then went deeper. Tommy was already splashing like a Labrador fifty feet out. Jenny cupped water in her hands, let it fall.

We dove out dog paddling, then turned onto our backs.

I felt the kind of calm that only arrives when the world stops making demands.

Jenny squinted at the horizon. "Do you think Thoreau ever just floated on his back here, staring at the clouds, and thought: Simple livin, that's the life for me?"

I smiled. "Probably. But, I think you are mixing in some of the *Green Acres* song."

I let myself drift, the sky a blue coin above me, Jenny's words sliding over me like the water. For once I didn't feel the urge to squint or look away. The world seemed unthreatening, briefly manageable.

Then Tom shouted from the deep, “I touched a fish!” He splashed furiously toward shore as if he’d been ambushed by Jaws. Jenny doubled over laughing.

“Paradise interrupted,” I said.

She smirked, shaking water from her ponytail. “Every Eden needs a snake.”

A week before Labor Day, Coach called asking if I was running cross country. He talked about morning practices, about the tradition of rotating breakfasts at each teammate’s house. That detail alone made me hesitate. Even with the so-called upgrades to Clock Lane, our place and our family couldn’t measure up to what the other boys had at their tables. I imagined pancakes in white tiled kitchens, bacon sizzling beside double ovens, orange juice poured from crystal pitchers. Ours would be weak coffee and toast, Ma trying meekly to be gracious.

“I’ll think about it.”

Then Danny called for me, eyes bright with news. “Wait for Ricky,” he said, “he’s the one who heard it.”

Matt and Ricky were both waiting on the Flannery front steps when I got there, Matt lounging like a spectator. Ricky straight to the point, voice low, too serious for gossip.

“You’re being cheated on.”

The words lodged in my ribs before the name even registered.

“Timmy Salinger,” Ricky said, regretfully. “Miglione, that instigator, asked him, ‘You lay Lahu yet?’—meaning his supposed girlfriend—Timmy said, ‘No. But, I laid Sutter. Jenny Sutter.’ He told us it happened in the woods by the public pool, behind the library.”

Timmy—Peach’s upstairs neighbor, living in the double-decker—was basically Michelangelo’s David, only pocket-sized.

Not marble, but flesh: taut, aloof, beautiful. One year younger than me, three years younger than her.

The humiliation was public, the kind you can't erase. Everyone knew. Everyone would delight in my comeuppance. I dared joke about their virginity? The one thing worse than a virgin was a cuckold.

I didn't believe it, not for a minute. I called Jenny right away, mouth dry.

"He's lying," she said without hesitation. "I love you. Why would I do that? I was babysitting at the tot lot. He saw me there, said something funny, then something stupid, and I told him to screw himself. That's it. I was with the kids."

Her voice was steady, but my mind split in two. The worst part was the ambiguity—her denial set against his boast, neither one fully provable. And, beneath it all, the potential betrayal, the publicity, what really twisted the knife was jealousy—not of him, but of her. Timmy Salinger, flawless and smiling, one of the boys who set something humming in me. She may have had what I wasn't even allowed to dream of.

And, what was all my effort to please her for, if she didn't love me?

I was soon strongly encouraged to behave like a *normal* aggrieved male.

Peach found me sitting on the swings later that week, staring at nothing. He plopped down beside me, eating from a bag of Red Vines.

"So, heard the news."

I nodded. "Yeah. Says he and Jenny..." I trailed off.

Peach made a low whistle. "Classic Salinger. The guy thinks the sun rises just to shine on his biceps. I asked him about it. He just told me to shut-up."

"He's not even—" I stopped myself, fumbling. "I don't get why he'd make it up. What's the point?"

Peach shrugged with a crooked smile and handed me a strand. "Same point there always is. Makes him look like a stud, probably. Simple math."

"Great." I dug my heel into the woodchips. "At my expense."

"Could be worse," Peach said. "Might be true."

I choked on the candy a little, despite myself.

Peach leaned back on his chains. "Look, Timmy's got the looks, sure. But, you know what else he's got? The attention span of a fruit fly and the charm of a broken lawnmower. Girls figure that out sooner or later."

I told him, "Jenny flat out denied it. Barely ever spoke to him, and it wasn't pleasant."

Peach listened, arms folded, face softer than usual. He wasn't secretly savoring it like most of the others. He almost looked sorry for me.

That's when Danny and Matt came striding up the walk, catching the last of it. "What's this?" Danny asked, eyes already narrowing like he smelled blood.

"Timmy," Peach said simply.

Danny turned to me. "You gonna let him get away with that? Or should we believe him and start calling her Jenny *Slutter*?"

I didn't answer.

"Whether he was talking trash or truthfully got your girl," Matt pressured. "You gotta go face him."

Danny piped in with a snort. "What if he admits it? He'll just smirk. Kid needs a punch in the face."

Peach, half-grinning again now, leaned close. "He's not home anyway. Over at his buddy's place a mile away. If you want him, you gotta go on a hike."

"No problem," Danny said, eyes lighting. "We march up there. He'll come clean when he's cornered."

I shook my head, but their energy was already pushing me.

That's when Matt Mundt and Bobby Sharpo came sauntering over, catching the vibe like dogs hearing a whistle.

"What's going on?" Mundt asked, an eager grin plastered across his face.

"Johnny's about to storm Timmy Salinger's castle," Danny declared.

Sharpo squinted, wary. "He got a dog? I'm not messing with some psycho German shepherd."

"No dog," Peach said. "Trampoline in the yard maybe. Worst you get is thrown up in the air."

Mundt clapped his hands together. "Then let's do it. If Timmy wants to play tough guy—"

"—We'll give him an audience," Matt overspoke. "This is John's fight."

Sharpo wagged a finger, suddenly solemn. "Just remember—once you throw the first punch, you can't take it back."

"We've got Ghandi over here." said Peach

And somehow, without me agreeing to anything, my legs carried me forward with them, a whole crusade gathering around me. Their voices rose—half comedy, half threat—while inside me all I wanted was clarity. Justice, maybe. Or maybe just silence.

By the time we got to Timmy Salinger's location, up toward Pershing Square, our group had ballooned with hangers-on. There were eight of us—maybe nine. I lost count after the girl with braces started tagging along. I didn't even know their names. People just sort of appeared once they smelled drama in the wind. I didn't say much. Didn't have to. I was the one walking in the middle. The other kid I didn't recognize nudged his friend and whispered, "That's the boyfriend." I felt like a sideshow.

The house was up on this slight rise, the porch tucked behind one of those stupid white lattices people think look classy. You could barely make him out at first—just a figure in a tank top, reclining like he was some kind of Roman god on a folding chair. He didn't even stand up.

"Yo, Salinger!" Danny called, cupping his hands. "You wanna come down here and have a talk?"

No answer. Just the faint sound of a screen door creaking open and maybe a laugh, or a cough.

"Coward," Matt muttered. "Doesn't even have the decency to gloat in public."

I don't know what I thought would happen. That he'd charge down the porch steps and beg forgiveness? That he'd scream something outrageous and get himself punched in the face?

Danny kept at it, throwing jabs from the lawn like he was auditioning for a soap opera. Peach, chewing on his knuckles like it was popcorn, muttered, "Someone get a mediator before this drags out all day."

Matt Flannery, ever the volunteer, stepped forward like some peace envoy from an ancient tribe. He made a big show of walking slowly up the path, hands out like he was proving that he didn't have any weapons. I half-expected him to be hit with a water balloon.

They talked. Couldn't hear most of it. Some shrugging. A few gestures. Then, Matt came back down the walk like he'd just returned from battle and didn't win.

"Says it was a misunderstanding," he announced. "He was just talking about girls he thought were easy when he was high. Swears nothing ever happened and he never said so."

Ricky wasn't there to clarify.

Peach leaned closer. "You want to believe Jenny, right?"

I nodded.

Sharpo chimed in with. "If he was talking about people who are easy when they're high, maybe he meant himself." And laughed hard.

No one else laughed, but we needed the line. It cut the tension.

Eventually the whole crowd sort of... dissolved. Like a broken Pixy Stick in the rain. No clear answers. No fight. Just that surreal ache of wondering what Timmy thought of me. Had the whole event made him respect me any more?

And, I guess, the one real thing I appreciated was what Peach had done for me that day. Staying steady and not being swept up by the frenzy.

For a few high-mileage months, cross country was my life—and Jenny's house was headquarters. Conveniently located right at the start of the course, her living room became our war room and recovery ward. Things between us weren't the honeymoon phase anymore, but they'd stabilized into something real: two loyal teammates trading energy bars instead of drama. The gossip mill had blessedly spun down. My weak yet steady efforts seemed to be succeeding.

Karl was technically on the team, but you'd barely know it. The cross-country roster with mixed years made him easier to overlook. Though, sometimes that was impossible.

Ron stationed himself along the course with a jug of water. "Hydrate or die-drate!" he yelled once, holding out a Dixie cup. I don't know if it helped my time, but it lifted my spirits.

At Jenny's, her mom handed out Gatorade and snacks like we were Olympians, offering soft encouragement about "pacing yourself" and "running your own race"—advice that applied equally well to relationships. Then, there was Tom, who had a talent for badly timed entrances, barreling into the TV room door mid-make-out session.

"You might want to knock!" I hissed once, fumbling under a throw pillow.

"What for?" he shrugged, grabbing the remote.

One day at school, Jenny showed up wearing my clothes—the jeans and red plaid shirt I'd left at her place. She smiled like we were sharing a private joke I didn't understand.

"I want to know what it's like to be you," she said.

I just nodded, speechless.

Danny Flannery found me on the side steps, face lit with that mix of gossip and glee. "It happened again," he said flatly. "Not just talk this time. They were caught with their pants down—woods by the tracks, behind the gas station. We got witnesses." My stomach turned before he finished.

That night, I rode my bike furiously, but didn't apply the right timing and speed to get up the hill at the end of the Lane in one swoop. My feet hit the ground just feet from the top, a very bad omen. I cornered Jenny outside her house, the streetlight throwing a yellow cone over her hair. I was almost yelling: "How can you lie like that? How can you say you love me and then..." I broke off, clenching my fists. More denials. She tried to laugh it off, but I persisted. "If a girl really loves her boyfriend, she doesn't spread her legs for his friend in the woods." Jenny froze, lips parted. Then, almost in a whisper, she said, "If a girl loves her boyfriend, she wouldn't."

"And, if a girl did that, that makes her a slut. Right?"

"Why are you making me say this? "

"Say it or I won't believe you."

"It would make her a slut."

The words hung there, echoing back like a statement she didn't really believe.

I should have felt relief, but instead the ground quaked beneath me. Hearing her delay was worse than any rumor. My chest ached with the contradiction: I did love her, platonically, with loyalty and tenderness. But, my desires were tangled elsewhere—even toward Timmy himself, of all people, the same boy who probably had no respect for me. Confusion surrounded me: betrayal, jealousy, shame, and a perverse recognition that my feelings had never aligned with what I claimed.

I wondered if all relationships follow the same arc as the seasons—bloom, blaze, cool, fade or crash.

Not two days later, Jenny's friend Kathy was waiting by my locker after school, arms crossed, staring at the floor. Her backpack hung off one shoulder like she'd been there a while.

"I need to tell you something," she said, not looking up.

I blinked. "Okay."

"Let's just get out of here. Away from people."

I followed her outside, down the brick steps, past the cafeteria loading dock, toward the corner where the sidewalk dipped into residential streets. She lit a cigarette. It trembled a little in her fingers.

"There are two things," she said. "One's bad. The other's worse."

I tried to laugh, but my throat didn't work.

She took a drag and exhaled slowly. "First: I guess you've already figured it out. Or part of it. Jenny... she did everything you accused her of. With Timmy. That time by the pool? That was real. The second day she saw Timmy, they went for a walk in the woods. I was watching the kids while she—" Kathy's voice cracked, just a little. "While she hooked up with him. She told me all about it after."

I stopped walking. Set my book bag down.

"All that time," I said, "she denied it, looked me in the eye."

"She was good at it," Kathy said. "I don't mean that as a compliment. But, yeah—convincing. She said she wanted both things. You, and... freedom, or something."

"But not honesty," I said.

Kathy wiped her nose on her sleeve. "I told her it wasn't fair. She said she couldn't help how she felt."

I looked up at the sky. It was that pale, coppery blue that only happened in October, like the air was losing color. I felt numb and full of static at the same time.

"She could've just broken up with me."

"She wanted it all," Kathy said, echoing my thought. "And, she didn't think about how it could affect you."

We walked in silence for a block. I tried to summon anger, but all I had was shock. Not surprise—just the cold, full understanding that there was nothing left to doubt.

"I'm sorry," she said.

"You said there was a second thing."

"Yeah." She looked down the street like she might run. "It's harder to say."

"Go on."

"I like you."

The words sat there, unadorned.

I blinked. "You what?"

"I like you. I know you probably didn't see it. Could you tell?"

I didn't know what to say. I kept walking, just slightly ahead.

"I'm not trying to cash in," she said quickly. "I'm not expecting anything. You don't have to say how you feel about me. I just didn't want it to be another secret."

She was right about one thing: I hadn't seen it. Not in her eyes, not in her shyness. I was too busy trying to love Jenny. And, I wasn't sure what love I had to return to anyone. I briefly thought of the benefits of being with a short, shy girl. But, no. Faking it wasn't working.

The thing about deception is, it never walks in alone. It brings its cousins—denial, corrosion, and pain. Jenny lied with her whole face, clean and practiced. She had nerves of steel. And, I... I lied with my absence, with the space between words. I let myself pretend I could be the boy she wanted, and I really wanted to be him for a while. But, that makes neither of us honest.

At the same time, my lie didn't justify hers. If I had a sudden opportunity with Karl or Peach, I would have definitely taken care of Jenny first to minimize her pain in the midst of my happiness. Setting the account straight does less damage than lying. It's the least a person who truly cares about you can do.

Maybe relationships turn with the seasons whether we want them to or not. Maybe some things bloom just long enough to betray you with their sweetness.

Maybe my facsimile of devotion and desire, left Jenny wanting. Maybe the biggest infidelity was me to myself. What was the point of playing a game with what I actually felt inside?

It was time to open my eyes to my own heart.

That's when Peach started popping up again. He'd transferred to Beaumont High from the trade school, and I ran into him during free periods. We left campus without permission to hit White Hen Pantry for donuts and jerky.

By the snack racks he said, "So, you and Jenny are done, huh?"

I nodded.

"At least you got some tail for a while."

I was glad he wasn't judgmental about how it all ended.

He shrugged. "Timmy told me she came over to the apartment a few times. For... you know."

He said it with the same tone someone might use to comment on a Red Sox game.

"His mom caught wind," he added. "She laid into him hard. 'Don't be sleeping with girls unless it's a real relationship, and you didn't use protection?!' She was on a roll."

I stared at the register's price display that kept blinking zero.

And, then outside: "They're not together now," Peach said, biting into a mini-muffin and talking with his mouth half-full. "Timmy's chasing some new chick. Jenny's old news."

On another day we were definitely late. The bell would ring in under three minutes, and we were still two blocks from school with Good and Plenty in our mouths and contraband snack cakes crammed in our pockets.

We started leaping over trash cans unnecessarily.

"Worth it," Peach mumbled around a mouthful of raspberry Zinger.

"I hope you choke."

We jogged the next block, then slowed when we reached the corner near the staff parking lot. Peach adjusted his shirt collar like that would convince someone of something.

We reached the final stretch. The school loomed ahead. No one had noticed we were gone.

"I should ditch more often," he said. "You make a good accomplice."

I looked at him. "You make a good alibi."

Sometimes, unpredictably, we'd walk the tracks home together. We never made plans. It was more like a slot machine—same three icons spinning, maybe lining up, maybe not. If Peach showed up in the hall at the right minute, we'd walk the tracks, stop at the gas station for soda, and drink them on the concrete ledge outside the Lions Club.

One afternoon, passing the empty playing fields, I asked,

"What's your favorite class?"

"Advanced basket weaving," he said. "Or really... gym. Obviously. Yours?"

"English. We're doing *To Kill a Mockingbird*. Did you see the movie?"

Peach snorted. "Why read that?"

"It's about people getting punished for being different but harmless. Good, even. Makes you think who gets to judge."

"Oh sure," he said. "Let me guess—you had a strong opinion in class."

"I don't really speak."

"You don't bring up Latin root words?"

"I save those for you. Still fascinated by *lunatic*?"

He grinned. "That moon-crazy spiel was wild. The rest? Embarrassing. This is why people think you live in the library."

"What's your reputation?"

"My reputation," he said, "is better than yours. I'm a stoner, a rebel, and classy as hell."

At the patched-over hole in the chain-link fence, he ducked through first, then held the slack open for me.

"Your Latin-speaking highness," he said, directing me up the path.

I stepped through. "That makes you my court jester."

We smiled—just not directly at each other. We never did.

Peach was a break from the muck. A crooked little light in a stretch of dim. He never tried too hard—never tried at all. Just jokes, stray observations, a smile that hit the spot.

Things with him didn't zoom like the others. They percolated in waves. He slipped past my guard without either of us noticing.

On the tracks later that day, the sun dropped low enough to make the gravel glitter. We balanced on the rails, arms out like tight-rope walkers, shoving each other off whenever one of us got too smug.

"I saw you talking to Jenny," he said, hopping ties.

"Correction: Jenny talked to me."

"You still carrying a torch?"

"No," I said. "I'm on to better things."

Maybe it was time to be faithful to my own reality.

Then, came that night that challenged my resolve, and had me scrambling. It started in the Flannery basement—Matt, Danny, Peach, and Ricky chugging beer while we waited to leave for the Battle of the Bands. I played pool badly, missing every shot. Peach and Ricky climbed onto a tall bureau and sat there for half an hour, heads brushing the rafters, whispering in tones I couldn't hear.

I watched from below, jealous of them both. What were they saying? Were they connecting the way I wanted to connect with either of them? The mystery of being excluded while standing right there was the worst part.

So I drank. Whiskey tipped into beer, swallowed fast. The room went soft. Voices blurred.

Next thing I knew, Matt was hovering over me, checking my pulse. "You're not going," he said. "Sleep it off."

They left. I stayed slumped on the couch—until stubbornness kicked in. Within five minutes I forced myself upright, shook myself off, and sprinted down the tracks toward the high school, lungs burning, refusing to be left behind. I had a plan that could lead to my redemption.

By the time I splashed water on my face in the bathroom, I'd sobered up enough to stumble into the cafeteria. The space had been transformed: tables pushed back, lights dimmed, a makeshift stage glowing at one end.

Danny later said the project kids tried to talk to me, but I ignored them. I don't remember that. All I remember is Karl, leader of Second Nature, behind his drum kit, sweat catching the light, and me dancing wildly in front of the stage—flailing, spinning, trying to merge with the beat. I was probably giving more eye contact than I had since I knew him.

When the floor cleared between songs, *Dancing with Myself* came on. Another boy stayed out there alone, kicking and jerking under the lights while everyone else watched and laughed. The song was about daring to be seen, daring the world to meet you where you stood.

There was a lesson in that. I just didn't know how to hold it yet.

Karl gave no indication that I wasn't invisible.

That night never made sense—why I shut people out, how I kept moving when I should have collapsed, what Peach and Ricky whispered about, why Karl stayed just out of reach. What I understood, dimly, was this: I had no outlet for what I felt, and that void had left me with a hunger that had nowhere to rest.

Time for a more realistic plan. You let go of Ricky, you're letting go of Karl... but, I still needed to figure this out. In the light of day, out of that chaos, I caught hold of one thought I could live with—that Peach, by some mysterious gravity, might be the one I could figure this out with, and that if I figured out how, maybe we could make something of it. Or at least I could find a way to understand and just be honest and real.

And, then came the thoughts. Not full-blown fantasies, not the hot, spiraling ones I'd had with others. With him, it was different. He wasn't handsome. Maybe cute, if you tilted your head and squinted. But, it wasn't his looks. It was his spirit—unguarded, crooked, lit from some strange bulb inside. What I really wanted was to tell him how he made me feel, how much I valued him, and say it like it was worthy to be heard.

I imagined how he'd laugh at that.

"Feelings?" I could hear him say. "No time for nonsense."

He didn't want that—not from a girl, not from me, not from anyone, maybe. Still, I was determined to find a way to say how I felt. I had one strategy that was completely silly, the other a little profound.

Each day, as we approached the turnoff from the tracks onto Clock Lane, I'd ask, "You going straight, or coming with me?"

It became a ritual. A riddle tucked inside a dare.

He had options: stay on the tracks, cut through the Town Yard, to get home. Or, veer with me down Clock Lane by my house, then through the projects and home.

He usually went straight. But, every so often, he opted for the route that gave us more time. And, every time he did, it tickled me—as if he were letting go of his "straightness" just a little, just long enough to walk beside me where the air softened and the street narrowed.

One day, I thought, I'll ask him in. Just for a soda. Or to play Pong. Or nothing. One day.

Did he ever get the play on words? I was never quite sure.

Then came an opportunity borne of tragedy.

The second teen death on the tracks in ten years. This time a foreign student. Headphones in, Walkman on, walking not on the tracks like us, but just across them—trying to get to school. He didn't hear the train coming. He never had a chance.

It shook the town. For a week, everything smelled like flowers and metal.

I took the moment to ask Peach, laughing but not really joking, "Would you be upset if I got hit by a train?"

He looked up from his Coke. "What?"

"I mean... would you cry?"

He shrugged. "I guess. I don't know. Maybe."

I nodded slowly. "I'd cry a lot if you died. I wouldn't be right for weeks. Longer"

He accepted that, didn't make a joke of it. Just sort of nodded.

Then, the following week, we were sitting on the concrete ledge at the Lions Club, where the wall across from us was covered in graffiti. Random stuff—phone numbers, doodles, "A/C D/C," which Peach once said meant "you go both ways." An idea jolted across my skull.

That night, I went back to the ledge alone with a Sharpie in my pocket.

Across from where we always sat—right there between "A/C D/C" and "Lick my ballsack"—I wrote: I LOVE YOU.

All caps. No name, no initials. Bold and waiting.

I had made up my mind it was time to confess, but not without an escape hatch. It wasn't just the fear of Peach cringing or pulling away. It was the dread of some new rumor storm about me rolling over our friends and the entire town.

If Peach didn't flinch when I said those words out loud, the moment could hang there—naked, maybe they would be well received. But, if he looked disgusted, I could just shrug, point at the wall, and laugh it off:

"Relax. I was just reading the graffiti. There's love in the center of all that smut."

Either way, I would have said it. And, for at least a second, he would know it.

We had a routine. Tracks, sodas, ledge, competition. Every time: He got Coke, I got Sprite. We'd sit and sip and I'd stare at the wall, heart pounding, searching for nerve.

We'd walk on.

As spring approached, when the thaw came and the valley below Serenity Drive filled with snowmelt, we upped the game. Each of us would fling our empty can into a shallow spring pond, and then the battle began: rocks flying, water splashing, each trying to sink the other's can first. Just two boys laughing manically as if it would actually prove something.

And maybe it did.

Peach lobbed a rock and missed. "If I sink yours," he said, squinting at my Sprite can bobbing in the pond, "I get your celebrity crush. Jamie, what's-her-name. The Bionic Woman."

I smirked. "That's Lindsay Wagner, idiot."

"Whatever. I'm gonna make sweet love to her."

I hurled the next rock. It plunked wide. "Fine. If I sink yours, I get Farrah Fawcett. The poster version. Red swimsuit."

We kept playing, laughing out loud, pretending we didn't really care who won—but both adjusting their aim with every throw, taking it just a little more seriously than we'd admit.

Peach hit my Sprite with a clean shot. It gurgled once, then went under.

I stood still, muddy and breathless. "Do you think anybody ever ends up with who they really want?"

"Most don't," Peach said. "They find someone they can stand— if they're lucky."

I watched the Coke can drift in circles, half full of rainwater, dented but refusing to sink.

Just as often I would win. He would exaggerate disappointment, or call me a cheater.

After a multitude of stalled opportunities, the school year ended. I let the plan rot. Never read the words aloud. Never tested the water, never gave Peach the chance to look at me and choose. I told myself it was caution, or timing, or wisdom even. But, mostly, it was fear. And, the three words stayed where I left them.

Weeks later, I returned to the ledge.

The wall had faded. I LOVE YOU was still there, barely. Not erased—just surrendering.

I walked down into the valley, now dry. The pond had shrunk to memory. Cracked mud, summer weeds, and the dozens of cans sat where they'd landed, streaked with dirt, mangled and cut in half by stones.

I stood in the middle of it all, and for the first time, it hit me: what I'd let happen. Each pair represented an attempt thwarted.

Some opportunities are like spring ponds—wide, bright, fleeting.

What was left was a brittle floor and the wreckage of what we once dared to aim at. That pond had shielded us. Kept the damage below sight. But, now the water was gone, and all the wounds were visible—the dents, the gashes, the ones we aimed for and the ones we didn't. Every toss and every miss had left a mark.

Maybe Peach and I sank each other, one stone at a time, out of fear of being judged weak the way boys do—never aiming at each other directly, only at what floats between them. Maybe, I was the only one with a loftier goal.

So much for my plan.

A confession with an escape hatch—clever, bold, deniable.

But, in the end, the hatch stayed closed.

The mission itself was aborted.

The lesson of *Dancing with Myself* is that life is too short to spend it paring yourself down to something safer or smaller. Let yourself be seen. Then, ask the world to meet you there. See if it does.

Easier said than done.

Jenny had been unfaithful to me. I'd been unfaithful to myself. And Peach? I'd never given him the chance to be faithful to anything—I'd kept the truth locked in my head.

Maybe that's what fidelity really is: not staying with someone, but staying true to what you feel, even when it terrifies you. Especially then.

16

Slow Departures, Strange Arrivals

At some point during sophomore year, it felt like people were slowly drifting out of my life. I was surprised when I realized the one who was leaving was me.

Sarah had opted out of the academic track entirely, announcing to our mother that she was "done with books." She enrolled at Regional Vocational Technical School, majoring in painting. Not portraits. Not seascapes. Walls. Trim. Commercial interiors. She was fifteen, cynical, and always had paint on her cuticles.

It might've been a social decision more than anything else. Up until then, she'd hovered at the edge of my social orbit, but something about the shared bus ride, shared hallways, and higher hormone levels shifted the dynamic. The boys—the Matts, Ricky, Sharpo, and Will—kept going to that school too.

For a short time, the second underground fort that we found—the little hideout tucked behind the treeline—took on a new identity as a kind of love shack. Someone (Ricky, probably) added class to the place by adding colorful pillows. Someone else (probably not Ricky) painted a few hearts on the inside wall, sloppy but bold.

And, then someone set it on fire (probably a parent.)

A kind of muffled silence fell over everything when I was around. The usual back-and-forth between the boys and me flattened out. No one talked about Sarah—not directly. But, I knew something had shifted. The way Ricky looked away so quickly when her name came up. The way Matt watered down his jokes around me, like I might catch on to the secret.

No one called her hot. No one dared mention her at all. But, there was no mistaking it: Sarah was suddenly in the picture. And, I'd somehow been cast as the chaperone nobody asked for.

I braced against the thinning connections by considering new friendships. Old echoes resounded as I added new music.

Seb Jenkins was an easygoing chap with the agreeable habit of rescuing failed joke attempts. If I tried something dumb and it fell flat, Seb would scoop it up, fix it, and extend it, or match the absurdity until we both crashed and burned together. Somehow, it made the failure funny instead of humiliating.

We shared a particular kind of dread: having to recite poetry from memory in front of the class. I remember us whispering before our turn, both of us sweating over Gerard Manley Hopkins.

"Margaret, are you gríeving / Over Goldengrove unleaving?" I muttered, practicing under my breath.

Seb groaned. "What does that even mean? Goldengrove? Sounds like a cereal."

I snorted, "Yeah, and unleaving must be when you return."

When it was his turn, he stumbled through and came out with a D+. Instead of slumping in shame, he punched the air. "Yes!"

The teacher blinked. "You're celebrating a D+?"

He grinned. "I was expected to fail."

That was Seb: he turned everything into a kind of victory.

Mark Zavala was different—short, quiet, shy, a serious face that made him seem older than he was. But, when he smiled, it was sudden and broad, and you couldn't help but catch it. He was a junior and my chemistry partner, and I was thankful to be paired with someone who didn't judge me when I fumbled through equations or spilled sodium all over the bench. He loved James Bond and Sherlock Holmes, and it gave me an idea: if he admired intrigue and spies so much, why not make him one?

So one afternoon, Ron made a call to Mark under an assumed name—"Ralph Furley," he announced, straight-faced, after I dared him. "Not my real name, just a cover." Ron told him he was being invited into a spy ring. He rattled off a few random "current members," slipping in my name.

Mark looked at me the next day, dead serious. "I heard about this... group. Are you really in it?"

I kept my voice low, trying to sound mysterious. "You might not want to join. The admission requirements are pretty steep."

His eyes widened just enough to let me know he was hooked.

So the game began. I gave him assignments: solve a math problem and a riddle to get the combination to a locker—what he didn't know was that it was a vacated student's locker, and everyone had the combo already. He retrieved a "clue" locked in locker #281 like he was holding the crown jewels.

Mark solved it in a day and retrieved a folded slip of paper that gave him an address and instructions to visit the women's restroom in the Unitarian Universalist Church annex after hours and find a package taped beneath the sink. He went. No questions asked. The package was a crumpled takeout menu with a cryptic note on the back: "Welcome. Your next mission will be real."

He glowed. Every time I passed him in the hallway after that, he'd give me this secret look, part gratitude, part anticipation. For the first time, Mark Zavala looked like he was starring in his own movie. And, I got to be the guy who handed him the script. I told him to stop thinking of it as a spy ring, just people helping people.

I saw Tom Sutter around from time to time. I'd gotten used to him with his sister around, with Jenny as the glue. Without her, he felt like a misplaced object from a set I didn't collect anymore.

Still, he was persistent. Not in an aggressive way. Just... present. Like a song you couldn't quite remember but somehow kept humming.

He caught me outside the entrance of the school one Tuesday, just after the last bell rang and kids were pouring out like soda from a shaken can.

"Any reason you're always in a rush these days?" he asked, voice light but not unserious.

"I'm just... I don't know." I said.

We stood there in a half-silence, punctuated by a passing shout and the slap of sneakers on pavement. I could feel the air between us trying to decide whether it was going to be friendly or tense. He didn't push, just waited. Unphased. There was so much unsaid about Jenny, and neither of us would go there.

"Anyway," Tom said, finally cracking the pause. "Just saying hey."

He gave a slight nod and walked off. I let out a breath I hadn't realized I was holding.

Jenny, meanwhile, had gone through her freshman footballer phase in what seemed like a blink. Some stocky boy with acne and red hair, always talking about practice and protein.

But, after that fizzled out, she settled in with a new guy. Soft-spoken. Possibly timid. He looked like he still asked permission to go to the bathroom.

They held hands in the lunch line and swapped notes in the hall. I didn't mind. Not really. But, every now and then, she'd still play along with our old rituals.

One day outside the auditorium, I exaggerated a limp and said, "Jenny. Payback time. My laces won't stay tied."

She rolled her eyes and knelt anyway, tying one shoe, then the other, like she was completing a sacred duty from a bygone era.

That's when we both heard it: a high, nasal voice behind us.

"What's wrong with you?" It was a chunky boy in an ill-fitting sweatshirt, standing with a crooked smirk. "You sucking another guy's shoelaces?" It was her current boyfriend's brother.

Jenny froze. Then stood.

"You wouldn't understand," she said flatly.

She grabbed my sleeve and tugged me away before the kid could respond. I let out a half-laugh as we turned the corner.

"Thanks."

"Least I can do."

We were smiling, but there was a distance to it. Some nostalgia on my part but, mainly relief that I could no longer be humiliated by the odd boundaries.

Apparently, Margaret was grieving over autumn and falling leaves. And, time passing, along with Margaret's passing youth. That's what we were told anyway. The motif was loss. And, now the assignment was personal.

"Write your own story of paradise lost, abundance turned to scarcity," Mrs. Slade said, stepping back from the chalkboard with a theatrical sigh. "Something you once had, that changed. Could be a person. A place. A state of mind."

I was ready.

I wrote about Jenny. A perfect beginning, an unraveling middle, and an ending that kept pretending not to end. I was sure to mention the infidelity and the drawn-out con-job that came before the truth settled. But, the ache was there, loud and clear. It was a clean enough version to hand in, but it had weight.

The day she passed back the papers, the teacher paused beside my desk. I felt her shadow before I saw her squat down beside me.

"Is it true?" she asked softly.

I nodded.

Her eyes lingered. Not pity, not surprise. Just... recognition. The moment was small, but she understood me.

She gave me an A for content, D for mechanics—"poor spelling, comma splices and sentence fragments galore," she wrote—and the grade averaged to a B-minus. But, it felt like success.

Seb was content with his C-minus. "I spelled *paradise* three different ways and was only marked off once."

That day, I told Seb the story behind my essay. I used low tones to relate the first part—the garden of eden—in class.

"I never thought you had it in you." he said, his voice caught somewhere between awe and amusement.

I spilt the rest in the hall by the school store.

"Yeah. Denied it at first. Then, her friend Kathy confirmed she was a liar and then she made a play for me herself. Turns out it was with full permission from Jenny. She wanted to hand me off to her friend."

"Damn," he said. "That's... cold."

"Jenny changed her mind and tried to win me back. I was done with both of them."

He didn't pity me. That wasn't his style. But, I could tell it hit him—the sex, the betrayal, the public wreckage unfolding frame by frame. It wasn't just heartbreak; it was the kind of thing that leaves you raw. And, yet, it left virgins like him dazzled—like watching someone else's roller coaster ride and thinking, maybe someday I'll get to buy a ticket.

We started eating lunch together more often after that. There was a certain rhythm to it—observational sarcasm mixed with eccentric trivia and the kind of ironic commentary that made school tolerable.

One afternoon, we were outside by the pond heading for the drinking fountain. I saw Jimmy Flannery sitting on the cement bench near the water.

"Oh, wait. I don't want him to see me."

Seb stared at him a while. "You know him? I've seen him sitting out there every day."

"Yeah," I said. "Lunch, free period."

"What's his deal?"

"Says he likes to clear his head."

Seb squinted. "Does he listen to music? Read a book?"

"No, he just colors in the little stones in the bench with a pencil."

We watched a few moments longer. Jimmy was currently engaged in the task—leaning over, tongue tucked to the side like a kid doing a jigsaw puzzle.

"Does he... talk to anyone?"

"Not much. As far as I know."

He tilted his head. "He looks like a gaybo," said Seb.

I gave him a look, but not too sharp.

"You think?"

"Not saying he is," Seb said, holding up his hands. "But, just look at him. Mannerisms. He prances around with a queer look on his face. The... artistic commitment to cement..."

We crossed over to the sidewalk next to the school.

"How do you know him?"

"Just one of the kids in the neighborhood. His brothers are cool."

I was glad I wasn't like Jimmy, but I wondered where the line was between acceptable and gay mannerisms.

And who got to draw it.

Jimmy Flannery had started showing up at my house before school. Out of the blue one morning, he was just standing there on the porch.

"I'm at Beaumont now," he said. "Tech school wasn't for me. Matt and them kept getting high and dropping trow in traffic."

Most mornings after that, he'd be there. Waiting. At first, I thought it might be nice—something familiar. But, we ran out of things to say by the beginning of Regal Road. We walked in long silences, broken only by passing trucks or the whistle from the tracks. Every now and then, I'd offer a half-formed comment about a movie or a class. He'd grunt or say, "Huhn," and that was that.

I couldn't tell if we didn't gel because we were so different or because we were so much the same. I think we knew each other's secret. We handled the situation the way boys handle a cracked windshield—by looking through it and never at it.

Oddly, it felt more awkward with him there than walking alone. With him, I felt I had to awkwardly pretend to be content—and it didn't help my social standing any more than being alone would have.

It was New Year's Eve again. By nine o'clock the Flannery basement was already dense with bodies: Matthew and Danny Flannery, Matt Mundt, and, in fits and starts, Jimmy Flannery, who drifted between the basement and his mother's kitchen upstairs. My sister, Sarah, was there too, not as a visitor hanging on the margins but as a full-fledged member of the night. She brought two of her friends—one of them Joanne—and the sight of them all together down there made my stomach twist. This wasn't like before, when we ran into the girls later when we were on the prowl or when they came around for one round of pool and then vanished upstairs out into the cold. They'd claimed seats, poured drinks, laughed too loudly, as if entitled to the same air the rest of us breathed.

No one had asked how I'd feel about it. Not the Flannerys. Not Sarah. It just was. There was nothing wrong with it per se.

But, I didn't like it.

The underage drinking, the sideways flirting, the electric possibility of someone leaning in too close, kissing in the shadows or in the hall. Sarah, silly and goofy as ever, tossed out weak jokes that Danny and Matt rewarded with laughter far louder than the material deserved. Their laughter grated. It was less about humor and more about her—about noticing her in ways that left me restless in my own skin.

I didn't last an hour.

I slipped out, past the furnace heat and the clutter of feet, climbing the narrow basement stairs until the night air opened around me. In the courtyard I ran into Joanne, who promised, almost conspiratorially, to tell me later how things went. That gave me cover: I could walk away without forfeiting my insider knowledge.

I couldn't return home that early though. It would look like defeat. So, I kept walking—down the Lane, over the bridge, out onto Serenity Drive, over to the houses of the historic district. Saranopoulos's porch light glowed faintly, Norman's curtains drawn against the cold. I had no real destination, just a determination to not be seen as the boy without a place on New Year's Eve.

The streets were nearly empty, until a couple appeared in the distance. My first instinct was to turn around. I hated feeling self-conscious—alone on this night, while they had each other. But, then I heard the girl's voice. Jenny.

She was surprised, maybe a little tipsy, and delighted to see me. She stepped toward me, leaving her new boyfriend lurking in the shadows. Her energy was urgent, as if fate had engineered the meeting. She asked what I was doing out here, and I gave her a patched-together story: a fight with Matt Flannery, an invented party on Beaumont Hill where I was headed to make an appearance. She believed enough of it to keep smiling.

Her boyfriend called her name. She raised a hand—Just wait.

Then, looked up at me, and said we had been good together. She wished me a very happy New Year. She hugged me quickly, warmly, before stepping back into her role as someone else's girlfriend.

I circled a few blocks after that, stalling, letting the night burn itself down. When I finally reached home again, there were still twenty minutes left in the old year. I didn't go inside. Instead, I tip-toed into the garage, stretched out on a stack of flattened boxes, and let midnight arrive over me like an impersonal tide.

Sarah had finally beaten me at something that mattered. Not a math test, not a board game, not some petty sibling contest but at the thing that actually channeled the river we swam in. Down in that basement, the balance shifted. Her sex appeal crowned her with a power I couldn't touch. It wasn't skill or intelligence or effort—it was something given, something automatic, something she had without trying much at all.

And I knew it would only get worse. Ricky and Peach, ghosts of lingering affection, were due to show up in that basement before midnight, and the thought of them walking into the kind of opportunities Sarah and friends now offered, made the contrast unbearable. Her life felt rigged to fall open in front of her. Mine was all sealed doors.

I couldn't stand the emptiness. I couldn't stand the sights I could never be seen in, the laughter rising, the bodies huddled together in that cramped room, a stacked deck of appreciation. So I withdrew.

And apparently no one noticed. No one ever asked where I'd gone or why. Not that night, not the next week, not ever. Even Joanne, who had sworn to report the night's secrets to me, barely remembered her offer when I questioned her later. She could only half-recall drinking too much and getting sick.

In that silence, I felt the truth—Sarah had won, not just the night but the game itself. And, I had lost, not just to her, but to the whole idea of adolescence.

I liked to imagine I needed a better caliber of company, though Ron made it clear that teenage vulgarity transcended class. So, I started pulling my school friendships closer.

Seb did winter track with me. The program was run by an older coach who taped daily drills and event exercises to the wall, then disappeared, leaving us to sort ourselves out. A solo sport somehow managed to feel even more solitary. Daily, the fluffy shot-putter tackled a cute freshman onto the pole-vault mat and wrestled him there long enough to make it clear that wrestling wasn't the point. *Light My Fire* and *Riders on the Storm* played in a loop as we ran loop after loop on the small indoor track. I didn't like the Doors. I thought it was country music. The field house was expansive and exposed. There was nowhere to escape.

Thankfully, as the weather improved, Seb and I were released to do our workouts on city streets. The long runs turned into long walks, and those into long talks. We traded jokes and odd confessions from our lives—funny in their smallness, freeing in their lightness.

I went first, as usual. "My job with Mrs. Saranopoulos is basically running an estate. She trusts me with managing her finances, the upkeep of vast gardens, negotiating with dignitaries, the whole thing." Seb raised an eyebrow, and I admitted the truth: I washed her laundry room walls and dusted her books.

"Sounds like something you might want to leave off your résumé," he said, smiling.

"At least I don't live on the Street for Gray People."

He blinked. "What are you even talking about?"

"That's what you said."

He shook his head. "I said the Street for GREAT people. Like me. Great!"

"It's definitely a street for old people or full of gray houses."

"Nope."

We argued it down the block, me sticking to gray, him insisting great, until it wore us both out.

"You might have just told me the real name of the street," I said.

On another stretch of road, I told him about Mr. Norman. "My mentor. Assigned to me by the government to foster my special talents. He could be the town's head selectman if people could hear him past his laugh. He was a seal with asthma in a past life."

"Mmhmm."

"Okay, maybe he was a grade school sub who pitied the poor. Your turn."

Seb's voice was more weary than annoyed when he opened up about home. His younger brother, Calvin, had just started middle school and cried almost every day. "He never thinks he did well enough, and worries he'll do worse in the future. I have a no-crying pact with him," he said.

Seb described his friends without judgment—an odd boy who trailed him like a lost puppy, another rough around the edges who seemed half-adopted by his family, and a third obsessed with withholding every penny from the government. He just let them in.

Then, "my best friends, the fun ones. Brothers from England," he said. Even-keeled, reserved but sharp when the subject was sports. They spoke in stats and scores, playing and watching like it was religion. Seb matched them stride for stride on the field and in conversation. "We have a great time and hardly ever have to speak."

It was an odd assortment, but he laid them out like it was nothing unusual. For me, it was proof that he carried a whole world around with him, a world that somehow made room for everyone. I couldn't understand why Seb wasn't an object of my desire. He was perfectly nice, perfectly friendly, not ugly—and yet no chemistry. That absence, actually, felt like a relief.

Mark was thoughtful, eyes always scanning for meanings others didn't see. He carried his obsessions like holy relics—literature, foreign films, a girl named Nadia—and shared them with a conviction that pulled me halfway into his world. Once he dragged me to see Ingmar Bergman's *The Seventh Seal* at the Brattle. He whispered the symbolism to me like gospel, convinced

Death himself was speaking directly to us from the screen. I admired his intensity, even when it creeped me out. Being with him was like sitting on the edge of a storm: you didn't know whether to run for cover or marvel at the sky.

Mark had already shaken my belief in God by pointing out how closely faith follows birthplace. Now he was saying all religions were true—just different attempts to reach the same wisdom he believed he had finally unlocked. If anything, that made me doubt God even more.

Tom was different. He kept circling me with a persistence I couldn't match, an eagerness that only made me fold my arms tighter. I didn't like it. It sat in an awkward region that made it difficult to politely drift away. Conversation sputtered and died, but he didn't seem to notice. His energy barreled through the dead air like a dog who keeps fetching even when you never threw the stick. Better than Jimmy, but not by much.

Things began to change the day he got his license.

"Hey, Lucky Lindy," he said, rolling the nickname out like he was testing it for durability. "We're going to the mall after school. Pizza. Maybe a little ho' hunting."

I made a show of grimacing. "That's exactly the kind of phrase my guidance counselor warned me about."

But, he had use of a car. How could I refuse?

He drove like it was an NASCAR event. Quick bursts of acceleration, deliberate slams on the brake, then that proud moment of shifting into reverse and threading the car into a space so tight I couldn't believe it fit. He'd throw me a sideways grin, waiting for applause.

I shrugged. "You parked. Congratulations. Millions of Americans do it every day."

“Yeah, but not like me.” He revved the engine twice, like a period on the sentence.

Independence is intoxicating, even when it’s borrowed. His enthusiasm was contagious.

I started using the two-for-one coupons that I saw in the paper, casually producing them when we were “deciding” what to do. Tom groaned like I’d forced him into indentured servitude, then pulled out a map and swung the car around anyway. We went through half the restaurants in the region like that.

Papa Gino’s became our default—partly for the pizza, partly because a classmate, Shawn Yong, worked the counter and we lived in hope of a discount. Sometimes it happened, sometimes it didn’t. The routine was more important than the food.

The awkwardness between us didn’t vanish, but it began to melt. He could find the fun in anything, even our own mistakes. Like the day we attempted a small prank that got out of hand. We let a little air out of Shawn’s tire. But, the nozzle jammed and hissed out more air than intended, all of it. Now we had to go find a pump.

Pumping it up again was only a temporary fix. Removing the pump would release the air again. Tom crouched down. “We’re a pit crew now,” he said solemnly, screwing the cap back on as if it fixed the whole thing. We both knew Shawn was driving off in a precarious state, but the absurdity broke me. We laughed despite ourselves.

There were other small revelations about Tom’s integrity. In math class, he could use extra time in free period to finish tests due to a learning disability. He could have used the situation for even greater advantage, by consulting the textbook in the intervening time. He refused to do that. There was unique honesty in that, something I respected.

At home, his parents were splitting, and the facade cracked. I went back to his place at the edge of Haver Hill, where the house sighed with the sadness of things changing. His mother thanked me in the kitchen for being supportive of her son, though I didn't feel like I'd done much. She had a kind of sweetness that made me feel warm and complete inside.

I thought of his father, rough and weathered. The summer before, I had worked for him mowing church lawns and polishing CCD floors. I remembered when he used me on the church's dime to mow a residential lawn for "Bambi," a woman he flirted with. I remembered overhearing them talk about me—joking.

"He looks the age when they start getting busy."

"He better not be. He's seeing my daughter."

That memory made the divorce feel even sharper. His mother, with her gentle dignity, deserved better. So, did Tom.

The divorce hollowed Tom out in ways he tried to mask with bravado, leaving him quick to joke but quicker to give up. Beneath the noise of cars and pizza runs, there was always the quiet tears of a boy who was losing his family as he knew it. He couldn't concentrate on much else, and no longer believed the future had a place for him.

One day we were parked at Beaver Brook, windows down, the air easy and warm. He closed them at some point, for no reason he said out loud. The air got warmer between us. Then, he cried—heavy and unashamed. I felt bad for him and didn't know how to help. He just suddenly said "that's enough of that." He drove extra fast after that. Later, he threw a tennis ball out the car window, down a steep hill and tried to catch up with it.

To balance out the way he called me Lindy, I started calling him Tommy, the way his sister did. It shifted something small between us, like we'd found a private exchange rate.

One night, parked in a lot at the mall, he told me flat out he didn't care if he graduated. "I'll just join the military. Forget college."

"That's the dumbest plan I've ever heard," I said automatically. But, my voice was softer than the words.

He shrugged. "Then, I'll be done with all this crap."

I thought of Ron, who once explained how college meant a chance to be an officer instead of a grunt. I passed that along, nudging him toward something higher. He half-listened, fiddling with the radio dial, but didn't push me away.

We limped through precalculus together, our one shared class. Tried to get him to care about English, though his track was different that mine, and he barely scraped by. We sat with open books, the silence occasionally punctured by a little nod of appreciation, like he knew this was sometimes more about me wanting to help rather than him wanting to succeed.

And, somewhere along the line, the awkward middle ground shifted. Something bloomed, not all at once but gradually, like realizing you've been warm for hours. He was nothing like the others—no skinny boy quick to laugh. He was tall, heavier, just starting to shape muscle. Blonde like many of them, yes, but carrying it differently. That smile, though—crooked, mischievous, a little dangerous—snuck under my defenses.

Tommy had an easy goodwill toward me that didn't announce itself—it just settled in. His laugh started somewhere behind his eyes before it reached his mouth. He was Teflon to my weak points. When I slipped into self-deprecation, he'd just grin and say, "Yeah?"—half acknowledgment, half dismissal—and the heaviness would lift. But, when I landed on something good, he was all in. I didn't have to engineer spending time together, because he kept offering me the right thing at the right time.

Most of all I liked feeling needed.

I remember walking with him through the new Arsenal Mall, the air still sharp with paint and popcorn, our sneakers squeaking on tile. We stopped at a window of teen mannequins dressed like adults trying too hard to be cool. "You can tell who picked the clothes," I said. "Someone who thinks teenagers dream about being adults, not about getting away from them. That's sort of your whole deal."

Tommy studied the display, then exhaled. "You're on to something," he said.

I looked at him.

"My father wants me right in the middle of their mess," he went on. "Like I'm supposed to pick sides, or fix something, or prove I'm okay." He nodded toward the window. "All I want is space."

"Getting distance doesn't mean you don't care," I said.

He smiled, relieved. "Exactly."

Then he looked at me the way he did when something clicked. "You pegged that one right, Lindy."

For a second, it felt like more than agreement. It felt like trust—like he'd let me hold something of his, and I hadn't dropped it. We had crossed into something mutual, unspoken. I had set out to tolerate him. Maybe to help him. Somehow, without meaning to, he'd turned into someone I loved.

Tommy was unpredictable. He had restless energy wrapped in a big frame. He'd call me "Lindy" with that smirk, blink fast when he had an idea, and pull me into schemes—attending country fairs, cruising to malls for the grand opening of new stores. We bought a couple pairs of parachute pants from a store called "Just Shirts."

He took Jenny's place in many respects, absent kissing and cuddling, of course. But, also absent the dreadful vagina dodging. His perseverance and motivation despite pain inside kept something bubbling inside me. I had tried to fake a relationship with someone I loved as a friend. Now, I had a real friendship that I tried to stretch into a relationship.

Tommy was waiting at the lockers when I came in from the track, already changed, jacket on, one foot propped against the bench like he'd been there long enough to get comfortable. Kevin Shea was pulling on his sneakers nearby, and when he saw us together he asked about Met State.

"Tell him about the guy," Tommy said, grinning before I'd even caught my breath.

So I did. We'd gone with the civic Beaumontian Club to a residential floor of developmentally disabled adults. The facility was old but clean. Some students held their own with the residents; others went quiet, unsure how to meet them where they were. The staff were kind. The residents moved through the common room at their own pace, some watching television, some just watching.

And, then there was the man in the corner chair who bore such a precise and uncanny resemblance to Governor Michael Dukakis that Tommy and I had spent the rest of the visit in a state of barely suppressed hysteria, each of us afraid to look at the other.

"The hair," Tommy said now, hands framing his own head. "Tell him about the hair."

"Identical," I said. "The eyebrows. The whole thing. Like a lost relative nobody talks about."

Kevin laughed and Tommy embellished, and for a few minutes we were performing the story together, one of us catching what the other dropped, the timing easy and unplanned. When

Kevin finally shouldered his bag and left, the locker room settled into its particular after-practice quiet—dripping somewhere, a distant door, the hiss of a radiator.

Undressing with someone watching, even casually, even with their eyes elsewhere, is different from undressing together. There's no mutuality to absorb the self-consciousness. I was the one getting naked while he remained exactly as he was— jacket on, arms crossed, comfortable in his own skin. I moved through it without obvious rushing, which took more composure than it should have.

Slipping out of my clothes and quickly wrapping the towel at my waist was easy, and then off to the shower room. The water was hot. *Would Tommy be waiting by my locker or out in the field house?* Under similar circumstances I would have waited outside. I dowsed myself with some cold water before returning.

Back at the lockers, he was already mid-thought, leaning forward now, elbows on knees. He'd been thinking about a camping trip. Not a casual one—a military exercise. Backcountry, minimal gear, the kind where you practiced actual skills. Fire without matches. Navigation without a map.

I toweled off quickly, back half-turned, working through the ordinary sequence.

“You'd have to learn to live without luxuries. If you're hungry, suck it up and stick with the rations. Pack out everything you carry in,” he said. "No cheating. That's the whole point."

“I can carry things,” I said, pulling on my Calvin clones.

He gave me the sideways look. "You won’t complain?”

“Practical complaints only.” I sat down on the bench and put on my pants.

He laughed, that laugh that started somewhere behind his eyes. "Three days minimum. Maybe four. You need that long before it actually starts to mean something."

I said that sounded right. We talked about when—not seriously enough to mention dates, but seriously enough that it felt like a plan. I didn't know if the trip would ever happen. Many of our plans were more like wishful thinking. But, for a while it lived in the future, whole and real, waiting for us to arrive at it.

All of my friendships were one-on-one, and that worked just fine. Still, I felt an urge to widen things out, as if I were trying to find a new group identity to replace what I was losing with the Flannery crowd. I started small, letting people get used to each other two at a time before bringing everyone together.

At Seb's front door on Beaumont Hill, I begged him to come out with Ron and me. He stood halfway in the hall, slippers on.

"Come on, just a quick walk."

"I can't," he said. "Watching *Heaven Can Wait* with my brother, and I want to see how it ends."

"I'll rent it for you tomorrow. Unedited. No commercials. I'll even rewind it for you."

He hesitated. "You really think it's worth it?"

"Snake Hill at night? Us? How could it not be?"

He sighed, grabbed his jacket. "Fine. But if I get attacked by a raccoon, I'm taking you two down with me."

Out in the woods, the snow was gone, the ground soft and spongy underfoot. Ron lit up, dragging hard like he had something to prove.

"This," Ron said, leaning against a tree, "is what separates men from boys."

Seb took a turn, coughed, and tried to be clever. "Or separates a fool from his money. Maybe an addict from an entrepreneur."

Ron didn't laugh. "Pot's not a gateway drug. That's a myth. That's just parents freaking out."

Seb's grin faded. He hadn't meant to hit a nerve, but Ron's jaw had already tightened. The chemistry was off before we made it ten steps down the path.

I tried to rescue things. "Relax. We can all agree that nothing we do here tonight is shaping anybody's future."

For a while we walked, smoke curling in the cold as each of us took a hit. Then I pulled Jenny's graduation photo from my wallet. She looked sunlit and alive, which was probably why I carried it around like evidence of something.

Ron studied it, grinning wide. "Great picture. If I were you, I'd show everybody and say—'I fucked her.'"

Heat rushed to my face as I snatched it back.

Seb just frowned. "Classy."

Later, the munchies hit and we ended up back at Seb's house, his parents still gone, the kitchen warm and crowded with snacks. Crayon drawings by the Jenkins siblings covered the cabinets. Seb's brother had illustrated a whole list of riffs on his name: *Where's Hobbs?; Hey, Calvin Klein, why no style?* Another showed his name scrawled next to a thermometer.

"Oh, Kelvin scale," I said quietly. "Science joke."

Ron was already rooting through the fridge. Seb looked tired.

"A little cream cheese between two pop-tarts would really hit the spot," Ron said, as if inventing a cuisine.

Calvin padded down in pajamas and muttered that he was trying to sleep. Ron puffed himself up, pretending outrage.

"You hear that? Kid disrespected me. Better go teach him a lesson. He took one step toward the hall, fists raised like a boxer.

"Knock it off, Rocky," Seb said.

Ron grinned like he'd scored, but the rest of us let the moment die.

The night fizzled after that. That didn't bode well for the experiment.

Then, I tried the friend group thing again with a different pair—Seb and Tommy this time. We went to a movie, *Fast Times at Ridgemont High*. The movie was a good break to the uncomfortable silence.

On the ride back, I told the others about Mark Zavala. Seb said he had a screw loose for believing in a spy ring.

Seb scoffed. "I'd never fall for that nonsense."

"I could've convinced you," I said.

"Not possible."

I took that as a challenge.

Tommy said, "That's the kid they call eraser face. He's different alright."

In the locker room, Tommy had warmth and timing. In the car, with Seb in the back, he just had opinions.

Back in town at the end of Seb's street, Tommy glanced at me, grinning. "I'm not stopping for him. I'll slow down, but he's gotta jump."

Seb reached for the door handle, half-ready. "Fine."

It landed with a thud, no laughter. Tommy shook his head later. "He was actually going to jump. Space cadet. But, not the fun, goofy kind, like Shawn Yong."

I learned something then—sometimes the chemistry just isn't there. You realize you've been running a centrifuge. Still, I made note: Tommy had standards. And somehow, I was the only element that bonded.

I never tried to bring Mark Zavala into the mix. He was too unique. The poor guy's extreme love of puns and obscure *Dr. Who* references wouldn't fly with anyone else, and besides, he was hopelessly lovesick.

He told me about it often, in that breathless way he had, like he was fulfilling a prophecy. He loved Nadia—a girl from my grade, taller than him, painfully thin, pale, blond with red streaks, the kind of aloof loner who lived exactly where you'd expect: the spooky Gothic mansion on Clock Street.

Mark watched her like a hawk, convinced he could decode her body language. "She smiled at her homework, John. That's when I knew."

"People smile at their homework sometimes. It doesn't probably mean anything special."

I saw that you shouldn't build a case from details that were never meant to be evidence.

He dressed for a special moment—black trousers, white dress shirt, a single red rose. He walked straight up to her, handed over the flower. She took it.

"I asked if she'd like to spend some time together. She said, 'Actually, my father doesn't let me date.'"

Mark shook his head as he told me, still half-smiling. "She would have said yes. Without her father."

I knew Mark was deluding himself, and I questioned whether she was worth all the hubbub. Nadia was shunned by pretty much everyone, maybe that was part of the appeal. I was overly harsh about her trying to dissuade him. I said she was "an unfeeling, whiny, nerdy gal. Quite plain with a nose too big for her face"—nothing like the princess Mark had invented. But, to each his own. I knew how precious things seemed when it came to obsession. I was no innocent.

Over the next few weeks, Mark really started to believe Nadia needed saving from that house on Clock Street, that her father was some shadowy threat holding her captive. With his graduation looming, he felt pressure to prove his undying love before time ran out.

He started walking long distances in her name, as if each mile was a brick in the foundation of their bond. One night he walked ten miles home from his job at the Charles Street Cinema, convinced it meant something—that the sacrifice would register in the universe, or in her. It was like a silent fund drive, with no donors but him.

Ron left for Texas for the summer, but this time he wasn't coming back. I wasn't happy about that. He was going to live with cousins and finish high school in what he called his "preferred terrain." I pictured him there easily enough: boots, dust, guns, loud religion. In Massachusetts his swagger had always been slightly out of tune—too much or too fake for the crowd he wanted to impress. He'd still come back to see his parents from time to time, but the cost of long-distance calls took him out of my everyday life.

Mark was leaving for UMass Amherst, his first time apart from his family. Before he left he told me, eyes shining, "I heard from Nadia. She loves me as much as I love her—it's forever, John. You can't tell anyone, promise?"

"Sure," I said, though my voice cracked halfway through. Something was off. He was ambivalent about the distance—Boston suburb to Amherst felt like a gulf—but hopeful about majoring in English Literature. For a moment I thought college might steady him.

A month later the phone rang with a new secret.

"Can I tell you something in complete confidence? "

"Of course."

"I'm back in town on a mission. My eyes are finally wide open. Can't tell you what it is over the phone. Meet me outside the main library."

I did.

Mark was more animated than I had ever seen him, practically vibrating. "Get ready for something that'll change your life. I've found another level to the universe. Numbers and colors—they have meaning on a spiritual plane, and I can read them now. Take a look at this."

He pulled out a map of the MBTA system and pointed to route designation number 74. "That is where Nadia lives. The same as my house number. Coincidence? I think not."

There was a flash of bright light from the library.

He smiled, "And, you know how in westerns the good guys wear white, bad guys wear black? That's not just a metaphor, it's real. More complicated than that. It's baked into the universe."

I tried for humor. "Does it hold true for horses?"

Mark didn't smile. His eyes burned too brightly for jokes.

He leaned closer. "Nadia's been sending me messages through Magic 106.7—love songs, dedications. She's a good witch, John. Her father's a demon."

I swallowed and tried a different tack. "Mark, you know you've never actually spoken with her, right? Not really."

He waved that away. "I don't need to. She's speaking through the air waves."

As he spoke, the lights in the library flickered again. He pointed like it was proof. "You see that? That's me. That's the electrical power underneath everything, and I'm flexing it."

Against all reason, I said, "Okay, that's...impressive," because for a split second, with his certainty, I almost believed him.

Then, he gripped my arm. "If you see Nadia, tell her I'll love her forever. All she needs to do is wait for me."

I nodded, but my stomach turned.

Later, I learned he had dropped out of Amherst and his family was pressuring him into treatment. When I saw him again, he laughed at my concern. "I've already had the cure, John."

I walked away shaken. I'd known obsession myself—how it warps the air you breathe, how it makes you delight in any meager sign that feelings are mutual. But, with Mark I saw the darkest side of it, a place that can lead to ruin.

Senior year, it took a Herculean effort for Tommy to care about school, and he needed every bit of energy just to clear that bar. We both dropped everything else—no more track, no more civic Beaumontian Club. Tommy was my after-school activity. With the exception of an appearance at the Halloween party, we declined the rites of passage. Pep rallies and senior slide shows struck us as reheated cafeteria food—lukewarm, over-salted, not worth one bite. Tommy even skipped Senior Skip Day, just stayed home instead of going to the beach.

Seb wanted all of it. He laced up for track, auditioned for the play, signed up for the winter carnival. His voice carried this pleading tone when he urged me to join, and he demanded an explanation.

I wasn't ready to tell him why it was so important that I did not participate, didn't know for sure myself. I took the opportunity to try and win the Spy Game Challenge. I told him "I don't care about anyone. Just what I can get out of them. Told him he had been helpful. And, everyone would soon be useless, so bah-humbug to the lot of them."

Eventually, the class president cornered us, clipboard clutched like a shield. "You guys should really find a way to get involved," he said, eyebrows arched with hope. "There are no more cliques."

Tommy smirked, leaned in close, and whispered our creed: "Turn off, tune-out, dead drop."

Seb rolled his eyes. "You're hopeless."

Seb didn't like my explanation. He liked it even less after the play.

Our class put on *The Good Doctor*, which was supposed to be high culture but played like a faint echo of last year's *Pink Panther*. The year before, we'd laughed at bumbling detectives who never solved anything, pratfalls masking failure with charm. That had been my life then: screwing up, but in ways that could be laughed off. Nothing was serious enough to matter.

Now the script was Chekhov by way of Neil Simon—parables of small humiliations, people yearning for dignity and tripping over themselves instead. That felt closer to the bone. I watched Seb and the other stagehands in their open vests, hauling scenery across the stage like a mute servants, while the actors stumbled through sketches about disappointment and fragile pride. It was my story too, only no playwright was around to dress it up as art.

On opening night, one of the chair legs cracked as they carried it across the stage, sending Seb and another boy into a frantic shuffle. The broken chair scraped a jagged line across the floor. Another stagehand tripped on a trailing curtain, vest sliding off his shoulder so far it looked like he was stripping. The lead actor tried to plow ahead, but his voice chirped when the broken chair collapsed under him with a squeal, dumping him to the floor.

I laughed until I couldn't breathe.

Seb spotted me in the audience and glared. Later, he cornered me, his face red. "You think it's all a joke. You don't care about anyone but yourself."

That's when I told him. "Remember the spy ring? Remember how you dared me to make you believe I had people working for me? I did. I repackaged it—called it disregard, opportunism—but it was the same deal. And, you bought it."

His face hardened. "That's not funny, John. That's low. All I wanted was someone to do things with, and you—" He shook his head. "You turned me into your experiment. Like Mark."

It wasn't a win. It was damage.

I tried to explain, fumbling for words. "Fake acceptance at the last moment won't make up for years of rejection. That's why I can't play along with all this. You understand that, right?"

He looked at me for a long time, then finally said, "Maybe a little. But, that doesn't make what you did right."

Mark believed he had received word through the spiritual plane: it was time to act. Nadia was waiting, imprisoned in her father's castle, and only he had the courage to confront the ogre who guarded her. So, he set out, love flashing in his chest like a lantern against the dark.

An aroma of disinfectant and overcooked vegetables wafted over us. Mark sat across from me, thin wrists folded on the table, eyes flicking to the window and back.

" I brought another rose to her house," he said suddenly. "Walked right up to the door like a knight at the gate. This time her father was stationed there."

I swallowed. "He answered the door?"

"He did. Invited me in, even. I told him, 'I cannot live without her.'" Mark's voice dropped to a whisper. "That's when I saw the sign."

"What sign?"

He leaned forward, almost smiling. "By the door, nailed right there. It said, *Abandon all trope, ye who enter here*. Clever, right? A supposed parody of Dante's Inferno. So, I asked him what it meant."

"And?"

"He said it was just nothing. Just a family joke. They fancy themselves to be above cliché."

Mark's hands trembled. "But, I knew he was lying. Because what is tr, but an h twisted and torn? Hope torn asunder. Don't you see? The house is a gateway to hell. I had already passed the threshold."

I asked, "if you are in hell, how could I be with you?" The fluorescent light above us buzzed, flickering in and out, and he glanced up at it as if it confirmed everything.

"They called the police," he went on softly. "Took me by force. Said I was a danger to myself." His eyes fixed on mine. "But, I'll still love her forever."

The nurse came by then, tapping her watch. Mark leaned back, calm again, as if we'd only been talking about the weather. I walked out into the corridor heavy with the feeling that I had glimpsed a fairy tale gone wrong—where the knight believed he was saving the princess, only to discover he'd been cast in the part of the fool.

Tommy was the director of our friendship, and his enthusiasm, the engine of my affection. I rarely initiated anything;

he appeared like a spark, grinning with a little eye twitch as he laid out plans, and I followed. Most days it was indulging in our grand discovery at the mall, one of those newfangled food courts, polished and abundant.

One week he said, "Lindy, we're going to Plywood Ranch for two-by-fours and paint. It's time for a build."

It turned out we were walling off part of his basement, a little chamber where we could hole up apart from the chaos upstairs. He positioned it directly beneath the TV room alcove. He formed a built-in sofa, mapping out a wall and a small secret peep door to spy on anyone daring to come near. It was ridiculous, resourceful, and entirely my kind of thing. I held a board in place when he told me to, I painted where he told me to, thrilled to be included. His energy carried me along, and my affection grew in the wake of his resilience.

Jenny and I even teamed up to buy him a drop-ceiling for Christmas.

My back went out at the Sutter house. A sudden sharp pain left me stiff, leaning against the wall like I was three times my age. Jenny hovered nearby with nervous sympathy, while Tommy moved with the calm certainty of someone who thought he had the cure.

"Wait. Trust me. I did this for my cousin once," he said. His tone was matter-of-fact, but his eyes had a spark, like he'd been waiting for a chance to show off.

Before I could protest, he stepped behind me, sliding his hands across my waist and drawing me back against the soft bulk of his Christmas sweater. The pressure of his arms and chest was both comforting and electrifying.

"Cross your arms," he murmured.

"No, wait—"

"Trust me, Lindy."

We argued back and forth, a playful exchange stretched into long minutes of contact, his hands steady, my breath shallow. Jenny broke the tension with a sing-song quip, "Have you hugged your friend today?"—her rewrite of that TV public service announcement.

I laughed, then surrendered. "Okay."

Tommy tightened his hold, lifted me slightly by the arms, and in one swift motion my back popped, the pain loosening. Relief spread through me, but the warmth of his chest against me lingered even more.

Mark's love for Nadia reminded me of my own earlier obsessions—grand, desperate, built more on fantasy than reality. What I felt for Tommy was just as consuming, but rooted in action and closeness: hammering nails, sharing rides, completing assignments being carried along by his positive energy. But, certainly something essential was missing. Tommy never suggested he was interested in anyone who wasn't a girl. Where could I find the remaining pieces or with whom?

I ran into Jimmy Flannery in the hall one afternoon. He looked half-proud, half-defeated, and said he might not graduate—gym was dragging him down. "I don't like the stuff," he muttered, as if lack of dodgeball were a moral failing. He owed two full years of make-ups for skipping class or refusing to dress. I only had one quarter to make up, so I doubled up for rescue swimming and jogging.

Although I pretty much knew Jimmy was gay, it never once crossed my mind that we could make something of it. No feelings, meant no experimentation. I was squarely focused on people in their totality, not body parts. And, his personality gave me no onramps.

The swim class is how I met Paul Erickson. He was the only guy in school with a pierced ear—a small silver stud that looked almost illicit in 1983, when earrings still belonged to girls and rock stars. Paul had a kind face, a solid build, and a gentle way of moving through the world. I asked, maybe too sharply, "What's up with the earring?" Which, translated, probably read as: "Are you gay?"

He just smiled and said he liked fashion and girls. Then, he was my partner. We practiced saving each other in the pool—chin tows, chest carries, awkward splashing maneuvers that left me dizzy. The feel of his stubble brushing my arm, the press of my hand across his chest—it was electric, almost unbearable. I was certain he'd be a prime candidate for my feelings if the universe allowed more reasons to interact.

But, desire at that level carried shame in spades—tenfold for every shiver. Could we have rescued each other? Or was I the only one in danger of drowning?

Reconnaissance and covert engagement took so much energy. So, I resolved to be happy with what I had with Tommy, to embrace it, and let it be what it could be without trying.

For a time, Mark believed he lived in the west wing of the White House, pacing grand corridors in his mind while locked behind hospital doors. When he finally agreed to swallow the bitter draught of medication, it was not from trust but from strategy—a reluctant spell to win his release. Freedom came at a cost. The potion dulled his spirit, drained the color from the air, and left him mourning the loss of his *joie de vivre*.

By decree he was forbidden from seeking Nadia, the princess he could not rescue. Without her, life seemed stripped of meaning. The law of the household was clear: compliance with the medicine was the price of staying under his family's roof. And, so he endured, working as a bagger at Sun Market, stacking bread and fruit with dutiful hands while inside he raged against the poison he was forced to take. In every conversation, he circled back to her name and to the potions that shackled him, as if both were the twin curses of his story—love denied and life diminished.

Some remedies hold you together just long enough to need a better one.

Tommy had started spreading his attention thinner—between me and a girl I didn't even know. He'd drive over to her house without warning, knock on the door, see if she wanted to go for a ride.

"She says 'no thanks' more than you do," he laughed one night as we drove along in his car in the mall parking lot, fast-food wrappers crinkling underfoot. "But, hey, one of these days, Lindy—we'll double date. Me with her, you with..." He trailed off, grinning at his own imagination. "Or maybe we just go ho' hunting for you first."

I turned toward the window, watching the streetlights smear across the glass as he drove. The smell of fry oil clung to my jacket. My throat ached with words I couldn't form.

He noticed. "Lindy, what's wrong with you? Cat got your tongue?" His voice was too loud in the small car.

I shrank in on myself, the air from the vent blasting my face, unbearable. Before I knew it, I'd thrown the door open, leapt out, and darted back into the mall. My sneakers slapped against the linoleum, echoing through empty corridors. I burst out the opposite side, the cool night air shocking me awake, and started walking—five miles home.

But, when I reached the corner, headlights flashed. Tommy's car idled there, window down. "Get in," he said simply. No grin this time. I did, reluctantly, the seat belt strap rough against my neck. He didn't push. He knew when to let silence ride.

Once, Shawn Yong saw me in one of those moods. "What's the matter, asshole?" he sassed, putting chapstick on his lips.

"Don't mess with him right now—believe me," Tommy cut in, quick, protective.

Later, it got even stranger. But, first we had to graduate.

Graduation day arrived in the echoing fieldhouse, the air thick with heat and ceremony. The bleachers were packed—families clutching cameras, younger siblings fidgeting in starched clothes, teachers standing along the walls like sentries. Jenny sat somewhere in the middle rows, camera in hand, cheering for Tommy and me at every opportunity. I could hear her voice cutting through the murmur, bright and certain, like she'd needed to be sure we stood out.

Karl sat at a drum kit beside the stage with a little pickup group tasked with punctuating the speeches with rhythm and flourish, and to accompany our songs. His sticks cracked like gunfire between the principal's words about futures and potential, sharp enough to make people flinch. He looked focused, untouchable, like he could handle being the entertainment at the same time as celebrating his achievements.

Most faces around me shone with pride and easy smiles. Mine didn't, if the photos have any say. I looked like I was bracing for impact, like I'd just been asked a question I couldn't answer: *What fate did love and life have in store for me?*

As rehearsed, we all stood and sang *Through the Years* and *Redemption Song* to the crowd—voices scattered but pulling toward the same refrain. It was supposed to be unifying, a last chorus before scattering to separate futures. The words affected me differently than they did the others: loyalty, secure love, freedom, release, escape. They belonged to everyone in the fieldhouse, but I couldn't make myself join fully. My lips moved, but the sound stuck in my throat.

For me, support and redemption had never been about linking arms with classmates who'd barely known me. It was about surviving them—slipping free of the years when their laughter had been the loudest thing in the room, when I'd learned to make myself small enough to go unnoticed. Now I was supposed to sing about togetherness? About bonds that would last forever? I mouthed the words and felt like a fraud.

Karl's drums punctuated the final verse. I watched his hands move—precise, relentless—and thought about all the times I'd stood near him and said nothing. All the races I'd run that let me stay in his orbit. All the silence I'd carried because speaking felt impossible.

The song ended. People cheered. I clapped along, hollow.

That evening came the lock-in—the sanctioned vigil meant to corral us from the chaos that graduation nights had been in the past. No booze-fueled brawls, no cars wrapped around telephone poles. Just a cafeteria, games, food, and us, sealed in until morning like lab rats in a controlled experiment.

Tommy and Seb stayed close by my side, though away from each other. We'd each had a reasonable amount to drink before arrival—enough to take the edge off, not enough to act foolish. Karl drifted at a distance, orbiting with the valedictorian, and that small gap between us might as well have been a continent. I told myself it didn't matter. That I'd moved on. That Tommy was the one who mattered now.

But, I still tracked Karl's movements like a satellite.

I moved through the night like a collector, asking people to sign my program, keeping my yearbook untouched and pristine. Some people scrawled jokes. Others wrote *Have a great Summer* or *Stay cool* instead of referencing a memory. I nodded and smiled and felt nothing. These signatures were proof I'd been here, nothing more.

In the auditorium, they played *The Warriors* on the big screen—gangs in vests, graffiti-tagged subways, a long journey home through hostile territory. Karl sat a few rows down with the valedictorian, head tilted toward her, the glow from the screen flickering across his face. I pretended to watch the movie from above, but really I was watching him. The way he leaned in when she whispered something. The way he laughed—a sound I'd heard maybe twice in four years.

Tommy nudged me. "You even watching this?"

"Yeah," I lied.

He didn't push.

By one o'clock, the cafeteria had thinned out. Some people had crashed on mats in the gym. Others huddled in corners, whispering about plan for college, for lives that suddenly felt too close and too far away at the same time.

I sat on a folding chair near the vending machines, program in my lap, and let the weight of it settle: *This was over.* High school. The script. The performance. The twelve years of pretending I belonged in a story I'd never had a hand in writing.

And Karl? He was leaving for college in the fall—some school three states away, engineering or pre-med or something practical that would take him far from here. I'd never told him how I felt. Never even hinted. Now it was too late, and he'd become another name I'd carry in silence.

Tommy dropped into the chair beside me. "You good?"

"Yeah," I said. "Just tired."

"Liar."

I smiled despite myself. "Yeah."

He didn't ask what I was really thinking. That was the thing about Tommy—he gave you space to be sad without needing to fix it. He just sat there, solid and warm, until the night started to thin and the fluorescent lights buzzed overhead like a question I still couldn't answer.

By the weekend, Ron was visiting his parents. Both of us eighteen now, legal on paper if nowhere else, he steered us straight to the Chinese restaurant that didn't bother carding. We ordered Singapore Slings like we'd discovered a magic elixir. The drinks were too sweet, too red, and went down easy.

"To freedom," Ron said, raising his glass.

I clinked mine against his. "To whatever comes next."

From there it was on to the Combat Zone—that neon labyrinth of adult entertainment wedged between Chinatown and the financial district, where the promise of entry felt like another diploma. We walked past strip clubs with names like *The Glass Slipper* and *Naked Eye*, past peep booths and XXX theaters, past men in suits who looked like they'd ducked out of board meetings and now stood smoking under marquees soliciting things I didn't want to say outloud.

Ron was giddy, electric. "This is it, man. We're adults now. We can do whatever we want."

I nodded, but I felt like I was watching the scene from outside my own body.

The peep booth was a scam. Tokens kept the light on, but real money had to be shoved through a slot before the girl on the other side took off her clothes. I hesitated, then slid two crumpled bills into the slot. Just as the paper left my fingers, the lights snapped out. Darkness. Silence. The sour realization that I'd been had.

I had no plans to buy more tokens. Even if the lights had stayed on, I wasn't sure I wanted to see her—thin, tired-looking, eyes averted like she'd already gone somewhere else in her head. Oh yeah, and female.

Ron bragged about seeing "live boobs" with adolescent glee, expecting me to match his joy. I nodded along, but the words caught in my throat.

We moved on to the theater, where XXX reels flickered in grainy color. The men onscreen were ugly but well-endowed, the women striking, their bodies gleaming under harsh lights. Watching, I felt a strange, inverted arousal—yes, I was turned on, but in a way that hollowed me out rather than filled me. My body stirred. My mind recoiled.

Somewhere in the second reel, I felt myself detach—rise up toward the ceiling and perch in the back corner of the theater, watching myself watch.

The reference group that had grounded me—my classmates, the world of Beaumont Public School—was gone now. I'd calibrated every move against their judgment. *What would they think? What would they say? Would this make me more visible or less?* Their opinions had been the gravity that held me in orbit, even when I hated them for it.

Now they were scattered—college-bound, job-bound, gone. And, without that tether, I drifted, surreal and unmoored.

I glanced sideways at Ron. His mouth hung slack, eyes glazed, caught in his own trance. He looked like he was witnessing revelation. For me, it was a reckoning.

If I wasn't performing for them anymore, who was I performing for?

If their judgment didn't matter, what did?

If I could finally stop pretending—would I even know how to start being real?

The film kept playing. Bodies moved on screen, mechanical and joyless. Ron shifted in his seat, mesmerized. I sat perfectly still, watching my own shadow on the theater wall, and felt the ground disappear beneath me.

This was supposed to be freedom. This was supposed to be adulthood.

But, all I felt was the terrible, weightless drift of a satellite cut loose from its orbit—spinning in the dark, searching for something to pull me back to earth.

Tommy began showing up at the softball games of Mark's younger sister, Amy. I'd met her before at Mark's house, and one weekend, side by side, we stripped and polished the CCD school floors—two atheists doing piecework for Tommy's father in the name of the Church. Small world.

Tommy showed up at my place still smelling like beer and cheap perfume.

"You're not gonna believe this, Lindy," he said, blinking fast. "Amy takes me to her softball game, right? They need an assistant coach. It's an adult league. Whole team's women in their twenties and thirties. Lesbians mostly. Afterward they go straight to this bar like it's part of the sport. And, I tag along."

"They just let you in?" I asked.

He grinned. "Not even a glance at our IDs. I'm sitting there with a glass full of rum and Coke, acting like I've been doing it since birth. They're yelling over the jukebox, pounding the table, and nobody cares that we are underage."

"Didn't you feel...out of place?"

"At first, yeah. Then one of them leans over and says, 'Drink up, Rookie. You're on our team now.' They call me Rookie or Mascot, Lindy. Next thing I know, they're buying me rounds of beer and daring me to sing karaoke."

I laughed despite myself. "You? Karaoke?"

"*Total Eclipse of the Heart*," he said proudly. "I get up there, my voice cracks on the first 'Every now and then I fall apart,' and the whole team jumps up behind me like backup singers. Bar crowd went wild. They treated me like I was family. You ever have eight women chanting your name? It does something to a man." I had a strange sinking feeling in the pit of my stomach.

Tommy smirked and looked off down the street. "Oh and – Mark's...different. You know that. He says things I don't always follow. Half the time I don't understand a word out of his mouth. He doesn't have the sense to clean off his glasses. Just let streaks sit in his visual field. Kid's not well."

"Love has broken his brain," I admitted. "He's lovesick, are you?"

"Amy and I are just friends, but she's alright."

What exactly did that mean?

"Really?"

"She looks good compared to those lesbians."

Two too many girls were coming into Tommy's life for my taste.

Seeing no other recourse, I asked Amy out myself. The words tumbled out, sharp with nerves, and she surprised me by saying yes. When I picked her up, Mark stood in the hall, awkward as I was, the layers of strangeness stacking high. We went for yogurt, but I was barely there.

Amy sat across from me in the yogurt shop, plastic spoon tapping against the cup. The place smelled faintly of bleach and semi-fresh strawberries.

"So...how do you think the floors look at CCD these days?" I asked, half-smiling.

"Shiny," she said flatly. "I mean, we made it shine, right?"

I laughed politely, feeling the air between us widen. I tried a bite of yogurt, but the cold dulled everything, the taste gone before I swallowed.

"You don't usually hang out with me," she said after a pause.

"I figured, why not?" My voice cracked on the last word. Why not? As if I'd flipped a coin. As if Tommy hadn't been the coin.

Her spoon hovered. "Might as well, yeah."

We traded safe small talk—school plans, Mark's quirks, stories from the bar. She described the softball team's third base, who'd once thrown a glove at the umpire and gotten a standing ovation from the opposing team's dugout. I laughed, genuinely for a moment. Then, I wondered if Tommy had already heard this story. Whether she'd told it the same way, hands moving like that, and whether he'd laughed in the same place I just had. Or had he actually experienced that event with her?

I felt the full, airless weight of the evening. She was right here. She was agreeable, pretty even, and she had said yes. Now, I was supposed to be happy about it.

Driving home, I still couldn't make sense of what I'd been attempting. Interference? Imitation? Some clumsy bid to insert myself into Tommy's orbit by proxy? Or just proof—to her, to him, to myself—that I could want what I was supposed to want, and act on it, and have it go somewhere ordinary and fine.

None of it had gone anywhere. And, the yogurt had tasted like nothing.

Tommy had graduated successfully, been accepted to college, and with that, the pressures had lifted. I needed to say how I felt out loud because it wasted so much energy keeping it in. And, in many ways, I thought it was unfair for him not to know. Our reference group scattered like loose papers in the wind. In the vacuum that followed, I carried a single mantra in my chest, louder and louder with every beat of my heart: *Tell him.*

We were alone in his car after a movie, headlights tunneling through backroads neither of us knew well. The mapless drifting only added to my unease. I gripped my arm rest, staring at the glow of the dashboard, until the words that I had long contemplated jumped out of me.

"We can't be friends anymore." The first step of a strategy that seemed logical, at least in rehearsal.

Tommy turned sharply, shoulders tightening. "Oh, this always happens to me." He let out a sharp nervous laugh. "I lose friends. Why? What did I do? You can't even say?"

Now, I'd have to tell him something.

"It's not about you," I muttered, but my hands wouldn't unclench.

He swerved a little around a curve, eyes flicking to me. "Come on, Lindy, you gotta tell me." The nickname carried a nervous affection.

"It's for the best," I said, looking out at the trees flashing by.

"Tell me." His voice had an edge now, almost pleading. "I'll guess, then. You're mad about Amy? You're mad about Jenny?"

I shook my head, mouth dry. Finally: "No. It's because of how I feel about you."

I went numb, unsure if I'd opened a door or slammed one shut.

He slapped the heel of his hand against the steering wheel, not hard, but enough to make the horn sputter. "Oh!—you're a fag?"

"Not exactly." My throat burned. "Just...missing you too much. Thinking too much."

Tommy leaned back, with a half-smile that didn't signal happiness. "I've had this happen before. What is it with me?" His hands tightened and loosened on the wheel. "That pervert at the library—he left me notes when I was eight. The blonde hair, the blue eyes...gets to people."

I didn't know what to say.

"How long have you felt that way?"

I swallowed. "Since the night you cried about your parents."

"That was a loooong time ago." He drew out the word, trying for humor, but the silence afterward was heavy.

"Maybe I can wear a mask," he joked weakly, his voice cracking.

He shot me a sidelong glance, brow furrowed. "Can we treat this like a joke?"

I didn't object.

"You need to get your hormones checked," he said finally, voice lighter, almost teasing.

Then, without warning: "Maybe I can beat it out of you." His smile was wide now, forced, hands drumming on the wheel.

I stared ahead. "Keep this quiet if you can."

The car filled with the sound of tires on gravel. My own questions echoed in my head: *What was I hoping for here? An end to the limbo? A firm declaration that we must remain friends? Some tender appreciation? A door cracked open?*

What I got was Tommy's shrug, eyes fixed on the road.

I wanted him to say *"Maybe it's okay, Lindy. We can still be friends...but not too close!"* I could accept that. *What if he said "You might as well blow me." Had I wanted that?*

The only thing I knew for sure was this: I had to begin with "We can't be friends anymore"—not because I wanted that ending, but because it was the only shield I could raise. A way to guard against him mistaking my confession for a come-on, and a way to soften the blow if he chose to turn from me in the end.

PART IV

Reckonings

17
Calibration

Mark was already bagging groceries at the Sun supermarket, so I figured—if he could, so could I. No bagger jobs were open, but the manager said, "You'll make more in the deli anyway."

I had only the foggiest idea what a deli was. My father avoided it on principle, steering us toward factory-packed cold cuts "priced right" in the meat department. The deli, in his mind, was frivolous. Suspicious. A luxury aisle best ignored. So, I went home and looked it up in the dictionary—*deli, short for delicatessen*—as if a definition might help.

It didn't.

The deli cases stretched along the wall like a small cathedral of glass—spotlit, orderly, and faintly ridiculous in their devotion to cold cuts. Deli was its own clan, complete with uniforms and dialect. Three slicers screamed at once, the air buzzing with motors and the smell of brine, beef, and cellophane. Customers lined up eight deep, shouting orders like auctioneers.

"Half a pound of imported boiled ham?"

"No—honey ham. Thin."

"Not *that* thin!"

Who knew there were seven kinds of ham? Four bolognas? Italian names that tied your tongue in knots—mortadella, capicola. Sale prices were taped to the wall. You were expected to memorize all the regular prices.

After a week of training, I worked days all summer, nights once school started. Most of my coworkers were engineers pulling second shifts, collars still faintly starched, talking about traffic flow or circuitry while slicing salami. One guy was a bailiff, trading the courthouse for corned beef without missing a beat.

In Deli, cleanup was constant. Officially, you were supposed to break down the unplugged slicer and wash every part. Unofficially, there was a shortcut: rough-cloth against the running blade until it gleamed. Dangerous, forbidden—and universally practiced.

"Just don't let the manager see," one of the engineers said, shrugging off his apron.

"What happens if he does?" I asked.

He grinned. "He gives you another slicer to clean."

That was deli justice—no punishments, just more work, measured out like meat on a scale.

One night, I was cleaning the uncovered running slicer blade the easy way. Mark came to me in a slump at the end of his shift saying he was going to kill himself. To me, it was more of his high-drama pronouncements, and I was worn out by them. So, I said, "There's the blade." He took a step toward it, so I snapped the switch off, slammed the cover back on. The hum stopped, but the gravity stayed. Calling *his bluff* didn't help. But, he said he would hold off for a week to give Nadia one last chance to contact him, one last chance for the universe to prove it wasn't stacked against him.

Mark had been kicked out of his house for refusing his meds, a tough love gesture that left him drifting. He landed with Larry Smart's family up on Haver Hill. Larry was a big and awkward, kind and fluffy teddy bear who I'd seen trying to spread cheer in the school halls. Now, he was suddenly cast in the role of caretaker.

Mark also found companionship in unexpected places. There was a guy in General who claimed psychic powers and fed him "reports" on Nadia's movements. Mark recounted them to me like bulletins from another world, eyes bright, voice rising as if the information carried cosmic weight.

The "informant" was hard of hearing, and we'd communicated for months through a mix of gestures, lip movements, and patience. It worked. That felt real—both of us making the effort. Now, he was issuing psychic updates about Nadia with perfect certainty. The contrast was too sharp: someone who knew the difficulty of real communication was now claiming special clarity.

I didn't know if he believed his own claims or was just enjoying having someone hang on his words. Either way, Mark was getting worse.

I confronted that dude as he was attending to a clean-up in aisle seven.

"Maybe stop stoking his fever."

I tried to spend time with Mark, to nudge him toward lighter talk—movies, music, the old inside jokes we still shared. Sometimes it worked, and he laughed, but the laughter never lasted. I wanted to believe my presence anchored him, but in truth I was only a bystander, keeping vigil as he walked a narrowing path.

It is a hard thing to care for someone whose world no longer meshes with reality. You keep hoping a hand on the shoulder or a shared activity will draw them back.

But, three weeks later, Mark leapt from the fourth floor of a business office, where his psychiatrist had his practice. There was a balcony—an easy hop over a rail. He survived, though barely, his body sustained by machines in a hushed hospital ward.

When I heard, a hollow ache opened in me. I kept replaying our last conversations, the outright statements of his intent. His parents knew more than I had realized, he told everyone and had for a while. But, I didn't know whether I was the crucial link that failed. I thought my voice should have saved him.

I wheeled the barrow of woodchips down from Saranopoulos's house, under the railroad bridge, heading for her church. My task was to refresh the beds, but my thoughts wouldn't stay put. They kept darting between two things. Mark was broken. Tommy was gone. I felt raw and reckless.

They said Mark would live, but he'd never walk again. How was he supposed to bear that?

The night of my big disclosure to Tommy was still burnt in my memory: the stilted goodbye, the surreal walk back into my home, staring into the dim bathroom mirror. I had finally said it—admitted attraction to another guy. Said it to someone else, the source, after containing it so long. The words made it real. I'd seen myself reflected back as someone new, almost a stranger, and it was spooky. This time there was no escape hatch.

Where one cross to bear was already too much, Mark was handed two. When your mind loses traction in the world, you at least need your feet to work.

What right did I have to grieve a friendship beside what Mark was facing? Yet the loss of Tommy came bursting back anyway.

A week later, still panicked by what I had done, I tried to take my straight identity back. I called Tommy and told him I had gone to a school counselor, who said I was normal.

"The counselor even envied how much I could care for a friend."

"Oh?"

"So, we can probably still hang out."

"Oh. Okay. I'm pretty busy with school, but there'll be time."

There had been no counselor. I had made the whole thing up because I wanted him back.

We agreed to let it slide. But, we never spoke again.

So, I worked, raking and spreading, trying to disappear into the mulch. I was so absorbed I didn't notice the man until he spoke.

"Mind if I take your picture? I've got a new camera—the red in your shirt against the gray stone in the building would be a good test."

He was nerdy, early thirties maybe, his voice casual but careful.

"I guess," I muttered, not stopping.

"Could you look up? Maybe smile?"

I looked up but didn't smile. The shutter clicked anyway. He snapped a few frames and walked off.

That was strange. If all he wanted was the color, why did he need my face? What was he after? Was he about to offer me five dollars?

Later, in the back of the church, I was spreading chips under a thin row of bushes when he appeared again.

"One last shot," he said. "Against the greenery."

I'd had enough. I knew what this was. The thought came suddenly, reckless: maybe it was time to play it out.

"Do you need any nudes for your portfolio?" I asked, my voice flat, daring.

He froze. His mouth opened, shut. For a moment his eyes flickered oddly.

Before he could answer, a man and his dog came through the hole in the back fence, from the path to the stream. The spell broke.

I dumped the rest of the woodchips, went back up the hill for another load, my heart thumping with a mix of shame, power, and something I couldn't quite fathom. Mark had telegraphed his love until it broke him, I had whispered mine until it disappeared, and then the photographer appeared with his lens, twisting my frustration into an offer of complete exposure.

Jake Green worked in General, a short Greek kid a year older than me. I admired the guys in that department. While I was anchored to one station, they moved everywhere—bagging for a while, spot-cleaning the floors, stocking lettuce in Produce, even jumping in Deli when the line got too long. They had the run of the place, slipping from aisle to aisle like they belonged everywhere.

Jake had charm. I saw him at ease with everyone, laughing with everyone. He zipped by the deli with a quick quip or a morsel of store gossip, maybe something about the girls in Courtesy or across in Cheese Shop.

The line at the counter stretched nearly to the bakery case. Doug was hunched over his slicer, one hand steady on a block of ham, blade whining. I was wrapping rotisserie chicken, my fingers clumsy with the cellophane, while Jake slipped in behind the counter, tugging his General apron straight like it might magically turn him into a deli man.

"Which one is the Genoa salami?" he whispered in my ear.

I pointed toward the top shelf in the cooler in front of us.

He darted in, came back with the wrong stick. Doug didn't even look up. "That's hard salami, kid. Genoa's softer. Smells like wine if you stick your nose in it."

Jake laughed and grabbed the right one this time. "See, I'm learning. Next week I'll be running this place."

Doug snorted. "Next week you'll be cleaning toilets."

A woman at the counter asked, "Is the honey ham that's on sale, Kirshner's?"

Jake looked to me like a student to a teacher. I whispered, "Golden Harvest—red stripe."

Jake turned back to her, confident now. "Red stripe, ma'am. Best price in town."

He awkwardly placed the ham on a slicer.

She grinned. "Guess you boys know your hams."

Jake winked. "We dream about 'em at night." He completed the order. The woman laughed and shook her head, walking off with her wrapped bundle.

Doug finally cracked a smile, shaking his head as he slid another slice of turkey across the cellophane sheet. "You're a damn fool, Jake. But you keep the line moving."

"High praise," Jake said, puffing up like he'd just been knighted.

For twenty minutes, he hustled with us—fetching cold cuts, asking questions, wiping down the counter between orders. Every time Doug chuckled at one of his wisecracks, Jake's face lit like he'd scored another point.

Jake grinned, satisfied, and headed back toward Produce. The deli felt oddly quieter without his voice echoing around.

It had been four months since I'd last seen Tommy. My well was bone dry the entire time. I told myself I was seared shut, but little feelings had started slipping through the seams again. Admiration toward Jake felt a shade too close to longing, and there was this tall, lean Italian guy in Front End who sent my heart racing every time he bent to load a bag of groceries into the trunk of some Buick. His face was strong-boned, hair black and glossy, his body trim in a way that made the uniform look tailored. Every customer's wife seemed to find a reason to chat with him while their husbands stared from the doorway.

The Front End itself was comic theater: bags of groceries rattling underground on the conveyor belt like coal on a mine shaft, red baskets popping out into daylight where the boys sprinted to cars, their aprons flapping like capes.

Jake's jokes kept things light, and everything between us was easy unless we were left alone—thankfully rare. Then, came the day of the provolone. The block of cheese was coming to an irregular end. I was cutting it precisely, trying to keep the slices whole. I had the guard off so I could apply needed pressure at the right moment. My hand slipped a bit as I sheared a slice. The tip of my pointer finger went with it.

I finished the order as if nothing happened, applying pressure on the finger in a paper towel pressed against my palm, my hand pressed against my leg. Someone fetched the manager, who, in a stroke of cruel comedy, ordered Jake to drive me to the ER.

It was awkward from the start. My hand throbbed, and Jake clearly had no idea how to treat a bleeder. He fiddled with the radio, tapped the steering wheel, said nothing. I stared at the window, trying not to faint.

At Mt. Auburn Hospital's waiting room, we waited awkwardly. After a while, Jake commandeered the television in the corner like it was his living room, his tie pulled loose, a gold chain catching the fluorescent light.

Doc said, "There's nothing there to stitch together."

On the ride back, I sat in the passenger seat, finger half numb, half burning where the doctor had cauterized the wound, watching Jake's profile glow blue in the flicker of the street lights. Neither of us said anything the rest of the way.

We were both still on the clock. So, it wasn't a total waste of a couple of hours. And, something in the air was beginning to simmer, and I felt the familiar bubbles arise: Not again!

Funny thing about slicers— they can give you perfect, even cuts right up until somewhere near the end when the guard is supposed to be applied but has to stay off just when there is the most danger, and then it wants a piece of you. Maybe that was the price of pressing too close: a little blood, a little scar, and a warning not to try again.

Outside the store, the rest of life kept moving. I'd had my permit since sixteen but never got the hang of driving. I couldn't read street signs; squinting was no longer enough. My timing never left room for a comfortable stop, and I overthought every sign. Backing up was especially disorienting. Maybe that's why I was so impressed with Tommy and Jake, who both had easy confidence behind the wheel.

Neighbor Bob, well over forty and practicing for his license too, let me use his car. Next to Bob, I almost looked competent. He'd finally gotten a lucky break: a relative he'd never met died and the state transferred over a sedan—but that didn't stop him from treating it like the cockpit of a spaceship. He'd flip random switches on the dash and say, "activate – activate." Nothing happened, but he'd nod solemnly: "Good. Cloaking device engaged."

Denny rode shotgun, sighing at every joke. "Bob, just keep it between the lines."

"Relax," Bob said, steering with one finger, "autopilot's deployed."

It was a good thing Bob had reliable transportation, because he had court dates piling up thanks to Owen's land-grab scheme.

That amateur developer, fueled more by his wife's Beaumont Hill money than his own know-how, had managed to cram a house too large for his postage-stamp lot, leaving barely a breath between the walls and the property line. He sought to remedy his mistake by claiming swaths of Bob's land. As if that weren't enough, he dusted off an old easement buried in the deeds—meant only as permission to cross Bob's land—and tried to rebrand it as 4 Clock Lane's private walkway to the tracks.

"Owen came to us talking about how he was going to beautify the valley," Bob said, tightening his grip on the wheel. "Turned out he was just a feudal lord in khakis. Now it's time for his comeuppance." Bob kept his eyes down the road, hoping his next break would come from justice, not another dead stranger.

By the end of the summer, Ron had a new plan: "Vermont. Drinking age, eighteen. Road trip!?" He'd rented a car and we were going to have our first nightclub experience. Club Mirage. Big opportunity.

We were in the car, Ron fiddling with the stereo, when he said, "So, I finally had sex without paying for it."

I tilted my head. "Congratulations? Want a medal?"

"No, seriously. Six weeks. A real relationship. She was in college, too."

"And what happened?"

"She stopped calling back. Wouldn't answer. So, I came up with a plan." He grinned, smug.

"Oh boy. What plan?"

"I left her a card at her dorm. Wrote a little cryptic note inside, signed it, and taped a penny right after my name."

I blinked. "A penny?"

"Yeah. See, curiosity is a powerful motivator. She had to call to ask what it meant."

I laughed. "You're telling me, she broke up with you but came back just to solve your riddle?"

"Exactly." He smacked the wheel, pleased with himself. "And it worked. She called. We met up, had one last night together. Then she was gone for good."

I shook my head. "Ron, that's not romance. That's...a cheap trick."

He chuckled, unbothered. "Hey, I got what I wanted. A penny well spent."

As we crossed the state line, Ron had one hand on the wheel and the other drumming the dash, buzzing with ideas like he was drawing up battle plans.

"So, here's how it works if we strike gold tonight," he said. "I mean if only one of us gets lucky, the other hangs back in the lobby—acts like a patient wingman."

I raised an eyebrow. "You realize the lobby is just two broken chairs and a Coke machine, right?"

Ron grinned. "Details. Now, if both of us score—" he shot me a glance, the car lights strobing across his face as we passed a truck—"then it's tandem, same room, different beds. Simple."

I laughed out loud. "We line up like synchronized swimmers?"

"That or you get the car."

I slumped against the passenger door, shaking my head. "More likely, we'll need to flip a coin to see who has dibs on the bathroom first."

"Exactly," Ron said, grinning wider. "What? So, you've met Jacquin?"

I groaned, sinking lower in my seat. "Never mind. Let's just say I finally gave in to one of those vibrating back massagers." I hadn't indulged at all until after high school.

Ron barked out a laugh, slapped the steering wheel. "Took you long enough."

We fell silent for a while and that got me thinking. I still had never let Jacquin intrude when I thought about someone I loved. That would have felt like a violation—like dragging something impure and raw into a space I wanted to keep solemn. I was sure they'd feel used. So, I turned inward instead, using only the mirror as stimulus, a whole facet of desire bent back on myself.

We hit the line outside of Club Mirage, people shuffling, everyone making a fuss about fake IDs. The whole ritual made me sweat, though I had nothing forged to show. We scooted past the bouncers, IDs checked, wrists stamped, the bass already in my chest. Hardly inside, a girl turned to me and said, "So, you finally got in?"

"Yeah," I said, forcing a smile. "Long line."

She nodded once. "Yeah, it was."

"Worth it, though. Music's good."

She tilted her head, like she wasn't sure. "I guess. It's loud."

I faked a laugh. "That's the point, right?"

I searched for another hook. "Uh...have you been here before?"

"Mm-hmm." She took a sip of her drink and shook the ice, eyes already scanning elsewhere.

She gave a polite smile, already angling her shoulders toward the crowd. A half-step back, and she was gone.

The music throbbed and my drink order became my anchor: Tom Collins. The only cocktail I knew by name and one I could tolerate without gagging. Ron went for Screwdrivers. We alternated payment, acting like gentlemen with a system.

Neither of us had the guts to ask a girl to dance, and without one we were too uptight to go out there on our own. So, we lingered by the railing, pretending to study the DJ booth. Then—splat.

At first it felt like nothing—just a drop on my head. Then a steady cold stream.

I looked up. A mezzanine. Some drunk idiot with good aim?

I froze, trying to maintain composure, pretending it hadn't happened, until Ron muttered, "You gonna let him douse you like that?"

"What should I do? Go wrestle with him and return the favor?"

"Yeah," Ron said, deadpan. "Or you could tackle him and make him buy your next Tom Collins."

We just moved out of his target zone, but I felt pathetic for not doing anything.

I overheard the girl I saw when I first entered say "So, you finally got in" to the next guy. She hadn't chosen me; the line wasn't casual; it was just her opener for every stranger who she thought might buy her a drink.

In the men's room, some guy in a mesh shirt cornered me at the sink.

"Mirrors in clubs make you look better, right?" he asked.

"Booze helps too," I said, studying my pale face and wet hair. "I think they make me look like I need a lawyer."

He chuckled, slapped my back, then leaned in again, squinting at our reflections. "Nah, man, look—we're movie stars in here."

I glanced at him, then back at my reflection. "Mutt and Jeff, The Movie."

He wheezed. "From the funnies?"

He called me a "comedian," and staggered out, leaving the sink running like it was part of his bit. Later, I asked myself, was that whole thing just guy talk or was that actually flirting?

By closing time, Ron was drunker than he realized. He still insisted on driving the two miles to our motel anyway, and narrated the whole ride like he was filing a report on himself.

"See, I can hold the wheel steady," he said, drifting into the opposite lane. "Only problem's the whole two eyes thing. Hard to keep 'em both working."

At the motel, he collapsed on the bed. Then, he was suddenly up rifling his pockets, then shot outside and then back. His face twisted. "My Rolex. Where's my Rolex?"

He tore through the sheets, crawled under the bed, checked the bathroom, opened drawers we hadn't touched. His voice cracked. "Somebody took my Rolex. I need to have my Rolex."

I tried to calm him. "Ron, we'll probably find it right where you left it." And to lighten the mood, "Or the DJ's wearing it now, keeping tempo. We can stop by the club tomorrow."

He sat on the carpet, tears cutting streaks down his face. "You don't understand. I need it."

I perched on the edge of the bed, useless, watching my friend mourn a watch like it was a limb. The night had promised glamour and delivered damp hair, lousy drinks, and Ron crying over an expensive watch, and time itself disappearing.

In the morning, we found the watch in his car. Turns out time and class hadn't left him—it had just slipped between the seats.

The next day it was back to work. At ten o'clock, the deli went down to one man. The place was quiet except for the drone of the cooler fans and the occasional splash of a lobster tail in the tank. I was halfway through slicing two pounds of domestic boiled ham when Jake drifted in from the back, apron crooked, with the smell of bleach and cologne clinging to him. He leaned on the counter like it was a pedestal.

He watched as I peeled the wrapper back just far enough to free the next few inches. "Why don't you just rip all the plastic off and get it out of your way?"

I kept the loaf steady, careful with the pressure. "Because then it dries out, and tomorrow it's my fault when it looks like shoe leather. This way it stays fresh. Like peeling a banana—one pound at a time."

Jake snorted. "Banana, huh? Never thought I'd see somebody treat meat like produce."

"Trust me," I said, sliding a neat stack onto the paper. "Plastic's the only thing standing between you and customers complaining about crusty provolone."

He smiled. "Man, you're too careful. Bet you even double-check your double-checks."

A customer wandered up, asking for hot ham. I shrugged. "Sorry, we're out of hot ham."

Jake gave me a look, then whispered in an odd voice, "You ain't got no hot ham, you ain't got no hot ham," ducking back like he'd said something scandalous. I strained to follow whatever game he was playing while I finished the order.

When the customer left, Jake leaned in again rocking his hips. "You ain't got no hot ham... you can't afford it... you're on duh welfare." He doubled over laughing, nearly knocking over a row of paper towels.

Twenty minutes later he was back, telling a story about a cashier who'd just been mistaken for pregnant. I was putting the gourmet turkey breast away when it nearly slipped.

"Put that turkey down, Gus—it's gonna end up on the ground," Jake slurred in a muffled accent, staggering like a drunken uncle.

I rolled my eyes but smiled. "Seriously, where do you get this stuff?"

He waved it off, still grinning. "My original material. Just know, I worked hard on that."

By eleven, Jake had punched out, tie loosened, gold chain catching the light as he headed for the door. Over his shoulder, he tossed one last line: "Goony goo-goo, Gus!"

That's when he finally clued me in—Eddie Murphy. He'd been quoting the whole time, mixing the bits with digs at my deli mistakes.

The deli felt twice as empty once he was gone.

By fall, we were scattering. Seb had sailed off to Cascade College in Oregon—private, small, the kind of place where everyone rock climbs before lunch. Not the Ivy he'd hoped for, but it had mountains, math, and just enough prestige to feel like he hadn't veered off course. Ron claimed Texas for himself, University of Texas Austin, the so-called Public Ivy, a place with stadiums that roared and a skyline that was expansive with promise. It was University of Massachusetts Boston for me. That one big underground garage with the academic outgrowths out the top. Commuter lots, concrete walkways, the harbor wind whipping papers out of my hands. No ivy, no roar, just the daily shuffle of bodies passing through. It was my only real option. My father would cover tuition, but only at a public college rate, and living expenses only as long as I stayed under his roof at Clock Lane, where food and housing came bundled with his watchful budget. Books were my responsibility. "Find them in the library," he said, as if that solved anything. In the real world, on the rare occasion that the library had the right textbook, it was checked out or due back in a week.

If I'd wanted to live away from home or reach higher for a private school, I would have needed huge loans or time at a job to bankroll the dream. Instead, I chose the path of least resistance—home for freshman year and half of sophomore, commuting daily. UMass was fine for classes, but a commuter school is no good for a social life. The real campus, for me, became the supermarket where Jake and I worked together. The produce department was our greenway, the aisles, our hallways, and the in-store Brigham's, our student center. Jake was possibly worse off. He went to Bunker Hill Community College, mostly on his own dime. His mother scraped together what she could to help with tuition.

And so, I had to live with my father's rules, Jake with his mother's limits—and maybe that's why the fluorescent aisles of the supermarket felt like our rightful stomping ground, where nobody cared where you went to school, only whether you were scheduled for the closing shift.

Bob and I both got our licenses—on the second try. Embarrassing. He was a champ about driving me to work, but getting home was another matter. Sometimes, I caught the bus to Twombly if the timing lined up, then walked the mile back. More often, I rode my bike the four miles, until one evening, I came out to find it gone except for the front wheel chained securely to the pole.

So, I walked. That night, I had *When Doves Cry* playing on my Walkman, sweat soaking my shirt, buttons undone against the heat. The music kept me in a trance until headlights slowed beside me. A car window rolled down. A plump older guy.

"You wanna earn five dollars?"

Again?

I told Jake people shouldn't bother propositioning me unless they started negotiations at twenty-five. He thought that was hilarious, shaking his head. After that, he took it on himself to drive me home, at first whenever he could but eventually only when the rain came down. It was out of his way. He only lived a mile from the store. When he did make the journey, he made sure to ham up some complaints and made it sound like a burden.

One soggy night, he said, "Come on, meet my mom." He pulled into a squat brick apartment complex and we climbed the damp stairs to a cramped two-bedroom. The place smelled like garlic and Pine-Sol. His mother was waiting, a short woman with quick hands and quicker words. She rattled off half a dozen things Jake needed to do—take out the trash, fix the dripping faucet, call his aunt back—and he rolled his eyes but didn't argue.

We sat at the little kitchen table while she warmed up leftovers. Spaghetti with chicken stirred in, scooped onto mismatched plates. We dug in like it was a feast, talking with our mouths half-full, while I tried to keep up with his mom's stories. It felt like something solid: the comfort of food, a roof over our heads while the rain hit the windows.

While we were figuring out school and work, Mark was fighting something else entirely. He finally escaped the long corridors of the rehabilitation hospital, though he did not walk out; he rolled. His chair became part of him, the wheels whispering against the floor like a reluctant steed. He and his mother moved into the high-rise at 47 Lark Avenue, chosen for its elevator, but to Mark it was an unlucky castle. He had left behind 74 Holly Road—where he had the best number, his charm against fate. "With Nadia, I am destined to live to seventy-four," he told me. "Without her I will see my death at forty-seven. We need to move out soon." Numbers were still his omens, and he read them as faithfully as scripture. Psychosis and head injury had rendered him Catholic.

The building itself added to the fairy-tale strangeness. From the deli at Sun Market, I could cross the street on my break and climb into his new world. He would be there, waiting with stacks of notebooks—pages crammed with sketches, equations, half-poems, his attempt to turn madness into order. "It's therapy," he insisted. "Better than the pills."

One night, visiting after my shift, he wheeled me to the window and pointed across to the flickering neon of the liquor store. "That's the dragon," he said. "Always hungry, never sleeping. It wants to keep me weak. But, I won't let it." He gripped his wheels hard, palms red. It wasn't clear whether he was taunting the sign or confessing to it.

And in quieter moments, he dreamed aloud of Nadia, still his princess in a different tower, unreachable but never gone. He spun plans despite the unlucky number that glared at him from the tin plaque by the entrance.

Back at the deli, the manager was Bobby Bongiorni, a bundle of nerves who'd explode at anything out of line—long queues, an absent clerk, a missing ham on ad. His hands fluttered, his lips quivered, and he'd chant, "Oh, I shake, I shaaake!" When I once asked for a shift off, he fixed me with a look and said, "You owe me, Lindy." From then on, it became his catchall phrase, taking the place of hello, goodbye, and gazoontite—like I was a walking debt he could collect at whim. He had a way of appearing mid-conversation, catching me joking with Jake and wagging a finger. "Too much talking! Too much laughing! This isn't social hour; this is food service! " Then he'd vanish as quickly as he came, leaving us cracking up.

Jake was in one of his phases—this time, weightlifting. He'd commandeered his neighbor's basement, laid down a bench, stacked mismatched plates, and hung a warped mirror that turned us into distorted funhouse twins: me stretched tall, him wide through the shoulders. The air was cool, tinged with iron and old damp concrete, the faint musk of sweat beginning to gather.

"Spot me," he said, lying back on the bench, the bar rattling in its holders. I stepped close, palms hovering under the grip, my knees brushing the edge of the bench, his eyes staring up. The setup always carried an awkward symbolism, like we both knew what it looked like but never said.

"Don't let me die, Lindy."

"You won't," I said, watching the bar quiver. "Unless you try to show off."

He grinned, teeth clenched, pushing through the last rep.

When we moved on to curls, he strapped on his wide black back brace, tugging it snug like it made him invincible. The heavy barbell pulled his arms down, and he called me in close. My hands held his elbows steady, my chest brushing his shoulders, my hip bumping his lower back as he fought the weight upward.

"Did I use my whole hip like that—when I braced for you?" he asked, breathless.

"Think so," I said, voice lower than I meant it.

Later, sweat cooling, we sat on the bench in the dim light. I pulled my tape recorder from my bag. "Let's do a news parody," I said, clicking record. My voice dropped into announcer mode: "This just in: local teen collapses under delusions of grandeur, saved by heroic deli worker."

Jake laughed, shaking his head, breath coming out in little bursts.

"Over to Jake for the weather," I dared.

"Forecast calls for sunshine. . ."

Right then the pipes above us shuddered, water rushing through.

"Really? I predict rain," I added, deadpan.

Jake doubled over, laughing his voice bouncing off the concrete walls. A bigger reaction than I expected. For a moment, the whole place felt like a secret clubhouse, bound together with muscle, jokes, and something unnamed running between us, warm and electric under the basement chill.

That semester brought its own lessons about belonging. I'd saved enough for a year's room and board in a dorm, a small fortune earned one shift at a time under the fluorescent hum of Sun Market. Dad, ever the accountant of my fate, finally agreed to the minor tuition bump at UMass Amherst, so halfway through sophomore year I switched. It was supposed to be an upgrade—better classes through the Five College Consortium, the allure of Smith and Amherst College. A higher caliber education, a shot at a normal social life, or at least the illusion of one.

The reality was snow. Endless snow. White drifts banking the walkways, salt eating through my sneakers. I was the new guy in a sea of faces already settled into routines and friendships. But, my roommate seemed like the golden ticket: connected, smooth, with a knack for parties and a weekend pipeline to college basketball. Just the wingman I thought I needed.

It all seemed cool until the second Saturday morning. He said, "Let's go—I want to show you the Biomed building. Perfect place to study. Nobody ever goes there at this time." We crossed the street in air sharp with frost and entered an empty classroom—sleek, modern, unlike anything in the older buildings. We studied together for maybe fifteen minutes before he got up, stretching. "You should stay—it's so quiet. I'll see you later." He left with a pat on the desk, and the click of the door echoed too long.

That's when it hit me: I was being handled. He hadn't wanted to study—he'd wanted space. From me. But, instead of saying, "I need a little time alone with my buddies down the hall," he orchestrated a polite exile. I sat there another fifteen minutes, staring at the notes I wasn't reading, the fluorescent lights buzzing, and realized I'd been played. Jenny had done the same thing before breaking up with me—handing me off to Kathy like an unwanted library book.

I wandered the campus for hours, my breath fogging in the air. Ended up at a dining hall I'd never been to before, smaller, with big communal tables. Two girls asked if they could sit with me—out of necessity not preference—but I spun it later into a fantastic tale, proof that maybe things were turning. "John's scooping. Two chicks at once." roomie encouraged.

The truth was simpler: I wanted clarity, not stagecraft. Why couldn't my roommate just say, "Look, we need to make a schedule for time apart. Let's figure out how to breathe in this tiny room and still enjoy each other's company?" That I could have respected.

Every other weekend I trudged back east, catching the long bus home for an eight-hour shift at Sun Market. Bongiorni, pulling his hair, allowed it with his signature line: "You owe me, Lindy." Jake was there too, working late, sometimes swinging back after his shift to pick me up at midnight. We couldn't hit the nightclubs—we weren't twenty-one—but it felt good just to ride around. Meanwhile, my roommate had every other weekend free, his buddies across the hall, his oxygen back. And, still he wanted more space. What was wrong with me? Extrovert versus introvert—that was the easy explanation. I was cramping his style. But, it didn't stop me from asking myself why I was always the one people wanted time away from.

I fixated on one guy down the hall. He had this sly confidence, this way of making poker into theater. "Play for money," he dared me. I tried. Suspected cheating. Lost. "Go back to your room in a huff," he teased. "No," I said. But I went anyway, retreating from awkwardness. Always retreating.

By then my roommate had a setback in his schedule. Classes he needed didn't pan out— courses suddenly canceled, waitlists depleted. One stray music class at Smith hardly justified staying. Rumor had it I might be reassigned, paired with a guy in the next building whose roommate had left. He was "the king of the gays," people said, as if it were a crown to mock. The campus was split on gays—some supportive others loud with Christian Coalition disdain. I was torn. I didn't like gay people—me included. But, maybe if I had a gay roommate there'd be some awakening, some solidarity. Was it possible for me to be out and comfortable, despite opposition?

I lived in that question until the very last second. The king of the gays? Someone had meant it as a warning, but what I heard underneath was: someone who had decided to risk the blade. Someone who had stopped pretending the guard was the point. I thought about the blade running clean and fast without its cover, how the danger and the thoroughness were the same thing.

Then, I thought about the Christian Coalition crowd in the hallway, loud with certainty. About my father's voice, still living in my chest even ninety miles west of Clock Lane. About Tommy, who I had told the truth and then immediately tried to take back.

The guard was safer. I knew it would cost me—the inefficiency, the incomplete cuts. I chose the hermit's path. Paid the extra hundred bucks to maintain a single room, my fortress of solitude. The irony was sharp: I had longed for connection, traded campuses for a chance at a "normal" life, and ended up more alone by my own hand. My best company was silence. But, it was also the only semester I ever earned straight A's. Solitude, it seemed, had its rewards.

The only other socializing I managed that semester was when Seb came up for half his spring break. I decided we needed a plan—something daring enough to justify calling it "college life." So, I set my sights toward something that glimmered across the quad: the girls' dorm.

My ex-roommate had once orchestrated a drunken night for us in the girls dorm focused on his crush, and I remembered her well enough to think she might be approachable. She had a roommate—less striking, but no less present—whom Seb and I had brushed past on the quad coming back from dinner. In my infinite wisdom, I picked up the dorm phone and spun a story: my very handsome friend (Seb, naturally) had found this roommate intriguing, and we had a bottle of whiskey available. The truth was Seb had barely glanced at her, but the bait worked. She was intrigued. She invited us over.

We arrived quite buzzed, and the evening unfolded in a lopsided rhythm. Lacy seemed amused by me, though God knows why.

We started the evening in the hallway with Lacy and her roommate, all four of us perched against the cinderblock walls, knees pulled up, red disposable cups balanced on the carpet with two Frisbees as coasters. It felt like we'd stumbled into a secret club where the only requirement was that you laugh loudly at nothing in particular.

The conversation ricocheted from dorm gossip to absurdities. Her roommate whispered, "You see this door right here? Someone lives in there. She never comes out? I think she's hiding from the human race."

Seb grinned, eager. "Maybe she's listening through the walls, writing a sit-com about all of you."

"Or cataloging your outfits," I added. "Day one: sweatpants. Day two: slightly different sweatpants."

We laughed too hard at that, the kind of laughter that comes when you're not just tipsy but relieved to be included.

At some point the group split—Seb and the roommate stayed in the hall, their conversation dropping to a hum, while my date tugged me into her room with another round. We sat on the edge of her bed with matching cups, passing the bottle back and forth, our knees almost touching. She was good at letting pauses breathe without panic.

Eventually we ended up standing on her window sill, heads out into the sharp March air, her hair catching the breeze like a flag of mischief.

"You know," I said, swaying just slightly, "if you were a bike, I'd step on your left pedal."

She burst out laughing, eyes crinkling, and shook her head. "That makes absolutely no sense."

"Exactly," I said, grinning. "It's so bad it might be poetry."

We both looked out into the darkness, the quad glowing faintly under the streetlamps. My laugh faded into quiet, and words came out before I thought them through: "Funny how everyone lives so close and still finds ways to hide."

She tilted her head, thoughtful now. "Yeah. Some people hide in their rooms. Some hide in noise."

I nodded, staring out at the lighted windows across the quad. "And, some of us hide in hints about bike parts."

She laughed again, but softer this time. And, for a moment, in that open window, with the night air on my face and the campus alive around us, I felt like we weren't just drunk kids. We were confessing, in clumsy code.

We lingered at the girls dorm for more than an hour, talking, half-flirting, half-performing, all while Seb struggled to manufacture some spark with the roommate. Suddenly, Lacy was gone; we had to go according to the roommate. In the hallway, on the way out, the air between them was dead flat. She had been expecting some exchange, some connection, and Seb had nothing to give.

Stumbling back, my thoughts sloshed in drunken loops: Had we actually hurt her, by showing up with false interest? Had I offended Lacy with my absurd come-ons? Or had they simply grown tired of entertaining two half-drunk strangers they'd never really invited over in the first place?

Whatever the truth, it qualified as a college adventure—quirky, embarrassing, but ours. One of those stories you file under "experience," whether or not it made sense at the time. It helped me put a cap on the idea of using women as camouflage. Although, that kind of pressure didn't dissipate easily.

A small black-and-white TV with rabbit ears and the hum of the refrigerator became my new roommates. I leaned into academics, burying myself in books, and for the first time in a while, I felt good about that choice. Every night at 11, I tuned into the reruns of *Dynasty*, the flickering picture washing the room in gray light. I watched Stephen—gay, handsome, and "normal" in his affectations—navigate a world that wanted him silenced. Sure, his father had killed his lover, but still he carried himself with a kind of integrity I couldn't imagine ever possessing.

In that glow, I told myself grades would be my armor. Integrity could come later. For now, I would settle for survival, with the hum of the fridge and the faint signal from a soap opera as proof that I wasn't completely alone.

Dorm life was supposed to be informal and efficient, so I fell into a hygiene routine: towel around the waist, soap and shampoo in hand, shuffle down the hall, shower, shuffle back. Most of the time the tiled room was empty except for steam and the thrum of pipes, though now and then I'd hear a burst of raucous talk near the doorway—some kind of joke or argument I wasn't part of?

Then, one day, halfway through rinsing the shampoo from my hair, the door creaked open and a male was suddenly outside my curtain. "You have to leave. This is the women's restroom."

I blinked through the space against the wall. "What? It's always been—"

"It alternates," he said flatly, pointing toward the door. "Check the sign."

I wrapped myself in my towel and shuffled out, dripping, only then seeing the "sign"—a limp piece of notebook paper Scotch-taped next to the door on the wall *Women's* scratched in fading ballpoint. For two months I hadn't seen a sign. I ignored random pieces of misshapen paper on the walls, assuming personal notes or similar. Two months of showering in the same stall, half the time in the wrong room. All the while oblivious. Why didn't anyone just tell me this could happen? I felt the sting of being out of the loop more than embarrassment. Group living, they called it. I'd never felt less included in a group.

Later that fall, I saw a crude drawing on a library table—a cluster of males in a tangle, sketched in pencil, in graphic sexual detail. Beneath it, in smaller letters: Basement men's room, Science Annex.

For weeks I carried that location in my mind like a dare. Finally, when I found myself near the building, I gave in and descended the narrow stairs. The men's room had little embossed plastic signs on the walls inside, official and severe: *Only toileting activities permitted*. The language was so stiff, so strange, it was almost comical, but also clear enough to hint at what it was prohibiting. A remnant of passed activity.

I stood there in the dim light, taking it in—the empty stalls, the echo of water in the pipes, the silence thick with possibility. There was a gay underground on campus. A mess of feelings pulsed in me. I was embarrassed. I was scared. And, I was excited.

It struck me as absurd: more effort had gone into warning strangers about what not to do in a hidden bathroom than into telling me which shower room I was supposed to use.

My short story class met in an ancient one-classroom building tucked into the School of Agriculture, a place that smelled faintly of oats especially when it rained. Every week we turned in reaction papers—our proof of attention. I always earned a check-plus, though the professor's margin note was nearly always the same:

Did you like this one? I never answered. I gave analysis instead: here's what the story set out to do, here's how it succeeded. Whether I liked it felt beside the point.

Several classmates—non-English majors, I assumed—didn't analyze enough. "How do you know what the author meant?" they queried. "It's not straightforward. It could mean anything." The professor, weary but sly, suggested an experiment: "Some of you write stories. We'll critique them, and see whether intent survives translation."

Three of us volunteered; mine was the only one not later withdrawn. I wrote about a boy on his first hunting trip, puffed up with pride until the moment he witnessed the kill. Then, shame, disillusion, a rejection of his father's idea of manhood. The class read it, and the discussion sharpened. "Loss of innocence," someone offered. "Masculinity redefined," another said. One voice, almost grudging: "This was the clearest story we read." I felt, for the span of that conversation, that maybe I'd spoken across the gap, made myself understood.

On the last day of school, the dining hall was shuttered without warning. No sign, no explanation. I was owed one more lunch before the long bus ride home, but when I hiked across campus to a second hall, I found only locked doors and silence. A few big clouds drifted across what had been turning into a sunny day.

I caught it first as a sweetness in the air—something faint. Then, a low thump, a sound that might have been a bass carried on the wind. Music? I pieced it together in my head like a riddle: the sun was shining, the walkways were sparse, the football field was the only wide open space, so maybe...a picnic? It seemed too hopeful.

But, when I rounded the corner, there it was. My imagined answer, real. Barbecued chicken glistening on trays, the lunch ladies stationed at the entrance with portable scanners for food cards. A line of students passed through like it was the most natural thing in the world.

I took my plate and sat on a log at the edge, chewing slowly while the scene unfolded. Little clusters of people scattered across the grass, some chatting, some laughing, a frisbee arcing overhead, a football thudding into hands. Everyone seemed to know, by word of mouth or instinct, that this was where you were supposed to be.

No one spoke to me. I was there but not of it, watching the brightness like a stranger. The same story as my adolescence: other people knew the script, and I was left to imagine it from the sidelines, surprised only when my guesses came true.

There was no sign on the dining hall door, no flyers given out, no announcement. None was needed—the picnic was a tradition, passed hand to hand like a secret map, its directions obvious only if you belonged. I had followed the faintest of signals—bass notes, a sweet smell—and found the crowd. But, finding it wasn't the same as being part of it.

That was how it always seemed. Straight kids got their instructions handed down—how to join, when to flirt. Permission to grow into themselves. And, then a chance to explore in the open. Gay kids were left to improvise in the dark, hoping instinct would be enough.

It was time to leave Amherst. Paying extra for more loneliness was no bargain.

Returning to my old routines felt like defeat—like stepping back into a room whose air had already gone stale. Near-full-time hours at the deli blurred the weeks, the smell of meat and cleaner clinging to me long after I clocked out. There was no plan of escape on the horizon now, just a faint ache where ambition had been.

I tried to make it feel like progress. I enrolled in a summer psychology class on Childhood Development at the meager downtown campus. Between lectures I drifted through Boston like a spirit, watching the swan boats churn slow circles in the pond, walking past Cheers where tourists lined up to photograph a facade from a TV show. Once, a small girl offered me a flower. I dropped a dollar in the wicker basket—grateful for the gesture—but when I reached for the bloom she tightened her fingers. It was bait. I hesitated, then pulled my dollar back, feeling like I couldn't afford to experience even the smallest unfairness.

By the river, men lay shirtless in the sun, their bodies stretched like exclamation points on the grass. I wanted to lie among them, to feel the heat of the day rise up through my back, but I kept walking. I told myself I needed more definition first—more muscle, more something—before I could take my place in their easy sprawl.

It was one of those drowsy afternoons at the deli when the line disappeared and all we had was the hum of the cooler and the squeak of shoes on tile. Joey, the new guy—handsome in a way that made customers linger—slid a radio out from under the counter and tuned it low. Baseball filled the lull.

Jake wandered in, apron loose, a red smudge still on his forearm. He leaned against the salad case, watching Joey fiddle with the dial.

"You ever settle on one thing, Joey?"

"Says the guy from General. Jack of all trades, master of none," Joey slid back.

Jake smirked. "At least I don't smell like bologna every day."

"Point taken," Joey said, chuckling.

Then, the radio shifted to a new song—the jangly beat of *Walk Like an Egyptian* was unmistakable. Without a pause, Joey laid down his knife and shot Jake a look. Jake caught it instantly, that spark of recognition between two hams who saw a stage instead of a deli.

They stepped toward each other rhythmically, arms bent stiff at the elbows, wrists flopping, faces dead serious as they stalked the length of the glass case. A dramatic squat. A sharp hand slice through the air. A customer blinked, unsure whether to order or applaud.

"Italian style roast beef?" an old lady finally asked.

"In just a minute," Joey said, trying not to break character.

I leaned back against the wall, arms crossed, smiling. These two had known each other maybe two weeks, tops. Yet, there they were, coordinating like vaudeville partners, fearless in the middle of a grocery store.

For days afterward I kept circling back to it. How did they just know the other would go along? How did they step into the absurd with such easy confidence, as if embarrassment wasn't even an option? I'd never been able to risk that much on instinct. Theirs was some secret handshake of boldness—an unspoken trust that, for a few minutes, allowed them to happily sync.

Jake couldn't get enough hours in General where only one or two guys at a time were scheduled, so he transferred into Deli. With four bodies commonly on the shift there were more hours available to work, and there was always someone to joke with or complain to.

Before long, he started bragging about a girl he'd met in one of his Bunker Hill classes.

"She's gorgeous," he said, puffing his chest like Doug did when describing a new ham special. "Beautiful, and we're exclusive now."

"Exclusive with who?" Tony teased. "Nobody's seen her yet. I'm starting to think she's imaginary."

Jake rolled his eyes. "You'll see. Just don't be jealous."

Then came the disclaimer. "She's a little overweight. But, you'll see—she's got it where it counts."

When Joy finally came to the store, the Front End guys and cashiers did double takes. She wasn't a little overweight—she was "Donahue-guest-level overweight." Doug, always the diplomat, muttered, "Well, she's pretty in the face," while wrapping some Venetian Salami.

"Thanks, Dougie," said Jake.

Not long after, Bob's case went to trial. I ended up being a witness, though "witness" might've been too grand a word for it. Mostly, I was backup—me and my dad, sitting stiff in the courtroom. I couldn't add much, since almost everything I knew was hearsay. What I could do was validate the shaky Video 8 tape I'd shot: Owen's crew lobbing Bob's lawn chairs and such over the fence like shot puts. The judge watched, frowning, as the chairs clattered on the grainy screen.

Then came the photos. Owen had submitted glossy prints of Bob's yard, his "evidence" that the man was hoarding trash. Each one had the same neat little caption: *Garbage!*

The judge squinted, lips pursed, then leaned forward. "I'm going to ignore these captions," she said dryly. "The labeling is prejudicial. What you call garbage, Mr. Masters, the law may well call property."

Bob shot me a look like he'd just won McDonald's for life. I almost laughed out loud—it was such a tiny moment, but you could feel the tide turn.

In the end, Bob walked out with a judgment of two hundred and fifty thousand dollars. Owen's "shenanigans," as the paper put it, had backfired spectacularly. Turns out overreach can be costly.

Bob wasted no time putting the money to use. The sedan he'd been nursing along was traded in for a gleaming new pickup truck—the kind of machine that looked just as proud idling at the lights as it did crawling curbside on trash day. He finally had the rig he'd always dreamed of, a proper chariot for salvage. A long way from the days of pedaling his black bike with a rattling trailer hitched behind him.

The key was good evidence. Law, logic, and the facts create winners even when the deck is stacked against you. I tried to keep that in mind.

I wasn't jealous about Joy that much from the start—and in the end less so.

An eight-hour shift beside someone in the deli is like being locked in a glass box with their true self. After a few months with Jake, the shine wore off.

When the store manager strolled by, Jake turned into a whirlwind—hands flying, voice loud enough to carry across the counter. "One pound of head cheese, coming right up!" he'd announce, stacking slices in record time, smiling like a pitchman.

The moment the coast was clear, he slowed to a crawl. Customers lined up, and Jake leaned on the back counter doing the chill side job, setting up the potato salad containers as if he were browsing at a yard sale. When I nudged him—"Hey, can you grab the next order?"—he pretended not to hear.

Instead, he'd socialize with the passersby, like when cute Kevin from Front End came through to punch out.

"What's that?" asked Jake, pointing to Kevin's crotch.

"My dick."

"Keep it under control."

On breaks, he took his time coming back, walking the long way through Produce like he was on parade. He usually grabbed baby oil from aisle eight and polished the chrome counter until it gleamed like a car hood—but when I asked if he'd used the sanitizer, he shrugged. "Looks clean, doesn't it?"

He thickly sliced the imported mortadella!

The worst was the slicers. By nine o'clock, when the customer flow wasn't really over, he'd already have one broken down for final cleaning. "No one else is gonna come in this late," he said, even as the bell dinged and another customer stepped up.

"Jake," I muttered, sharper than I meant to, "could you not shut down the whole deli when we still have a line?"

He gave me a lopsided grin, trying to brush it off. "Relax. You're way too uptight. One slicer's plenty. I want to get out on time. Early if possible."

"Yeah," I said, stacking slices with two customers waiting, "great customer service."

One Sunday I was stuck on shift alone for seven hours. Jake had withdrawn his usual availability.

He showed up as a shopper at about 4:00 pm.

"Jake, why are you scheduled for only two hours at the end of the day?"

"Holidays approaching. Sunday is supposed to be a day of rest. I still get in a couple hours when it's less busy and take advantage of time and a half."

"They couldn't find anyone else so I am alone, been getting slammed all day. Could you come in early?"

"For you, Lindy, of course. I'll head home for a quick shower and be back here to rescue you."

Jake saw the line I was contending with and only managed to arrive five minutes early, and took his sweet time putting on his tie. He acted like he gave me a big favor.

The admiration I'd felt was turning inside out, like what happens when you stay at the beach a long time. Not a wave breaking but a tide going out: you look up and the waterline has simply moved, and you can't say exactly when it went. I'd never experienced love in reverse before—not a sudden crash like Bruce, who could win me back at any moment, but a steady unraveling, as if the person I thought I'd found never really existed at all.

Second thoughts weren't just about changing your mind. They were about seeing the distance between expectation and reality. Jake taught me how deceptive partial knowledge could be. Mark taught me how intoxicating—and unstable—it was if you fed the expectation with twisted hope. I trusted evidence. I had not yet understood the essential thing that must live beside it.

18
Paradise Found

Jake and Joy made me wonder whether longevity was ever possible. They fought like it was a well-practiced hobby. One week they were inseparable, the next they were airing dirty laundry loud enough for the whole supermarket to hear. By Friday, they would be back together, swearing it was different this time."

Their most dramatic round came on a Saturday night. Joy pulled into the Sun Market lot in her dented sedan, climbed out, came in the store to dramatically buy a carton of eggs, and then started pelting Jake's car in full view of the Front End late shift. Splat after splat, yolks sliding down the windshield, shells cracking against the hood. Customers slowed their carts just to watch.

I found Jake leaning against the soda machine, arms crossed, not even pretending to intervene.

"Uh, you're just gonna let that happen?" I asked.

He smirked, half-proud. "She loves me."

By the time Joy drove off, leaving streaks of yellow dripping down the side of his car, Jake was laughing. "It's passion. Messy, but it's passion."

I didn't argue, but I couldn't shake the thought: it looked a lot like hate.

Joy talked to me about Jake's charm, his promises, his disappearances, the miscarriage he refused to acknowledge, and whether any of it added up to love. I told her what I believed: Jake was brave at the beginning of things, but weak at carrying them once they got heavy.

She thanked me for listening, and that was the strangest part. It left me feeling oddly useful, but not moved. Whatever they had, even at its hottest, struck me as exhausting rather than enviable. I didn't want love to feel like cleanup after an explosion.

One day, Ma said almost giddily, "A girl was here to see you." A few minutes later Denny saw me in the hall and chimed in too: "Some girl called for you." Multiple reports for such a rare event, like a UFO sighting.

Soon enough I found out it was Joy.

Later, she was outside, idling in her car by the winter driveway, cigarette glowing. I peeked through the window like I was checking on a wild animal in the yard.

I went to Dad, who was sunk in his chair by the front door, half-watching TV, half-reading the paper.

"If a large woman calls for me, just say I'm not home."

Ten minutes later he knocked on my door, deadpan. "Joy's at the door."

I sat up, glaring. "Why didn't you cover for me?"

"You need to see girls," he said. "Don't you like girls?"

"I don't like anyone," I said, unable to think of anything more specific without lying.

He shrugged and went off to tell her I wasn't available.

Joy's visits made less sense the more I thought about them. Was she really after counsel about Jake? Testing me out as a backup plan? Trying to make Jake jealous by parking under my window? Whatever the case, even a drama fan has a breaking point, especially when someone else is writing the script.

Wasn't there such a thing as a soul-mate where things just went well, where the drama was replaced by something steady and reasonable?

My friendship with Seb was easy and chaos-free. He was the kind of friend who seemed plucked from a different genre than mine—raised in a house of worn grace and quiet grandeur. Summers there weren't just endured but curated to happen—long, loose days composed for ease and whim. Pepperidge Farm cookies always open on the counter, Cape Cod chips crinkling in their glossy bags. Lemonade pitchers, fresh fruit, and popsicles melting faster than we could eat them.

Seb had sturdy shoes for the trail; I had sneakers worn thin. Yet somehow we came to the same crossroads. Small rituals grew between us, fused from heat and habit: four runs a week on the Snake Hill par course—a loop of weathered but well maintained wooden stations with signs urging pull-ups, sit-ups, or to hop, dip, or curl—which we ignored. For us it was a race track. Seb ran two full laps, clocking them with precision to maintain his collegiate training; I cut across the middle of the second lap, our agreed-upon handicap. The point was to finish in range to see who would win. Afterward, he stretched like an athlete, hands on his hips, chest rising in practiced rhythm. I was still gulping for air, half a lap lighter and twice as spent.

To get to Seb's house was a workout in itself. First, the easy stretch along Serenity Drive, then the calf-burning climb up Old Serenity Place Road—half a mile straight up. From there you traversed the narrow paved footpath called Angel's Way, which spilled you into Seb's cul-de-sac, a road bent like a question mark curling into a circle. Seb would usually be waiting in the front yard. We'd cut through the day school, stop at the outdoor bubbler, and then get on with it.

"You've got potential, John," he said between gulps of water. "If you'd just...you know, keep running."

I smirked. "With a life of leisure, you get good at pastimes."

Seb laughed. "Exactly. We'll both make it to the Boston Marathon, someday, though." He went on to meet that goal. I didn't.

If Snake Hill was where Seb outran me, the deli was where he tried to catch up. Seb heard many of my absurd deli stories and one summer, decided to join me there. Doug was handling roast beef, Tony weighed out salads, and Seb worked the slicer with me spotting him. He hovered by the ham like it might explode.

"You've got to use pressure as you push it through," I told him.

He gripped the meat gingerly, slicing disjointed half sheets, some meat sticking to the blade.

"I'm more of an athlete, not a carpenter," he muttered.

Doug raised his eyebrows. "Guy's afraid of the blade."

"I'm just...respectful," Seb said back, smiling. "Besides, you don't want me bleeding all over your bologna."

When the line thickened, Tony shook his head. "Man, John, is this your buddy? Did you know him before? He's like you, but...the turtle version."

Later, when the rush finally slowed, Seb leaned over and whispered, "Honestly? My parents keep saying, 'Don't work if it's too much.' But, I like this. I like the challenge. You and I, we're in the trenches together."

I smiled. "Trenches? Well, you are creating a field of carnage. But, trust me. It gets better."

Seb chuckled, clapping me on the shoulder with faux camaraderie. "Hey, every soldier needs a general."

That summer with Seb at the deli was easy in the way good things sometimes are, unforced, without agenda. New Year's would test whether that ease held up under a little cold and expectation.

At seven o'clock sharp, I dialed Seb, the receiver heavy in my hand.

"You want to head to First Night? Fireworks, music, booze?"

There was a pause, the faint sound of a ping pong ball clattering in the background.

"Maybe," he said. "Depends what Rob and Thomas want to do. We've been playing hockey all day, now it's ping pong."

I rolled my eyes. "So...can you ask them?"

Another pause. "I don't want to pressure them."

On the bus to Harvard Square later, I tried to untangle the logic.

"You've been best friends with them since you were eight, right?"

Seb nodded, his winter hat slipping over one eyebrow. "Yeah. Rob and Thomas. We play sports, watch sports, talk sports. It's perfect."

"Too much sports?" I teased.

"Nope. Sports make life worth living." His tone was final, like a referee's whistle.

"And, why couldn't you just ask them what their plans were for tonight?"

Seb shifted in his seat. "Thomas's so sensitive he barely talks sometimes. And Rob?—well, I didn't want them to feel awkward. If they wanted to leave, they'd leave. If they wanted to stay, they'd stay."

"Not very practical," I muttered.

When we got to Boston, First Night unfolded like a dream kaleidoscope—performers on stilts, ice sculptures glowing blue, brass bands spilling out of church doors. We drifted through the streets, not quite together, not quite apart.

Seb stopped to watch a fire juggler, transfixed as if each torch was a planet in orbit. "This," he said quietly, "is the real New Year. Boldness. Light against the dark."

A block later, he pulled me into a tiny tent where an avant-garde puppet troupe was re-enacting the birth of the telephone using sock monkeys and a rotary dial. Seb laughed until he cried. "This is art, Lindy! Pure art!"

It struck me then: one moment he could be almost serious, and the next, completely undone by sock monkeys. Seb lived close to the surface of things—light and buoyant. Going deeper was dicey.

Nanny died at ninety-two. The "funeral" was nothing like what I'd imagined, just family gathered in the newly renovated attic of her house, a white cardboard box of ashes set on a small table.

Dad cleared his throat, picking up the box casually, like he wasn't sure what weight to give it. "Nanny," he said, using the term that had replaced all other designations. "Never found a need for medical services since the day she delivered me. She was a Christian Scientist through and through. Lived her whole life on faith, and maybe that faith gave her the strength over so many decades."

He glanced down at the ash box, then back up with a half-smile. "Now, if you look you'll see there's a lot of soot in here, and then some big chunks. It's not exactly the tidy picture you might have in your head. But, it's her. It's what's left on earth."

His voice softened. "She was strong, practical, and maybe stubborn. She raised us with little more than her wits and her belief that life has its own healing in it. And, I suppose, looking around this room, she did alright. We're here. We've kept going."

He set the box down gently, his hand lingering on it. "So — here's to her long run, to a woman who left us all a little tougher, whether we admit it or not."

We all shifted in our chairs, Denny tearing up, Ma clearing her throat, Sarah staring at her shoes.

A week later, Seb and I ended up back at Nanny's place, two four-packs of wine-cooler smuggled in. We climbed to the attic, the air close and still, the scent of new cedar and saw dust lingering like a memory.

We sat cross-legged on the carpet, the furniture gone, drinking from the bottles. At first it was light—Seb telling stories about a girl on the next floor of his dorm who lent her hand to the guys quite liberally. But, the alcohol burned a hole in my restraint, and soon grief pushed through.

"I keep thinking about her," I said, voice thick. "And now she's soot and chunks. Like she was nothing."

Seb shifted uncomfortably, staring at his drink. "She was old. That's what happens."

"No, it's just that. . . She mattered. And—" My throat caught. "She was set to go to a doctor the very next day. Now it's just an empty house. Feels raw."

I opened one of the small doors beneath the eaves and crawled deep down into the narrow tunnel space that ran the length of the house. I lay flat in the dark for a while.

Days later, I mentioned that Seb was a little insensitive that night.

Seb fidgeted, drummed his fingers on the table. "C'mon, don't do this. It was supposed to be fun. A drink, a laugh. Not tears. Not..." He gestured vaguely. "...all that heavy stuff."

I stared at him, stunned. "So, we're only friends when it's fun? Not when it's hard?"

“Friendships are supposed to be fun,” he said firmly. “That’s the point.”

“Not to me.” My voice dropped. “To me, they’re supposed to be about life. Support. Sometimes fun.”

He looked away, jaw tight. “Anyway . . .”

Whatever I'd been looking for in those years, Seb wasn't it — not because he wasn’t a good friend, but because friendship was already the ceiling of what he could inspire in me.

For the longest time I hardly saw the inside of Seb’s house. It was just a spot where to meet-up, a landmark. Then, one afternoon we ducked in for sodas and a quick game of ping-pong. After that it became a regular station on the journey. One day Calvin was there.

I knew him from years earlier. Four summers back Seb had invited me to swim at the day school pool. I remembered Calvin then, braces flashing under the sun, hanging back at the shallow end while Seb and I raced the length. I couldn’t get my bearings and kept crashing into Seb using contact as a guide rail. He shoved me under, exasperated, and swam ahead. Calvin had watched, and when I returned to the shallows, coughing, he pointed at me with a smirk and said, “You lost because you stopped in the middle of the pool.”

That voice had deepened now—no more kid’s pipe. Crisp, confident, easy. The braces were gone, his teeth now very straight, white as fine porcelain. His lips were a flush of rosy red, his skin burnished gold, and his mind alive with light. Seb had once described him as shy, even anxious. The boy in front of me wasn’t that. He looked at me with a confidence that was almost theatrical, as if he’d rehearsed in private and was now trying it out on a live audience.

“Hey,” he said, stepping forward with an easy smile. “I don’t think we’ve actually met properly. I’m Calvin.”

“We did once,” I said. “At the pool. I’m John.”

“Seb finally let you in the house,” he went on, amused. “You must have passed the test.”

I laughed, caught off guard. “What test?”

“Endurance. You survived Old Serenity enough times. Most people stop coming.” His tone was crisp, yet a playful smirk tugged at the corner of his mouth.

He had a way of speaking that made ordinary remarks sound clever, as if he were letting you in on a private joke. He asked about my summer class and job, listened with real attention, then tipped his head and said, “So study, and work—and you still have energy to practice with my brother?”

“I fake it,” I admitted.

“Good strategy,” he said lightly. “I stick to lazy summers. Books, TV, eat, sleep, repeat. I think I’ve perfected the art of doing nothing.”

“That actually sounds like vacation,” I told him.

He smiled again, not smug, just bright and certain of his place. He was friendly, polite, engaging—the kind of small talk that felt like an invitation rather than an obligation. For a second, the room softened. Seb and I had our rituals, but Calvin was something else entirely.

At the finish of the next run I broke ahead and touched the end post first.

Back at the house, Calvin was waiting on the porch. “So? Who won?”

“I did,” I said.

“Because he took more of a shortcut,” Seb muttered.

“Because I out-kicked you,” I countered.

Calvin grinned, not taking sides. "You two need a referee. Or a psychologist." His eyes flicked, sharp with amusement.

He opened the door to the kitchen and a new topic. We drifted into talking about psychology.

"It's not real science," Seb said with a snort. "More like astrology for people who think they're smart. Horoscopes in a lab coat."

"That's not fair," I countered. "Psychology uses controlled studies, statistics. It's built on data, not magic."

Seb rolled his eyes. "Sure. But, you can prove anything if you play with numbers long enough."

Calvin leaned forward. His tone was lighter than mine but more pointed. "I don't know, Seb. My friend's sister was in treatment this year. She was pretty much frozen up before—couldn't sleep, couldn't get through a day without breaking down. Now she's back, laughing again. That doesn't feel like astrology to me."

Seb shrugged. "Placebo effect. People believe, they get better."

"Or maybe," Calvin said evenly, "it works because someone actually listened and knew what to say. That's worth something."

He glanced at me then, and I nodded, grateful. My arguments leaned on books and studies; his landed because they were alive.

I told them about the playwriting class, I'd had to drop. "I was adapting *King Lear* and *Othello* into a corporate boardroom drama, only to have the professor scribble on my outline: *Why would anyone want to watch this*? The comment killed my motivation."

Those words had stayed with me, blunt and dismissive. As if to rub it in, the professor turned then to Roger—the golden boy in our section, handsome in a way that made everything he touched seem brighter. “Let’s see what’s going on with these hot shots,” he’d said. Roger had written about fighter pilots, and in that moment it was clear the professor loved it. And, maybe he loved Roger too like I was starting to. I dropped that class to avoid painful public humiliation.

Calvin listened with attentiveness to the part of the story I was willing to tell. “By the way,” he said after a pause, “I think it’s unfair you couldn’t go to the school you wanted. That shouldn’t happen to someone who actually cares.”

Seb added, “We are both very sorry for your plight. Moving on.”

“Actually, I appreciate what you said, Calvin.” And , then looking at Seb. “Some people can see the point of view of others.”

“You don’t get it. Calvin spends his energy avoiding stepping on ants, there are limits.”

“That’s what you say, “ said Calvin.

“Remember the deer?”

Calvin stiffened. “Don’t.”

But, Seb was already telling it. “Family trip, somewhere in the Midwest. Deer runs out—bang. Down for the count. Calvin starts bawling. And, then down the road he goes running into the rest-stop station, tears streaming, begging them to help. He tells them someone needs to go back right away.” Seb’s smirk widened. “And the clerk just blinks and says, *Don’t worry, you’ve got first dibs on the body.*”

I had written about this once—the moment when a boy sees something die and refuses to pretend it doesn't matter. Calvin hadn't read that story. He didn't need to. I could imagine it: Calvin’s panic, his bravery, his words tumbling out, his meaning lost on someone who lived in an alien rhythm, where deer were only venison instead of unique, majestic individuals. The misreading belonged to the clerk, not Calvin. And, even as Seb turned it into a laugh, what stayed with me was Calvin's instinct—that flood of care for a creature no one else thought twice about. It melted something in me I hadn't realized was frozen.

There's no better springboard than a common enemy. Not that Seb was so bad, but Calvin and I found a strange kind of closeness in validating each other against his criticisms. After one of those talks, Calvin admitted he wanted psychological testing—not for curiosity's sake but, as he put it, "to find out what's wrong with me."

I saw absolutely nothing wrong with him. Everything about him seemed super-right. But, I also wanted to help and to understand him more deeply. I told him I'd look into what sort of test might be self-administered. "In the meantime," I said, "list your favorite films. Humor me."

"I'd have to think about it. But, I'll do it. I'll write them out."

I gave him a look—half a smile, half a dare—and I wondered whether he actually would. I wondered a lot about Calvin. Each little turn of his mood, each new answer, I tried to read like a code, as if the detail would tell me how he felt about me.

The next run day, Seb said Calvin wouldn't be around. I lost the race by far, but when we came back to basecamp, Calvin was just leaving, a friend's mother idling in the driveway to pick him up. He spotted me, doubled back into the kitchen, and returned with a folded sheet of paper. "Here," he said, passing it to me before running out again.

I stood there frozen, Seb prattling on about something, while I unfolded the list. It read:

Fast Times at Ridgemont High

Caddyshack.

10

Anything with Bo Derek or Nudity and lots of sex.

And, then, at the bottom, in smaller writing: *for your eyes only.*

I'd been hoping, maybe, for chick flicks or musicals—though I didn't even like them—something softer, something that might have signaled a different story. Was that simply his unrestrained list of favorites? Was he screaming, *I'm straight, leave me alone!*? Or was he trying to throw me off the trail, prove his straightness at all costs?

But, that last line—*for your eyes only*—sent a current up my scalp. Not a flutter, but a sharp, intense tingle streaming in all directions. I thought my head was going numb. I tapped the top and what happened then felt like a cerebral orgasm—something electric and entirely new.

Seb's voice broke through as if from far away. "John. John. You're not even listening."

I wasn't. Possibilities were churning too fast in my head.

I read the list again at home, this time as if each line spoke volumes. I was mesmerized.

Fast Times at Ridgemont High. A teenage free-for-all, famous for that one topless scene. Every guy in America pretended to like the comedy, but what they really liked was Phoebe Cates stepping out of the pool. Was Calvin just demonstrating that he was a normal high school guy all along, nothing unusual, nothing suspect?

Caddyshack. The safest pick in the world. Every basement wall had the poster, every guy knew the gopher dance. It wasn't about romance, it was about belonging — the language of Bill Murray quotes and locker-room laughs. Maybe Calvin wanted me to know he was fluent.

10. Bo Derek running on the beach. An older choice, more adult. Did Calvin simply lust after her, or just know he was supposed to? It was the kind of movie a father or older brother would point to with a nudge: This is what a ten looks like, son. Writing her name felt almost desperate, like saying, See? This is what I like. Exactly what you expect me to like.

Anything with nudity and lots of sex. The bluntest line of all, as if to slam the door shut. I imagined him writing it quickly, maybe with a smirk, maybe with a sigh. The overkill made it feel less like a preference and more like a performance.

And then, at the bottom, the words that outshone the rest: *For your eyes only.*

That was rapture. It was an invitation, a signal that the list wasn't about the movies at all. It was about the fact that he'd given it to me–only me. I was valued and trusted. Or did he just want me to make sure his mother didn't see it? I pushed that aside almost immediately.

When Denny purchased a camcorder, I saw a golden opportunity: a way to satisfy my creative yearnings and orchestrate time with Calvin at the same time.

I brought it up as casually as I could manage— "What if we turned my screenplay into an actual movie?"

Seb said, "No way!"

Calvin said, "Why not!"

Seb crossed his arms.

Then, after looking at Seb, then at me, Calvin concluded, "We've got nothing else going on this summer."

Seb feigned being personally wronged. "We'll be occupied on Nantucket."

Calvin shrugged. "That's one week." Flat and obvious.

"Absolutely not," Seb insisted.

Filming began that next Tuesday.

So, with renewed purpose in the air, I drove my newly acquired Ford Pinto, a car fit only for short pilgrimages through familiar streets. Its rusted belly and infamous gas tank made every ride a gamble, rattling as if it resented the road. Still, it had a sunroof—a square of sky that turned even the smallest errand into a kind of escape. It was coffin and chariot at once: doomed beneath me, but glorious above. I drove toward their house with the windows down and the future wide open feeling like something important had been opened, something more pressing could be redeemed.

I hauled out the large Video 8 camcorder, and just hit record on them at the kitchen table.

"You're recording?" Seb said.

"Yup."

"Why?"

"A little screen test."

Calvin stepped forward for a little improv. "I'd just like to say that John here is about to direct a movie worthy of an Academy nod."

"That's true," I said. "Keep going."

"And, John will likely go on to be one of the best psychologists in the world. Either that, or an accomplished civil rights attorney."

That tickled me—a comic flourish, hammed up and tossed off in the moment. The joke ran in the opposite direction from what I was used to, not cutting me down, but lifting me up. And, Calvin didn't mind that it was carved into a permanent record. It landed sweetly in the moment, and then again, just as strong, each time I replayed it.

On the other hand, the first scene went terribly. Poor lighting, my own nerves, dialogue that didn't want to leave my mouth. Seb, behind the camera, growing impatient. In the scene, Calvin was the son of the departing CEO, heir to the company, while I played the Iago figure—pretending loyalty but scheming to be CEO myself. The lines were stiff, impossible to say naturally. I had to trim them down as we went along.

When Calvin's close-ups came, I insisted on taking the camera. Seeing him through the lens mesmerized me. It gave me permission to stare into his eyes. I zoomed in without purpose, just recording his face. Later, in my attic, I watched the dailies projected huge against the screen—Calvin's face larger than life: laughing happily, laughing nervously, embarrassed but never angry, never frustrated like Seb.

On that screen, Calvin was both things at once: handsome like a movie star, pure like a saint. Innocent, and—this was the part that mattered most—he always seemed glad to see me.

Everything else receded. The deli job became a painful slog, flattened into two dimensions. What mattered was the next scene—*how to make it work, how to make it real. How would I edit this? How could I make it high quality for Calvin, something worthy of his effort, something that proved I was an artist?*

Their mother's office was perfect for the confrontation—dark wood shelves crowded with history books, a brass lamp casting shadows that looked professional. Calvin sat behind the desk, while Seb paced in front of him with a manila folder full of blank paper that was supposed to be damning evidence.

I framed the shot: Calvin centered, Seb entering from the right.

"Action."

Calvin turned to Seb. "We need to talk. Something odd is going on."

Seb waved the folder. "Don't even start. I see what you are doing. Making me look bad in your father's eyes."

He stopped, squinted at the bookshelf behind Calvin, then pointed. "Is that *The Rise and Fall of the Third Reich*? Mom actually read that whole thing?"

"Seb—"

"It's like a thousand pages. Who has that kind of time?"

"Cut." I lowered the camera. "Can we please just get through one take?"

"Right, right. Sorry." Seb reset his position.

I raised the camera again. "I am changing the angle so you can continue. Go back where you were. Action."

Calvin continued. "We need to talk about these discrepancies in the quarterly reports."

Seb blinked, found his place again. "Right. The numbers point straight to your department."

"My department is beyond reproach," Calvin said smoothly. "Perhaps you should check your own ledgers before balancing my books."

I thought it was a good line—one I'd labored over. But, Seb wasn't listening. He'd picked up a small bronze bookend shaped like an owl and was examining it like he'd never seen it before.

"This thing is so creepy."

"Seb!" I called from behind the camera. "Come on!"

"What? It's staring at me!"

Calvin reached across the desk and took the owl from Seb's hands, setting it deliberately out of frame. "There. Crisis averted. Can we continue?"

"You're not even staying in character," Seb complained.

"Because you keep derailing the scene!" Calvin shot back, grinning now. "I'm trying to be an unfairly treated executive and you're giving me a tour of Mom's office."

I was grinning too, the camera still rolling. "From the top. Last time, Seb, or I'm writing you out."

"You can't write me out. I'm the whistleblower!"

This time he made it further. The folder hit the desk, the accusation landed, Calvin delivered his denial. Then Seb leaned forward, placing both palms flat on the desk in what I assumed was meant to be intimidating.

"I have proof," Seb said, voice low and threatening. "Documented proof of—"

He froze, staring down at his own hands.

"Of what?" Calvin prompted.

"I just realized I have no idea what self-dealing actually means."

Calvin's face didn't move, but his eyes went bright with mischief. "It means I'm dealing with myself, obviously. As opposed to dealing with you, which has been excruciating."

I cracked up behind the camera, the frame shaking.

"That doesn't even make sense!" Seb protested.

"Neither does your performance," Calvin said sweetly.

"Okay, but, at least I am not a Nazi. Just look at the books you have in your office!"

"Just saying my lines." Calvin's smile was pure innocence.

I loved him for it—that quick wit, the way he could spar without malice.

"Reset," I called, still grinning. "And Seb, self-dealing means using company resources for personal gain."

"Oh. Right. I knew that."

"Sure you did."

We started again. Seb entered, did the whole routine, actually made it to his mark. "I have proof. Documented proof of your self-dealing. Money, contracts awarded to your friends—"

He paused, sniffed the air. "Do you guys smell popcorn?"

Calvin lifted his head, looked directly into the camera with an expression of profound suffering. "This is where my character turns evil. This exact moment."

"What?" Seb looked genuinely confused. "What'd I do?"

Calvin was smiling—that smile, the one that made the whole disaster worth it. And, when he glanced at me, still behind the lens, something passed between us: a shared joke, a mutual recognition that Seb was hopeless and hilarious and completely impossible, and that we were the only two people in the world who understood exactly how to balance fun with progress.

The camera kept rolling. I kept it on Calvin's face—the exasperation melting into laughter, the way his shoulders shook, the brightness in his eyes when they found mine again. He caught me staying too long on him unnecessarily, but just laughed and smiled more intensely as he picked up a rubber band and shot it at the camera.

The scene was ruined. But, Calvin's smile was perfect.

The third act wasn't even written yet, but the urgency was overwhelming—urgency in slow motion, stretching the summer into a reel I never wanted to end.

The answer was to rewrite the beginning of the movie. What we needed was comedy, action, and most of all sunlight. The camera loved the light, and outside it made us feel less like amateurs and more like filmmakers.

So, the new opening was a lunchtime bet between co-workers—a footrace, twenty dollars on the line. Seb and I lined up, dead serious, though both of us were already planning to cheat. When we tore off across the field, the script called for us to slip into different shortcuts and barrel back together for a photo finish. Seb went off-script at the end. We crossed the line. He refused to admit defeat, and the next moment we were wrestling in the grass beside the archery range, two giant bullseyes looming over us with unplanned symbolism.

Pinned to the ground, Seb gasped, "Now, what are you going to do—mate with me?"

"Whatever comes next."

We all cracked up, Calvin loudest of all behind the camera.

He was more relaxed that day, steadier, though every now and then he asked if he was doing it right. It meant something to me that he cared, that he wanted to be good at it. Between takes he even gave Seb a lesson in "looking sneakily around" before cutting a corner, teaching him how to telegraph the cheat so the camera could catch it.

There were loads of laughs that spread, the kind that leave your ribs aching. And, I realized that being with Calvin nourished me. Prepping for the shoots and editing them later sustained me. Everything else— the rest of the world—just annoyed me by comparison.

In the third week of my movie-making bliss, one of their Siamese cats—Stripey Cher— started coughing, her breath coming in ragged pulls. Seb tried to get a parent on the phone, but panic was already rising. I grabbed the keys, directed Calvin and the cat into my car, and tore down the hill to the nearest vet which was a mile down Serenity Drive.

"Don't worry about the cost," I told Calvin as we sped along. "I'll cover it." I wanted to help him, be the one who comforted him, his mentor, his friend. I wanted to be his hero.

In the waiting room, Calvin began to tear up. I steered him outside. "Cry as loud as you want out here. Waiting is hard, but save the full sadness for if the worst actually happens. It's normal to feel anxious, out of control." He nodded, and I gave his arm a small pat, trying to anchor him.

Cher was transferred by ambulance to the animal hospital. Later, Seb asked why I hadn't just driven there directly. "I went to the nearest professional," I said, though I wish I had thought of that.

Cher didn't make it.

And, to tell you the truth, she wasn't stripey at all. A single color variation on her foot had been enough for their mother to imagine a tiger.

Events didn't end the way I had hoped. I realized then I couldn't be Calvin's hero, if I couldn't stop his sadness.

The week the Jenkins went to Nantucket, I felt an intense withdrawal. I'd grown used to filming three days a week; going cold turkey was harsh on the system. No fun little interactions shooting. No new material to review at home made time feel empty. When they came back, I felt a rush of overwhelming joy. They came back with a few stories. Only one of them mattered, though, and it shot me into the stratosphere.

Some girl on the island had become enamored with Calvin, trailing him along the beach and refusing to take a hint. "I should have just told her I was gay," he said. Said it casually, in front of Seb, playing it for humor. But, allowing yourself to be perceived as gay wasn't a joke. It was big. For me, it was one step closer to believing he might be teasing me—maybe even signaling something real. And, it didn't stop there.

The living room was dim in that late-afternoon way, sun slanting through the maple outside, casting everything in amber. Calvin and I had claimed opposite ends of the sofa, legs stretched out, feet nearly touching in the middle. Seb was upstairs somewhere, rifling through drawers for his running shorts. We were headed out for a run after the shoot.

"So," Calvin said, tilting his head back against the cushion. "Any luck with girls?"

I hesitated, then decided to go for it. "Actually, yeah. There's this girl at the cheese shop."

His eyebrows lifted. "Cheese shop?"

"Yeah, she works across from the deli. I've been helping her with her UMass application."

Calvin shifted to face me more directly, tucking one leg under him. "She asked you to help her? Or you volunteered?

"She asked." I tried to sound casual. "Her name's Maria. She just broke up with her boyfriend—this really handsome guy, like movie-star handsome. I don't know what she sees in me, honestly."

"Maybe she's tired of handsome," Calvin said, half-smiling. "Maybe she wants smart."

The comment landed warm in my chest despite the half-insult. I looked down, picking at a loose thread on the couch. "She invited me over to see her apartment last week."

"Oh?" Calvin's tone sharpened with interest. "And?"

"It was... nice. Small place, but. . . We just talked, mostly." I paused, then added, "She told me this secret. Something pretty dark about her family. And, some surprising stuff about her ex. I can't say what, but—it made me realize she trusts me, you know?"

Calvin nodded slowly, his expression serious now. "That's big. When someone shares something like that.

"Yeah." I met his eyes. "She's really sweet. Genuine. And, she has a sister—just your age, actually."

"Are you suggesting a double date?" Calvin said.

"Sure. Why not?"

"Are you more than friends?" Calvin asked, leaning forward slightly. "Maria, I mean."

I rubbed the back of my neck. "I don't know. Maybe? I keep thinking, wonder if I'm just... I don't know, a study buddy to her. Someone safe."

"You're not that boring," Calvin said quickly, then grinned. "Well. Mostly."

I laughed, shaking my head. "Thanks."

"No, seriously. If she's telling you secrets and inviting you over, she's interested. Girls don't do that with guys they're not interested in."

"You sound pretty confident for someone who said he can't talk to girls."

Calvin's grin faltered for half a second, then came back softer. "I can give advice. I just can't take it."

Before I could respond, Seb thundered down the stairs in his running shorts looking between us with mock exasperation.

"Jesus Christ, you two," he said, tossing his hands in the air. "You can't stop talking. What is this, a reunion? You missed each other *so much* during that one week?"

I felt heat rise in my face, but Calvin didn't miss a beat.

"Yeah," he said flatly, deadpan. "I've had blue balls."

The room went silent for half a second. Then, Seb barked a laugh, and I laughed too, sudden and startled.

"You just made it weirder," added Seb.

"That's my job as the little brother." Calvin kept his face completely straight, blinking innocently at both of us like he'd just commented on the weather.

"You're a goofball," Seb said, grinning as he headed back toward the kitchen. "I'm gonna hit the head. Don't get *too* excited while I'm gone."

When Seb's footsteps faded down the hall, I glanced at Calvin. He was still sitting there, arms crossed loosely, the faintest smirk tugging at his mouth. I wanted to know what he meant by these references.

Calvin reached for the remote, flipping on the TV like nothing had happened.

The moment slipped away, and I let it, filing it alongside all the other moments I didn't know how to read.

A couple weeks later came the phone call.

A male voice, no name. Just: "Are you gay? I am. We've talked before."

"Shut up, Jake," I said automatically. It was just his kind of practical joke.

"I'm not Jake."

The voice was calm, steady. I couldn't place it, but it wasn't a prank.

"I don't appreciate the call," I said, and hung up.

But, it didn't leave me. The words looped in my head: *Are you gay? I am.* I heard them while facing the salad section at the deli, while brushing my teeth, even in the middle of sleep. Who was it? Jake? The actor playing the departing CEO—Larry Smart? Someone else? I started hearing it in Calvin's voice. Over and over, like the needle caught on one groove.

Later, when I told Seb and Calvin about it, before I even finished, Calvin cut in quickly, "It was me. It was me."

I laughed, but the sky seemed to open for me. He'd said it so fast, almost gleefully. Did he just want to see me squirm? I did squirm. Of course, in the moment, we laughed it off. Upon reflection later, I saw it as a line too sharp to laugh away, lodged somewhere I couldn't fathom.

What I wanted to say, what I should have said was: *If it was you, I'd be tempted*. I should have said it proudly, out loud, in front of Seb. Instead, I said nothing. It would have been perfect just returning the exact same energy, the exact same ambiguity Calvin had lobbed at me. But, mine would have truth behind it, and I did not know where his truth lay.

It was Calvin's *It was me* that now kept repeating, looping, overlapping in my head.

By mid-summer, Calvin had become the measure of every hour, though I couldn't have explained why in words that would satisfy anyone—even if there were anyone to tell. Maybe it was that he seemed to sound the same notes I'd heard before—Eric's quick mind, Ricky's steady warmth, Karl's drive, Peach's lightness, Tommy's fire—but now they harmonized, like a chord struck clean and full. With Calvin, I suddenly realized how much better it all felt when the pieces played at once. He was kind without being dull, playful without turning cruel, ambitious without belittling anyone. And now, that his presence was regular and predictable, I felt less like a listener chasing echoes and more like a player in the song itself, part of something shared, mutual, and alive. Every time his laugh sounded, or his eyes locked into mine as we worked on the movie, I thought: *this is the music I'd been waiting for.*

Meanwhile, my technical skills were lacking. Our VHS deck didn't have a flying erase head—whatever that was—but Denny's Beta machine did. I began the clumsy work of editing, splicing, trying to match jump cuts. I reminded myself to tell the others: *wait a few seconds after "action" so there's room to edit later.*

We had other outdoor scenes—messy but thrilling in their way. There was a rooftop confrontation where Calvin's character plummeted and I ran to his aid, only to abandon him. A hunting sequence turned murder, a wheelchair scene gone half-slapstick. I learned quickly how hard it was to make a thriller with amateurs.

The best parts weren't the scripted scenes at all. They were the outtakes—the laughter, the stumbles, the unscripted glances. Those were the moments that gave the film life. Many of those moments made the final cut.

I showed Dad the dailies of the rooftop scene. He watched it in silence, then asked, completely serious, "Why didn't you grab him when he started to fall?" He didn't get the difference between reality and fiction.

He hadn't realized Calvin was scripted to fall. But, his question stayed with me—it meant the scene had looked real enough to trick him. Real enough that he thought Calvin was really in danger and that I'd failed in my duty.

How could I script things so Calvin could stop me from falling?

The hunting sequence was supposed to be tense, all shadows and menace, but it ended up more comic than chilling. Calvin was behind the camera, crouched low like a pro, whispering "Hold still, hold still" whenever Seb tried to overact his way through loading the prop rifle. Jake was one of the hunters, stiff in his stance but clearly enjoying himself.

“Don’t squint so much,” Calvin told him gently from behind the lens. “The camera already makes you look intense.”

Jake laughed, relaxed his face, and—just like that—the two of them clicked. Calvin asked him to adjust a line, suggested he pause before the final word, and Jake followed every note like he was taking direction from a real director. Between takes, Jake leaned closer, curious about the camcorder, and Calvin walked him through the buttons, even letting him shoulder it for a practice shot.

That was unwise, actually. Jake ended up recording ten minutes of random panning and zooming, searching for a plane in the sky.

Watching them, I realized their rapport wasn’t as strong as what Calvin and I had, but it was closer than I had imagined it could be. Maybe Calvin was just that way—a little charmer, kind to everyone, generous with his attention. And, if he could do that with Jake, then maybe I wasn’t as special to him as I wanted to believe. But, I pushed the thought aside. *We had something different. The way he looked at me proved it.* I needed to believe that.

I was content with the friendship I had with Calvin, but come August, part of me kept circling back to the question of what would happen when the movie ended and Seb returned to college.

It was time for The Wheelchair Scene, though it looked more like office-park farce than high drama. The script said Calvin’s character was paralyzed, betrayed by my character, who was now cooling his heels in jail. Calvin settled into the wheelchair with mock dignity, his hair catching the late light, as if he’d been born to deliver lines of noble suffering. Seb was the dutiful assistant, rolling him past rows of concrete planters.

"Never should've trusted him," Calvin muttered, half in character, half about me. "That double-dealer sold us out."

Seb nodded solemnly. "He played us all."

"You are welcome to come back into my company," said Calvin.

Seb leaned closer to Calvin, dropping his voice into the sort of register he thought sounded sinister. "I took a position with the competition. Eligible to become their CEO after a couple years."

And with that, Seb gave the chair a playful shove. Calvin shot forward like a shopping cart with a busted wheel, careening off the edge of the walkway. My camera shook from laughing.

Calvin tried to rally, dragging the wheels against the curb, determined to hoist himself back onto the sidewalk. Every time he got close, Seb darted in, blocking his progress, pushing him backwards or into the grass with theatrical cruelty. Calvin cursed him in a perfect mix of character and real frustration.

What ended up on tape was better than anything I'd written: betrayal, sabotage, the noble crippled hero rolling uphill against impossible odds. Off camera it wasn't much different—Seb restless and needling, Calvin steady and determined, and me behind the lens, pulling strings from my "cell."

Finally, Calvin stood up. The performance was over. He walked away, and for a second I kept filming, as if the scene weren't finished.

Seb was leaving but Calvin wasn't, but it amounted to the same thing, unless I could find an avenue.

19
Undue Influence

When Seb left for college, and the days without Calvin started to mount, my stomach began to hurt and my head ached. My one nonpathetic way to see Calvin again was to show him the finished movie. So, coming up with a final cut was imperative. Editing the film had become both a distraction and an obsession. I thought that if I could arrange seeing Calvin just once a month after that, I could almost tolerate his absence.

I skipped some final touches and the end credits because I couldn't wait any longer. I picked him up in my worn-out Pinto with its clunking leaf spring and the hole in the driver's side floor. I drove him down the curved hill road into Beaumont Center, under the railroad bridge, up Regal Road, and very slowly down Clock Lane, trying to minimize the noise and vibration. I wanted to impress him but felt deeply embarrassed at every rattle.

Taking him up to the attic meant exposing everything: the chaos of our house, like my brother's makeshift bedroom in the dining space, the wall unfinished on one side, studs showing with egg cartons jammed between them for soundproofing. It would be unbearable if a train happened to go by during his visit.

The rapport was meager on our journey down. Without Seb there to riff off of, the silences stretched. I told myself after the film we'd have plenty to discuss.

Things fell into place when we focussed on the big screen. Calvin laughed in the right places. He seemed to have a good time. Talking about the mess-ups, the botched continuity, and how we'd tried to create special effects with no budget felt satisfying. For a little while I felt a small tingle.

I started building the chain, and worked rungs into the conversation.The next one came easy. His mother, ever polite, said she and their father would like to see the movie sometime. Perfect, I thought: a family screening. Film going wide.

Next, I wanted the cloak of doing something *for him*, or better yet getting together by his initiative. Otherwise, I was almost due to feel like a tag-along. Like the girl who followed him on the beach. And, that was a very bad feeling.

So, I offered: "I could videotape one of your track meets, you know. Repay you for being in my movie."

He grimaced. "I don't need a highlight reel of me sweating. My parents already know what I look like red-faced."

"Come on, I'd make it cinematic. Maybe a slow-motion finish line."

"Right," he said, smirking. "And then we can dub in music from *Chariots of Fire*."

We both laughed, but later he leaned closer. "Look, if you really need footage, we can do Private Calvin Running Sessions. Just you, me, and my world-class form. But, I get editing rights."

I couldn't tell what to make of it. Was it pure jest tossed into the air, or a veiled admission that he'd go along with me, even into the absurd, as long as it was private and I led?

I brought him home afterward feeling steady, almost normal. Not elated. Just even. For the rest of the day, I carried that balance, but the next morning, I woke up queasy, the unease spreading as if my body knew something my mind didn't.

Senior year pressed down like a weight. I had loaded myself with one manageable course and three brutal ones—Satire,

Shakespeare II, and Personality Development—the latter run like a graduate seminar, all theory and no handholds. Concentration was beyond me. Reading Aristophanes–*Lysistrata* or Voltaire–*Candide* felt like staring through fog, and when it came to writing papers my mind locked up entirely. Every play, every tangle of lovers in Shakespeare, sent me back to Calvin anyway, as if the syllabus had been designed to mock me.

I started hanging out with Jake more, hoping for distraction. He was acting strangely that fall, like every conversation was a dare. He was set to transfer from Deli to Loss Prevention, and maybe the change had him restless.

One day, while he was wrapping ends in trays, he said out of nowhere, "I have this female friend. Totally platonic. She shops for cucumbers, you know...for personal reasons." He smirked, waiting for me to react. I didn't.

Another time he leaned in, lowering his voice like he was confessing. "I rented some bisexual porn. As soon as I got it home, the guy from the rental store called me. Like he was testing me. Creepiest thing." He seemed half frightened, half thrilled by the story.

Then, there was the Garfield incident. I kept a little Garfield figurine on my Pinto's dash. One morning it was gone. Later I found a Polaroid in an envelope on my windshield: Garfield inside a microwave, beside a half-burned sign with cat footprints and the words, *Don't let me burn! Return what you took from my car.* I hadn't taken anything from his car.

When I asked, he grinned, shrugged, and acted like he was innocent. "Not me," he said. "Someone else must've done it."

Seeking an outlet, I tried edging closer to the truth with Jake. "I'm bisexual," I told him, letting the word hang there, a half-step past silence but not the full truth.

Jake tilted his head. "Yeah? Uh. Doesn't shock me." His tone was more curious than concerned, like I'd just told him I preferred Pepsi to Coke.

"So...you've been with a guy, or just thinking about it?"

"Mostly thinking," I said, and then added, "I can't stop thinking about Calvin." The name slipped out before I could take it back.

Jake's face stayed blank. "Calvin? Your buddy from the movie stuff?"

"Yeah," I said, hoping for something—advice, a joke, even disapproval.

But, Jake just nodded once and changed lanes. "Well. Anyway, Joy and I are looking at a place near Worcester. Cheap rent, thin walls, though. Could work."

And that was it. My confession sank without ripple, my storm reduced to background noise against his plans with Joy.

The Red Line subway car pulled away from JFK/UMass with its usual groan, the lights flickering overhead as if the whole train were dozing. I had my Personality Development binder open on my lap, though I wasn't reading, just staring. The words felt flat, useless against the heaviness in my chest.

"I think we are coming from the same class," came a voice across the aisle.

I looked up. He was sitting straighter than anyone else in the car—dark overcoat buttoned neat, hair combed with purpose, parted on the left. His briefcase rested against his leg like a loyal pet. He looked a lot like Eddie Murphy with glasses.

"Oh, yeah. I heard your comment about the workload," I said, tapping the book but not quite making eye contact.

He smiled—not warm exactly, but sharp, like he knew something. "The guy thinks he is teaching graduates. Last time I checked, I'm still four courses shy of my degree."

"I only have ten classes left." I said, forcing my voice steady though it sounded like a complaint even to me. I looked back down at my book.

"I work in administration at the school," he continued. "Registrar's office. I'm finishing a degree in psychology. Started at Penn State, got...detoured." He let the word hang, as if it were a confession. "Now, I'm wrapping it up here."

I straightened a little in my seat. It was the first time in weeks, I'd talked with someone from school.

He came across the aisle and sat next to me, voice casual but carrying over the rattle of the tracks.

"Did you take Social Psychology yet?"

I nodded. "Last semester."

"Which teacher?"

"Dr. Fitzpatrick."

He smiled. "Oh, Fitzpat. I graded your paper. I was his TA."

His words were strange: half boast, half connection. For a second I tried to recall what I'd written, if I'd been careless, if the grade had been fair.

At Andrew Station, the doors hissed open, and a group of loud kids spilled in, reeking of beer.

"You're stressed," he said eventually, like he was diagnosing a sprain. "Most students are. But, you—the way you said *ten classes*. You are overwhelmed. And, I saw that you seemed preoccupied in class. Sad maybe."

"I guess you're aiming to be a counselor?" I asked, more to deflect his scrutiny than out of real curiosity.

"No, no. I am not patient enough for that. Psychology helps, but it's an imprecise tool. You got to know when to use it, and when to put it down. When to splurge."

I leaned in, lowering my voice. "You're kinda right. I've been... off. Love sick."

His eyes flickered. "Love sick."

"Yeah," I admitted. The train rocked, and I gripped the pole attempting to calm myself. "I don't know what to do with myself. Feels like withdrawal. Like it's physical." Saying it out loud made me feel lighter.

He nodded slowly, as though he'd been expecting me to confess something, and now I had. "It eats at you, doesn't it? The wanting. Most people drown it with distraction. You—you're built to stare at it."

Broadway came and went. The train plunged into a stretch of darkness, lights flickering out for a few seconds, the roar in the tunnel drowning us both. When they returned, he was still watching me, unblinking.

By Charles he'd steered the talk into his favorite waters. "If you're going to be taking Psych Testing," he said, "you might be interested in something I've been working with: The Color Test. Quick to administer, but it gets right down to the personality issues. Could even shed light on your... troubles." He said it softly, like he was letting me in on a secret.

"Maybe, as long as you're not a Scientologist." I joked weakly, trying to sound lighter than I felt.

"Gary McKay," he said finally, extending a hand. His grip was dry, precise, the kind of handshake that let you know he was confident.

"John," I said.

"Well, John," he said, voice steady, "if you ever need a conversation, or want to look into that test, find me. Registrar's office. Or in class. I'm usually buried in psych journals."

When the train screeched around that long curve coming into Harvard Square, he rose, briefcase in hand, and before the doors opened, Gary glanced at me like we were already in on something together.

"I'll be happy when I can skip this subway altogether—walk from the condo straight to class at Harvard, no obstacles. "

"More school?" I asked.

He nodded. "It'll be *hello Harvard University* when I graduate. Masters in Public Policy. Big step. Different focus."

The doors slid open. He stepped forward, adjusting his overcoat with one smooth tug. "You better take my card. Don't lose that number, John. There's a reason when two people meet."

And, then he was gone, swallowed by the Harvard crowd, leaving me with the card in my hand and the uneasy relief that came with being affirmed—even if I couldn't quite say why.

I called Gary, we had a few conversations on the phone and around class. I actually told him about the source of my love sickness. He was not shocked it was a male. He said, "don't worry, everyone is bisexual. You know Freud said that?"

"I showed my film to Calvin's parents last week," I told him. "That was my last excuse to see him."

Gary chuckled. "And?"

"They were polite."

Later, he invited me to his office and closed the door for a private chat. I laid out the evidence: Calvin's comment about telling a girl he was gay, the anonymous phone call he'd claimed credit for, the movie list that screamed straight but maybe too loudly, the recording where he'd praised me unprompted. Gary listened, nodding at each piece. "The movie list is the tell," he said finally. "The louder they protest, the less certain it usually is. And jumping in to claim that phone call? He's starting fires on purpose." He leaned back. "He likes you. The question isn't if Calvin could love you—he can. You just have to know how."

"So, what do I do?"

Gary leaned in with the answer. "Could even be that he is gay, but only sees you as a friend. Don't worry. Even if he sees himself as straight. Like I said, everyone's bisexual. Most guys express it through slapping each other's booties after sports or wrestling around. Many have the capacity for a lot more than that and don't fully realize it. And so, the question isn't if Calvin could love you, he can. Just stop trying to bond with him through the front door. You just have to know how."

How else can you bond with someone?

The condo was eight blocks west of Harvard Square, tucked into a row of new-looking buildings that didn't match the older houses around them. Snowbanks lined the walk, bright white, the kind that looked clean after a storm. His place was crisp and modern, like it had been pulled from a catalog.

A roommate opened the door—a tall guy with round glasses, already deep into a textbook at the dining table. "John, meet John," Gary said quickly. "He's at Harvard grad school." John gave a nod, polite but preoccupied, as if he was trying to adjust to Gary's revolving guests.

We went upstairs to Gary's room. He sat me down with a pad of paper. "First, the interview," he said. He asked about relationships, attractions, early experiences. Questions I hadn't been asked before. I answered so much and so fast, the way you do when you think honesty itself will yield karma.

"You are a few years behind in your psychosexual development."

Next, came the Color Test. He handed me six cards, each a different color, and asked me to put them in order of preference. He made notes, nodding like it confirmed something.

"Your pattern is more typical of women."

Then, came what he called the Trust Test. He asked me to declare that I trusted him. Then to stand, then to close my eyes. His voice was calm, steady.

He had me recline. When he placed his hands on my shoulders, I flinched, but the pressure was firm, not rubbing. It felt less like massage and more like being held in place, pushed into awareness of my body without telling me what to do with it. *This feels chiropractical,* I thought. I had no other word for it.

Time blurred. He took off my shirt. Now more like a massage. He removed clothing slowly piece by piece. I didn't know if I wanted him to stop or keep going. He said to open my eyes if I wanted. My eyes stayed shut.

I wasn't physically aroused, and I was glad. *It really is only for special people.*

I thought he might be disrobing as well, but I wasn't sure.

At some point I realized there was no fabric left between us. The body heat was noticeable. The pressure on my back and arms deepened, steadier.

Then, he moved off of me. His voice cut through: "Open your eyes. Be a man and look."

I hesitated. For a moment, I didn't know what I would see or what counted as trust and what counted as trespass.

I opened my eyes. Gary was standing above me, closer than I expected, his face steady, not smiling, not mocking. He was bare, the way I was, but he carried it like it was nothing. His body wasn't a secret to him. Mine still felt like one.

The light from the window hit his shoulder, and I realized I had never seen a man this way outside a locker room, never on purpose, never held my gaze so directly. He didn't cover himself or gesture. He just waited, as if the real test wasn't color or trust but whether I could hold the look without flinching.

He looked good without clothes.

I wanted to look away, but his words echoed. So, I saw all of him. For a second, longer, I looked. And, in that stillness I couldn't tell if I was being taught something or stripped of something. But, I felt open and unashamed.

On the drive back, the Pinto felt smaller than usual, the heater blasting against the windows, making the glass fog up until the wipers squeaked. My body still hummed from the pressure of Gary's hands, but my mind kept circling the last command—*Be a man and look.*

I tried to convince myself it was nothing, or maybe something useful, a kind of training. Gary hadn't touched me in a sexual way exactly. That was true. But, there was body contact. He did put his full weight on me for a while. Skin on skin.

The thought slid in, quiet but sharp: I was meant to take his role. To do to Calvin what he had just done to me. The interview, the color cards, the pressure, the test of trust. It all lined up now, like steps in a routine.

Gay guys need a catalyst to get by their hang-ups, I thought. Breaking the ice was no easy feat.

I gripped the wheel tighter. Part of me wanted to believe it was a gift, that Gary had given me a map I hadn't had before. But, another part knew maps didn't detail road hazards. Still, I couldn't stop thinking: if I repeated the process with Calvin, maybe it would unlock the door I'd been knocking on so desperately.

The cafeteria smelled like steam trays and coffee. I followed Gary through the food line, both of us stacking plates without much thought. He talked in phrases that seemed vague at first, like he was testing whether I could keep up.

"It's all about momentum," he said while ladling soup into his bowl. "Small steps, each one a little more bold than the last. Not much by itself, but it builds."

I nodded, pretending I fully understood.

By the time we sat down at a corner table, away from the noise, he leaned in and dropped the abstraction. "We call it the pup situation."

"The what?"

"Pups," he said evenly. "I have dozens, close to two dozen over the years. I carefully select them. It has to be people with merit. All but one became partners. One even reversed the whole arrangement on me. That's okay. I love them all. Partners are equals. A few of my partners have pups of their own. The bond is so great that even if we're apart, we're family. If one calls, we answer. That's how it works."

He watched my reaction as he chewed.

I tilted my head. "Sounds a little like a pyramid scheme."

He set down his fork sharply. "Don't say that. This is about trust. And, there is nothing more sacred than trust."

Two women walked by, one waving at Gary.

When they were gone, he continued. "For you New England guys," he went on, "it's broken into two steps."

"So, I've already had the first step?" I asked.

He smiled faintly. "Yes."

I shifted in my chair. "So… all males?"

"Yes."

I squinted. "So, you're gay?"

"No." He shook his head like it was obvious. "I had a girlfriend living with me last year. But, I don't want a woman hanging off me all night. It's a different thing."

I stared at him, not sure what to make of it.

"The second step," he said finally, "is a climax. No other way to put it. Giving a pup a climax facilitates the bond."

I felt the word hang in the air, heavier than anything he'd said before. He took another bite of food, as if the conversation hadn't changed at all.

We came up out of Harvard Station, the wind cutting hard along the brick. Gary fell in step beside me. He hip-checked me lightly, grinning. "You're such a pup."

The streets were alive with students in coats, scarves fluttering, everyone looking like they were heading to a party I hadn't been invited to. Gary gave me a pat on the back as we dodged a puddle of slush. "You had a question?"

"For an introvert—two steps. For an extrovert, just one?" I frowned. "You just move into…?"

"Most of the time, I top them," Gary said without lowering his voice, as if the pedestrians were part of his audience.

"Sometimes it's oral. Depends. And if you want to become a partner—which you really should do if you want Kevin's affection—"

"Calvin," I corrected automatically.

"—Calvin, right. Anyway, you need practice. Confidence. A partner gives you that." He swerved toward a café window, checking his reflection, then back to me.

I stepped over a small snowbank, boots squeaking. "I don't want to do this with you. Or with Calvin unless he . . ."

Gary laughed, a quick bark. "You want to do it with Calvin. Drop the holier-than-thou garbage. Sure, you love him, but you also want his body. Admit it."

We crossed under a streetlamp where icicles dripped in the evening light. I kept my eyes on the sidewalk, but Gary was already half a step ahead, tossing out comments like confetti, as if the rhythm of the walk itself was carrying me toward something I didn't know how to stop.

The snowbanks out front glowed under the streetlamp, crisp white edges already dirtied by passing cars. Gary unlocked the door and looked back at me.

"Stop your worrying. I don't have step two planned for today. Just come in, have some dinner, and relax. My roommates are away."

Inside, the condo was unnervingly new. The carpet didn't have a single stain, the couch looked like it had just been unwrapped. He tossed his coat over a chair and headed for the kitchen.

"Chili," he called out, clattering bowls. "Best food for three reasons. It tastes good, it's hot, and there's plenty of it."

I hovered in the doorway, rubbing my hands. "Can't the last two apply to any kind of food—if you wanted them to?"

He barked a laugh. "This is why you can't get laid."

I changed the subject, blurting, "I have my movie, if you want to see it."

Gary poked his head out, smirking. "Calvin's in it. I need to see it."

We settled on the couch, chili steaming between us. The glow from the TV flickered across the white walls.

"Yes," Gary said, leaning forward. "I see it. I see what you see in Calvin. He's amazing. Smart. His brother—not so much."

I forced a laugh and said. "He's a good friend, I'd like to keep."

He waved it off, eyes on the screen. "Too bad I can't see them just talking. All this dialogue's getting in the way."

He left for the kitchen to grab another drink. While he was gone, a gun fired in the scene. I hit pause, waiting.

When he came back, I said, "You missed something. We have to replay it."

Gary rolled his eyes. "It's a gun. Of course it's going to fire."

"You have no idea how hard it is to dub in the sound at the right spot," I insisted, fumbling with the remote.

"Oh, you got any cash on you? Rent's due and I'd hate to have to go out again. I need about forty."

I hesitated, my wallet already half-open. "Forty? Right now?"

"Yeah, I give my roommate cash and he writes a check for the landlord."

I pulled out two twenties. Gary glanced at my wallet. "You're doing pretty well. Better make it sixty. I have to factor in what I spent on the Chili."

I handed him the money.

"Pay you back on pay day. At school."

Later, at the door, I pulled my coat on, the air sharp again from the hall. Gary leaned on the frame, casual. "Parting question. You gonna be down for step two?"

I tightened the scarf around my neck. "I don't know."

"The more intimate we are, the more I'll understand you," he said. "It's not mind-reading exactly. Just hit me with key words and I'll get you." He paused. "Or a third option—spend the night with me. Just cuddling, the whole night. Fall asleep, wake up together."

The silence stretched. Snow hissed against the street outside.

"I can probably do that," I said finally.

A week later, it was already strange enough when Calvin's father pulled up to the bus stop, window rolling down with a friendly wave. He was a quiet man, set in his ways—the sort who jogged in a dress shirt no matter how many athletic tees the family bought him, convinced comfort and sun protection mattered more than fashion.

"Need a lift? I'm headed toward Harvard."

"Wow, yeah. I'd be grateful. I am actually running late."

I slid into the passenger seat, my book bag wedged between us. The heater breezed warmth, smelling faintly of pine-scented freshener. There was some awkward silence.

"I teach at Tufts, but I'm part of a panel today."

We talked about Seb, and exchanged a few quick updates, nothing worth remembering. When he turned the questions back on me, I mumbled something about UMass and felt the hollowness of the words. Harvard and Tufts—those names carried weight. UMass sounded plain, mediocre, like I'd shown up to a banquet in sneakers.

"Calvin thinks he wants to go into psychology," he said after a moment, eyes on the road. "Don't think it's for him."

I nodded, but inside I thought: *Too much of a soft science for you? Isn't that ironic coming from a historian? Isn't that softer still? And, Calvin loves psychology. Support him!* My thoughts burned in me, but I said nothing.

He shifted to current events. "Their mother has a convention we have to go to this weekend." She was a professor at Tufts as well. "Calvin's on his own for a few days."

The words dropped with a strange weight. By chance, he was telling me exactly what I most wanted to hear—and what I most feared to know. Was this the universe opening a door, or was some other evil force setting a trap?

Gary picked up on the first ring, like he already knew I'd call.

I told him about Calvin's father, how he'd mentioned the house would be empty.

Gary let out a laugh. "Well, there you go, pup. Step one's in your lap. If he's got a little extrovert in him, move right along to step two."

"I don't think—"

"And, if he doesn't have a little extrovert in him, and wants one? I'll tag along."

I sputtered. "What? No, I—"

Gary chuckled, low and pleased with himself. "Relax. I'm kidding. Mostly. Look, don't just jack him off. He's got hands. He doesn't need yours for that. What he needs is to lean on you for something he can't do himself. That's how you start the bond."

My face burned, but he kept talking, smoothing it over like nothing was strange about the words tumbling out.

I tried to change the subject. "The snowbanks today were huge. I almost lost my boots stepping off the curb."

"Pup, focus," he purred. "You're getting lost in a drift while he's alone for the weekend. Connect the dots."

I bit my lip, but the fantasy unspooled anyway: Calvin choosing me, not as a joke, not as a dare, but in earnest. The two of us having one life for a while, not public or overdone, but simple.

Gary broke the silence. "You see it, don't you? Good boy. Now quit worrying. The universe just threw you a bone."

The phone rang twice before Calvin picked up, his voice as casual as ever.

"Hey."

I gripped the receiver tighter. "I was thinking... I've got a few tests you might like."

"Tests?" He sounded amused.

"Yeah, you've always said you wanted to know what makes you tick."

He gave a quick laugh, but there was no denial. "Yeah. Still true."

Maybe the Color Test, maybe the questions, would point to something. Something I wanted it to point to. Me.

"Anyway," I hurried on, "I thought I could bring you some Chinese food."

There was a pause, then Calvin said, "Only thing I really like is lobster sauce."

"Never heard of it. I don't mind," I said quickly. "I want to repay you for helping me."

"Okay then," he said lightly. "Bring lobster sauce. I'll eat it."

I hung up with my heart pounding. In my head I still saw the take-out menu at Aku-Aku, with its big cartoon dragon and the heading "Pu-Pu Platter." That was all I really knew. But, lobster sauce—I'd find it. Even if it cost a fortune. I heard Gary's voice—*This boy needs chunks of tender lobster in a rich, savory sauce to be happy*. But, the thought didn't slow me down—I'd have paid any price for it gladly.

By Wednesday, I was already erupting with nerves; excitement, then dread, the days slipping past in chalk dust and cafeteria steam. Everything felt like an obstacle course. I usually liked Satire, and *The Death of Peregrine* had real spark: usually great fun lampooning pretentious posturing. But, now, I thought maybe I was the pretentious one.

Thursday slid into Shakespeare. *Troilus and Cressida*—a play, if *Cliff Notes* are to be believed, about messy romantic overtures that rot when distance and politics get in the way. I had no patience for deciphering who loved whom and who betrayed whom. I only wanted the clock to move.

By the time I got to the deli Thursday night, the hours were molasses. Pastrami was on sale, which meant order after order, all shaved paper-thin. Cutting a pound like that feels endless, each strip a flimsy curl of fat pretending to be meat, the pile on the scale creeping up like it had no intention of ever reaching a pound. Jake and I tried to stem the tide, but nothing sped the time.

Friday was still out there, waiting, and everything between now and then was just something to be gotten through.

Jake and I both clocked out at ten. He surprised me outside, saying he had something urgent to talk about. Perfect, I thought—maybe it would pull me out of my own head.

But, what he said wasn't a distraction. It was a collision.

Jake drove me back to his place, that squat brick apartment building with a patchy lawn crusted over in frost. We stayed in the car, motor idling, breath fogging the windows. He had a bottle of vodka wedged between the seats, unscrewed it, and took a swig before handing it to me.

His shoulders were tight, hunched forward on the wheel like he was bracing against something. "Joy's been on me," he started, voice flat. "Always circling, always picking. I'm getting tired of it."

I nodded, not sure what to make of it.

He tapped the wheel with one finger, then took another drink. "I keep thinking... maybe I need new paths. Try different things." His tone was casual, but his eyes kept darting at me, quick and nervous, like he was checking if I was keeping up.

"Like what?" I asked, watching the streetlamp throw a dull yellow over the cracked sidewalk.

"It's not that I want to break up with her, yet," he went on, "But, it's getting old." His voice dropped lower, almost conspiratorial.

Then, out of nowhere: "I want you to top me. Down in my neighbor's basement. The workout room. I'll go shower then meet you."

The words landed like a barbell to the chest.

"Right here, right now?"

"I mean, you're bi."

"It doesn't work like that."

"It can."

"That's flattering," I said, because it was. "I even felt some energy between us when we first met. But, that was then, this is now. And, I am really into someone else."

"I just need to see what it's like, so I can let it go."

"Don't cheat on Joy," I added. "I know what that's like."

The whole week felt staged—Calvin's empty house, Jake's unexpected confession—all converging like the universe was conspiring against me for a laugh. Maybe I should have gotten Gary and Jake together? This was truly bizarre.

Jake dropped me back at my car saying he would never open the offer to another guy.

Really, go ahead. You can.

I had all Friday until six to perseverate. Shower, shave, the right shirt—not dressy, not sloppy. Jeans without holes. I plotted the time it would take to pick up the food, how long it would stay hot, how fast I could get from Aku-Aku to Calvin's house.

By the time I rang the bell, the bag of Chinese food was warm against my palm, grease soaking the bottom.

"Perfect timing," Calvin said, swinging the door open. He took the bag with both hands like it was treasure.

Dinner was right away, because the food wouldn't just keep steaming for long. He led me to the dining room, which was easily the prettiest room in the house. The table was mahogany, and the walls carried Asian prints and carved wood panels. I'd convinced myself he'd love Chinese food here, surrounded by this kind of art.

As we set the cartons out, Calvin gave me that sideways grin I remembered from months before, the one that made everything feel like a private joke. I could feel the old rhythm slipping back into place.

"Want some wine with dinner?" he asked, halfway to the door.

I hated the taste of wine, but I smiled like it was obvious. "Yes, of course." *Wine would loosen us.*

He disappeared into the basement and returned with a bottle, dust on the glass. He poured generously.

I tasted it. "Smooth," I said. It tasted like metal and sour fruit, but he looked pleased enough.

"Are you going to have some?"

"No, not old enough."

Calvin opened the carton of lobster sauce, spooning it onto his plate like he'd been waiting for it all week. "You actually found it," he said. "You're a hero."

"Not hard," I said, though I didn't admit I'd checked three menus to be sure.

"Try some?"

"I actually don't like lobster, the texture."

"Well, there's actually no lobster in lobster sauce. Weird, I know."

Through dinner we poured on the charm like old times, joking, asking questions, pushing back with just enough sarcasm to keep us leaning in.

He held up the plastic fork like it was a trophy. "Best meal I've had in months. Sorry, Mom." He nodded toward the empty kitchen.

Then he shifted: "So, how's the deli?"

"Pastrami's been on sale all week," I said. "I've practically lost my soul to the slicer."

"That's cruel and unusual punishment."

One of their Siamese cats waltzed by.

"I still feel bad about your cat—Stripey Cher."

Calvin paused. "Yeah. That was sad."

"I should've paid for the ambulance."

"No, don't feel bad about that at all. You were great."

We talked classes. "You took more Shakespeare?" he asked, rolling his eyes.

"Unrequited love everywhere," I said.

"Sounds like high school with fancier words."

We both laughed, but I felt heat rise in my face. He knew how to land a joke, but he also knew how to hold eye contact, making me wonder if it was still a joke at all.

"Do you like English? Writing?" I asked.

"I do, when it's over."

"You ever do creative writing, or analyze fiction?"

"I have some reaction papers I did well on, some persuasive essays."

"I'd love to read some of those."

He disappeared upstairs, and was back quickly.

"I was putting together a writing sample for college applications."

I wanted to read them all right there, but I wanted even more to keep chatting. "Mind if I take a few home? I really want to concentrate on them."

"Okay."

At one point he refilled my wine glass, brushing close enough that I could smell his cologne—something sharp, citrusy.

He didn't have to try, and I didn't know how to stop trying.

I wish I could go back in time, pause right there, and do things differently from that point forward. Instead of opening the fortune cookies, which were real duds, I could have said:

"I figured something out this summer, partly because of you. There have been a lot of jokes. Truth is I really am gay—and I now understand what the word really means. I was just about as happy as I have ever been. Thanks for the time you gave me.

Now, I am going to go, unless you want me to stay a few minutes more."

Instead, when the plates were cleared, I pulled out the colored cards, laid them carefully on the table.

He looked at them curious but amused.

"As you might have guessed this is the Color Test," I said, arranging the squares in a neat row. "You put the colors in order — the ones that appeal to you most, then least. It's supposed to say something about personality. State of mind."

"State of mind?" He raised an eyebrow. "Like a mood ring?"

"Kind of," I admitted. "But deeper. It can show how you see yourself... even stuff you're not conscious of." I didn't add what I was hoping—that maybe it would suggest something about who he wanted, what side of himself he leaned toward.

"So, if I pick blue first, what does that mean?"

"Blue is... stability, harmony. A need for peace."

"And if I pick black?" He tapped the darkest card with his finger, eyes mischievous.

"That's a rejection. It usually means you want to push something away. But, if I keep telling you what it might mean, we are going to invalidate the results."

He smiled, slow and teasing, "What happens if I am color blind?"

I forced a laugh, but my stomach turned. "Just pick your true preferences in order without thinking about what it might mean."

"Okay," he said. "Let's see how screwed up I am."

I wrote down his sequence and flipped to different pages in the book.

"You want others to see you as calm, balanced, and capable of keeping things together—even if you don't always feel that way. You really feel a pull toward closeness and understanding, but you also guard yourself, because you don't want to be hurt or judged." It got more and more generic sounding after that.

He took a sip of water. "Doesn't tell me anything I don't already know."

"Sometimes it is much more revealing, I've seen it." I hesitated. "Any luck with girls lately?"

"No." He said it flatly, then glanced away. "That's my biggest problem."

I swallowed, feeling my pulse pick up. "I could take a sexual history from you. Sometimes it helps."

He laughed softly. "But, I'd have nothing to report."

"It goes into fantasies, internal stuff too," I said. "So, if you're game, we can give it a go."

"Why not?"

I flipped open my pad. "Okay, um... when did you first hear about sex?"

He answered the first half of the questions like you would think any heterosexual male would.

I wrote quickly, trying to keep it clinical.

Then.

"Ever felt... unwanted thoughts or dreams, violence, same sex?"

"No."

"When did you start masturbation?"

He paused, the air stretching between us. "Never."

I tried to smooth the moment. "I didn't either at your age."

He gave a half-shrug, reached for his glass. The room felt smaller now, the mahogany table and carved panels closing in.

We finished up the questions. *Seems like he didn't want to be very open, which is fine.*

"You told me more racy stuff than this when I asked you about your favorite movies." I joked.

Moving into the Trust Test after his stilted reaction seemed unwise.

"You want to play ping-pong?" I said suddenly, pushing back his chair. "Need to stretch."

We volleyed a few rounds in the basement, the sound of the ball clicking against the paddles filling the quiet. The volleys lasted longer than usual because neither of us was trying to win. His energy was fading. Mine too. The Color Test hadn't hit on any real answers; my interview had gone nowhere.

I set the paddle down. "Well, there is one more test," I said, almost to myself. "But, that one's different. I know less about it."

Calvin looked up, curious again. "The experiential test you mentioned?"

I nodded.

He tilted his head. "How are you getting all this info? A class?"

"There's another student. Very knowledgeable about people."

He smiled.

"He could tell a lot about you just by looking at you, let alone talking with you."

Calvin's eyes sparked with new energy. "Well—let's go see him."

I blinked. I'd thought he was winding down the night. Now, he was talking about going out? Was he just trying to get us out of the house? It didn't make sense.

"You serious?"

"Yup."

"Maybe," I said, already reaching for his phone. "I could call him."

The air shifted. My stomach lurched. The night wasn't over after all.

I dialed Gary, half-hoping there'd be no answer. He picked up on the second ring.

"You got any time?" I asked, trying to sound casual. "I have someone here interested in meeting you."

There was a pause. Then a chuckle. "You're kidding."

"Nope."

"Well then," he said. "Come by."

Driving the Pinto felt like steering a roulette wheel. The catalytic converter had the engine choking on exhaust; sometimes the car died at stoplights. Other times it wouldn't start at all—just a dry clicking under the hood. And, bald tires and ice patches were the worst kind of combo. My palms were slick on the wheel.

Calvin, though, was lit up like it was Christmas. "So, this Gary guy—who is he? What's he all about?"

"He's... sharp," I said carefully. "Knows people. Reads them."

"Reads them?" Calvin leaned toward me, elbows bouncing with the rhythm of the Pinto's cough. "Like how? Psychological experience?"

"Some, but more like great intuition," I said.

He grinned. "Sounds cool."

The Pinto lurched through a yellow light, engine whining, and my stomach tightened. If it died here, we'd be stranded with no one at home to rescue Calvin, except the Chinese cartons and ping-pong balls. Car trouble could mean real trouble.

Calvin didn't seem to notice. "You know, I get nervous around the girls I like. Can't get words out. And, thinking about something I have to do stresses me. I hate deadlines."

"But you—you're fluent. Always talking."

"You've only seen me at home," he said, matter of fact.

He rolled down the window, letting the cold air rush in, cheeks flushed with the wind.

Gary ushered us upstairs, into a narrow room with a futon, a desk piled high with books, and a lamp with a crooked shade. Calvin hung back a little, glancing around.

Gary looked straight at him. "Did John tell you I was Black?"

Calvin blinked. "No."

"Well, that's good. It shouldn't matter. Doesn't matter." He dropped onto the futon, patting his knee. "So, you're stalled about meeting girls?"

"For sure," Calvin said, settling into the chair by the desk.

Gary smiled, wide and knowing. "I can see right away you're a virgin. Don't need no sexual history to see that."

Calvin's ears went pink.

"Not much masturbation either," Gary added, turning his eyes toward me.

"None," I blurted, my throat dry.

Gary chuckled. "Oh, a late starter like John here. That's fine."

"I never had the impulse. I just... don't," Calvin said, almost apologetic.

Gary shrugged. "You might test the equipment someday, but no rush. I've been hitting the ceiling since I'm twelve."

He stood, heading for the kitchen. "You guys want anything to drink? Beer?"

"Maybe a soda," Calvin said.

"I've got Coke." He disappeared for a moment, doors creaking open.

Calvin leaned closer to me, voice low. "He seems nice."

Gary came back with two cans, handed them off, and sat again, stretching out.

"So," he said, eyes on Calvin, "what do you think is holding you back?"

Calvin started to answer, but Gary's eyes narrowed suddenly. "Oh God—what just happened? Now you look like you been banging regularly." He barked a laugh. "How did that happen? Maybe I misjudged you. You been holding out on us?"

"No," Calvin said quickly, almost laughing at himself.

"You sure?"

"Yeah."

Gary shook his head. "Man, it's like you just got laid twenty times."

I held up my hands. "Don't look at me."

Gary leaned back, pleased. "You guys are pups." His tone made it sound like both a tease and a diagnosis.

Then, casually, he shifted: "Calvin, take off your shirt."

The air thinned. Calvin glanced at the floor, then back at Gary.

I felt my chest tighten. "No," I said, sharper than I meant.

Gary's eyebrows lifted. "Do you think anything wrong is going on here tonight?"

"No," I answered quickly.

"Well," he said, voice softening but with an edge, "you're sure giving that impression."

I fumbled for something to say, my eyes flicking toward Calvin. "It's just that... he's got SAT review early tomorrow."

Calvin nodded. "Yeah."

Gary sat back on the futon, studying us both.

"We just wanted to stop in and get your impressions real quick, we got to leave in a few minutes." I said, trying to keep my tone light.

Calvin echoed me, his voice steady. "Right."

Gary leaned back, folding his arms. "My only other impression is that Calvin is wasting his potential with false beliefs about himself. The main person holding back Calvin... is Calvin."

Calvin straightened in the chair, eyes narrowing slightly. "What can I do about it?"

"Get into therapy," Gary said with a shrug, "or just keep good company with John."

Calvin looked over at me then back at Gary. "Anything else?"

Gary's grin tilted. "Isn't John good enough for you?"

"Yeah, but—"

"Surround yourself with people like John who can see how impressive you really are."

That seemed to settle it. Calvin pushed back his chair. We gathered our coats downstairs, the quiet of the stairwell surging. Across the room, as Calvin slipped an arm into his sleeve, Gary caught my eye.

"The window is open," he said softly, "but it's temporary. It will close."

The words trailed after me out the door.

The ride home was mostly feeble small talk— the snowbanks, the Pinto's precarious state. Finally I blurted, "Why do you think he thought you stopped being a virgin?"

Calvin stared ahead, a crooked smile playing at his lips. "I just opened my legs wider and wider."

I laughed, though my stomach knotted.

As we pulled up to his house I said, "I'll drive you to Central Square tomorrow, so you can sleep in a little more before the review."

"That's okay," he said.

"I don't mind," I added quickly. "My way of making up for tonight's lateness."

He nodded, hand on the door handle. "Sure. Thanks, John."

I sat in the car a second, thinking about Gary's words. *The window is open, but temporary. Did that mean tonight?*

Calvin's porch light threw a pale glow across the snow. He was already entering the doorway when I caught up.

The outer door had started to close. I let it swing in front of me refusing to enter like a vampire waiting to be invited. Calvin pushed it wider. But, his face wasn't happy. Awkward.

"Let's finish the Trust Test," I said, following him into the kitchen. "It won't take long."

"I don't think we have time."

"Well—driving you in tomorrow will give you an extra hour of sleep," I reminded, trying to strengthen the proposal.

He shook his head. "What is the test, anyway?"

"I have to show you, not tell you."

"I need to go to sleep."

The window wasn't open at all.

I felt desperation edging my voice. "It'll take five minutes or less. Please—let me just show you it's nothing." I decided I would just have him lie face down on the sofa to prove trust. And, to prove that the test and my intentions were nothing too weird.

"I'm all talked out."

"It doesn't involve talking."

He looked shocked by that. And, turned away.

"I mean, we can talk," I said quickly. "What are you thinking?"

He looked toward me. "I don't think you have homosexual tendencies."

"Okay. Do you trust me?"

"No!"

The word cracked something in the room. Calvin's eyes watered; a tear slipped down.

"I'm sorry," I said, heart pounding. "I'm going."

He walked deeper into the living room, facing away from me. His shoulders were tight, his face to the wall.

I followed, placing a hand gently on his shoulder. "The last thing I wanted to do was hurt you. I want to be able to help you. I love you."

He didn't turn.

I retreated through the kitchen as he went upstairs. Dirty dishes crowded the sink. Without thinking, I began washing them, tears slipping down my cheeks, mixing with the suds.

The rhythm steadied me: rinse, scrub, rinse. I clung to the work like a lifeline. By the last plate I was shaking, crying outright.

The kitchen light snapped off, then on. I jumped. Calvin was behind me, hand still on the switch.

"You don't have to do that," he said softly. "We just use the dishwasher."

I turned, the wet plate still in my hand. "Now you see. I'm crying too."

He looked at me, blank.

I set the plate in the strainer. "See you tomorrow."

He hesitated, then said, "Bye." And, locked the door behind me.

Saturday didn't improve anything. I'd hardly slept — tossed, turned, rehearsed lines I might say to Calvin, only to abandon them before they finished forming. At dawn I was already up, pacing, nerves electric. By the time I went to pick him up, my own restless energy pulled him out of bed too early.

I wasn't going to take back what I'd said. But, I wanted him to know the shape of it—that all I wanted was his company, now and then. That when he was gone, I felt a hollow ache, and when he was near I felt back to normal. I wanted to ask if there was room for me in his life as something good, a steady force, but I had no script to draw from.

We drove through Beaumont Center, the brick facades and bare trees blurring by. I gripped the wheel and began.

"I want to talk about our relationship."

He didn't hesitate. "We don't have a relationship."

"A friendship is a kind of relationship," I said, voice rising, desperate.

He turned his face to the window. "We should bag it."

The words struck like a stone. "What?"

"We should bag it. You ruined it."

"I just want to go back to how we were in the summer."

"Okay." His voice was flat, more like a door closing than an answer—a syllable meant only to silence me.

Still, further down the road, I leaned forward, into my own needs. "Just... call me on Thursday. Please. Just to check in, to let me know how you're doing. That you're okay."

The plea hung in the air, heavy as the frost outside. If he followed through, it would steady me, like a small anchor in rough water.

But, even as I said it, I knew what I was doing—laying a burden at the feet of a senior in high school, still retaking SATs, still learning how to shoulder his own weight. I was years older, and yet in that moment I felt like some needy housewife begging not to be abandoned. And yet, I felt no choice.

We reached the SAT review class half an hour before the doors even opened, leaving him to wait on the street or in a sterile lobby all alone.

20
Chekhov's Promise

I worked eight hours in a fog, slicing and bagging cold cuts, more pastrami, the hum of the slicer drilling into my temples. By the end I didn't remember half the customers I'd served.

Sunday and Monday vanished into thick air. I slept until two both days, stumbling from bed to fridge and back again, no one at home noticing. Many more inches of snow had accumulated, and my Pinto was rendered useless.

I refused to call Gary. *Let him stew. If he wanted to reach out, he could.* But, he didn't.

By Tuesday I couldn't take the silence anymore. I caved and dialed Gary, just for a sliver of feedback. I didn't hate him then. That would have made things simpler. What I felt was worse—dependence threaded with suspicion; gratitude laced with dread. I wanted part of what he seemed to have. He maneuvered where I waited and hoped.

He answered on the first ring, cheerful, as though he'd been waiting. "Good news. My car's back in town. It was down in Pennsylvania with one of my partners. See what I do for partners?" His voice had that showman's lilt. "I'll swing by. We'll go over everything. Make a new game plan."

I hesitated, the receiver slick in my hand.

"Don't stall," he said, firmer. "You need this."

Really, what else could I do?

I agreed.

The old Chevy's headlights glared by the winter driveway an hour later. He leaned over, grinning as I slid into the passenger seat.

"Don't even think about blaming me for what happened," he said as I shut the door. "You didn't do what I told you to do anyway."

I didn't argue. It was a web of my own making.

The car smelled like leather cleaner and something sharper—aftershave, maybe. My chest tightened.

"No teenage male wants the pressure of being loved," he went on, voice calm, steering us into the dark. "They want a release, if anything."

I stared out the window, watching telephone wires dip and rise. "I'm done with the back door," I muttered. "Front door or no door."

"Stay outside then—with the cat." He gave a little laugh, one hand loose on the wheel.

My throat closed. "What's the difference between your pup situation and... approaching someone while they're asleep?"

He hesitated, then said quickly: "Being awake!"

Gary braked at the light, tapping the wheel as if weighing whether to gun it through. He stopped short instead.

"You've got the same problem most women have," he said easily. "You tie sex too tightly to love. They don't have to go together. It's nice when they do. Sometimes it's better when they don't."

I shifted in my seat. "Maybe men have trouble the other way—can't manage both at the same time, see how they work best together."

Gary grinned sideways. "Don't fight your nature. Sex is like a spark. Sometimes it builds into a fire when you kindle it right, sometimes it's just a sparkler. Either way, you get to enjoy it. Maybe you need to set your sights–differently. I was watching your movie again. The brother might be more realistic for you."

That's when the tears came, sudden and hot. I blinked hard, but the sting only spread. The idea of swapping—just trading Calvin for Seb—was absurd. They were nothing alike, and I'd known Seb for years without a flicker of what Calvin set off in me. This person didn't have the answers.

"If he doesn't call..." My voice trailed.

Gary's eyes flicked toward me, then back to the road. "If he doesn't call—what? Finish it."

"I don't know."

"You give this kid so much power," Gary said, softer now. "When you could have been in charge."

The dashboard lights painted his face an eerie green. I pressed my palms to my eyes, wishing I could vanish into the night's darkness.

We pulled into the icy lot outside the condo. The building's windows glowed faintly, a warm grid against the cold night. Gary cut the engine but left the lights on, and for a moment neither of us moved. I thought for a second, *I should just march away to the bus stop and head back home.*

"I need to know what's going on with him," I said finally, my voice thin.

Gary tilted his head, watching me. "You can't wait 'til Thursday?"

"No." I shook my head. "He might not even call. Wondering if he will is half my thinking right now. The other half is *did I hurt him*? *Does he hate me*?"

Gary smiled faintly. "Just come in—come in." He reached across and opened my door for me. "Daddy will make it better."

The words landed heavy, half joke, half something else. The glow from the condo's windows spilled over the dashboard, casting

Gary's face in shifting light. Then, I felt the urge to run; instead I stepped out into the cold and followed him up the stairs.

Inside, the air was warm and faintly sour, like old coffee and radiator heat.

"How old are you anyway?" I asked, trying to lighten the mood.

Gary grinned. "How old do you think I am?"

I squinted. "Anywhere between twenty-seven and forty-seven."

He shot a look at me. "That's racist."

Before I could ask what he meant, he flipped on the television. The theme from *Growing Pains* chimed through the room, — "*Show me that smile again…*" .

"Oh great, Calvin's favorite show."

"Relax," he said, stretching out on the sofa. "Just watch for a while."

My leg bounced restlessly.

"You know. I think you are dealing with a people-pleaser. And, there's no pleasing them. They sacrifice so much energy trying to look acceptable that they end up resenting the same people they tried to please."

I shook my head. "Calvin really cares about people. Creatures, the whole damn ecosystem—he cares when no one's watching." I was reaching.

At the next commercial, I got up to pace.

"You got his number?" he asked finally. Gary gave me a sly look. "Maybe I'll give him a call. Put your nerves at ease."

I gave him the number. He thought it through out loud—what to say, what Calvin might say back. Then, he picked up the phone. I sat forward, heart pounding.

"It's Gary," he said into the receiver. "Just checking in. I know that night got out of hand..."

A pause, his eyes flicking toward me. Then: "It's like that show, what's it called?—you guys are just going through *growing pains*." He chuckled at his own joke. "He's crazy about you."

Another pause. "Good, sounds good. Just say hi."

Gary set the receiver back in its cradle, leaned against the arm of the chair, and looked straight at me.

"Well," he said, drawing it out, "good news. He doesn't hate you. Doesn't think you're crazy, either. Just... says you came on too strong. Needs a little air."

My chest tightened. "He said all that during your pauses?"

Gary added, softer now. "Said he'd call on Thursday. That's as much as you can ask of a young guy with AP classes breathing down his neck."

I exhaled, shaky. Half-relieved, half-hollow.

We watched *Back to the Future*, and I felt better. I used the zoom function on the remote when Marty's mom had her sweater off in the car. Gary was puzzled by that. His reaction amused me.

"I don't think you know what you want."

His roommates came home. Gary seemed disappointed.

"They're home early," he said as he got up to intercept them in the kitchen.

"No late class?"

"I thought you said you were tutoring him." his roommate said in low tones.

"Yeah, he is my student. But, John and I are also good friends."

Gary came back and said, "There is more to come with you and your buddy, Calvin."

Three calls came and went between Calvin and me.

The first was his—Thursday, just as he'd promised. I was in my room when the phone rang. I ran downstairs hoping upon hope I wouldn't hear a different voice.

"Hey," Calvin said. "Just saying hi."

His voice was careful, a little distant, but he'd called. That was something.

"Hey," I said back, trying to match his tone. "How's the week treating you?"

"Fine. Busy. SATs coming up again." A pause. "I just wanted to—you know. Check in."

"I'm glad you did." I gripped the receiver. "Thanks for calling. Hope you're doing well. Call again if you ever want to talk."

The line went dead, but the promise hung there a moment longer. He'd kept his word. Maybe that meant something. Maybe it meant nothing.

The second call was mine. A few weeks later, high on nothing more than a good haircut and a pretty stylist who laughed at my jokes. I'd felt almost normal that day—lighter, less haunted. I wanted Calvin to hear that version of me.

"Guess what," I said when he picked up. "I got a girl's number."

"Yeah?" His voice perked up, genuinely interested. "The one from the cheese shop?"

"No, my hairstylist. We were talking and—I don't know, it just happened."

It hadn't happened. But, I wanted him to believe I was fine, that I wasn't still circling him like a moon with no other orbit. Of course, I wouldn't be calling if I didn't want contact.

"That's great," Calvin said, and he sounded like he meant it. "You should call her."

"Maybe I will." The conversation lasted three minutes. When I hung up, I stared at the receiver. *Was feigning heterosexuality really a good way to win a guy's affection?*

The last call was his. He caught me at the deli, mid-shift, Doug yelling about chicken roll in the background.

"John?" Calvin's voice cut through the noise. "Do you still have my essays? The ones I gave you?"

My stomach dropped. The essays. I'd meant to bring them home the night of the Color Test, the night everything fractured. I hadn't.

"I am pretty sure I forgot to take them. Did you look around for them?"

"I will," he said simply. "I need them for applications."

"Right. Of course. I'll look for them too just in case."

"Thanks."

A pause. I wanted to ask: *Why are you calling me at work? How did you even know I'd be here? Is this just about the essays, or is it something else?*

"Are you doing okay?"

"Yes."

"If I find them. I'll get them back to you, right away."

"Okay. Thanks."

I went into a trance waiting on customers. *Maybe he had the essays, and this was just a polite excuse to reconnect? Yeah, right. Maybe Gary had put him up to it? Maybe I was losing it, spinning out like Mark?* It was probably a straightforward ask and I was reading shadows again.

I hated not knowing.

Later, I came to a stark realization. *Calvin deserves none of my crazy. More from me would probably annoy him, maybe hurt him. Time to let him go—not to see if he would return, but to release him entirely. To love him was to want the best for him. And, in a world where straight paths promised safety and my kind led only to risk, it was time to just leave him pointing in the right direction.*

I felt depleted, yet resolute—at least for a moment.

Just as I was starting my break and heading to see if the essays might be in the back seat of my car, a runner from Receiving burst in from the back: "Someone tried to break into your car!"

Out in the back lot, I found the trunk door pried upward at two corners, bent like crooked wings. I pushed them back down, but the ugly creases remained. Nothing stolen, but just senseless vandalism.

And, no essays in the car. *Where are they?*

My face went hot before my heart went cold. I thought of Calvin crying that night. I made him sad, and I had lost him. I felt just like the Pinto looked. Bent at the edges, marred in ways I couldn't smooth away. I wanted to be Calvin's hero but ended up his villain. No matter how I tried to press it flat, I carried the creases. I couldn't help but look the part.

The semester was collapsing around me. I'd dropped the hard psychology class, with Gary's help. My English work sagged under the weight of Shakespeare, my thoughts derailed easily, procrastination stretched to the limit. The deadlines stacked like bricks. Two papers, both due the next morning: *Hamlet*, where I needed just one more page; and *Troilus and Cressida*, which I hadn't really read. What I could already read was people's thoughts about me: finally stumbling academically. An F would dash my GPA and make it impossible to graduate on time.

Gary appeared with his usual grin, a plan in his pocket like a magician with a trick card.

"Time for an old-fashioned all-nightah," he said. "You'll get access to cutting-edge word processing and a laser printer. We order pizza, count on a two-hour power nap, and mush on. We're in this together. The pizza will invigorate us—it's all in the dough."

The registrar's office was a hollow shell in the storm. Fluorescent light hummed against the dark glass, turning the windows into mirrors, the kind of light that makes every face look pale. Outside, snow swirled like static. The roads were becoming as white as the snowbanks.

I bent over the keys. *Hamlet*. One more page to construct, eight to apply hunt and peck. The words came haltingly. I wrote about the danger of delay, of thought stretched so long it strangles action. Hamlet had wasted hours, days, whole acts debating the best course of action while the ghost stood waiting. To be or not to be? Endless looping or peaceful nothingness? Each similarity gave my stomach a twist.

Wasn't I the same? Stalling, circling, weighing everything until nothing moved? Even now, writing this page at the edge of midnight, I was only one night away from failure.

Somewhere between keystrokes, I'd knocked the computer into a strange mode. The typeface ballooned, words scattered with dots and odd little symbols where spaces should have been. Each sentence looked diseased, infected with marks I hadn't meant to make.

I wrestled the mouse, inching it across the desk, trying to land the cursor on the exact spot I wanted. A twitch too far and the whole line slipped out of place again. My hand cramped. It was a test of precision, and the more I tried, the worse it got.

This was harder than the typewriter—at least on that machine the keys would hit solid and true. Here, everything felt slippery, mocking me.

My mind flooded to my other failures. Calvin. Failed to read him, failed to stop myself, failed to be what he needed. And, now I was failing at school too. Gary kept offering me shortcuts—with Calvin, with classes, with everything—and every time I took one, I ended up more trapped, more compromised, more lost.

Gary propped his feet on a desk and flipped open a pizza box, grease shining on the cardboard. "Don't lose it. You were doing so well," he said, chewing with relish.

I forced down a slice, each bite swelling like paste in my mouth, sticking to my teeth.

"Now, don't start thinking about Calvin again. I can see the sad sack version of you creeping back. Are you letting him interfere?"

My throat worked. "Things pop into mind because of what I'm reading!" I grumbled back. The lines on the screen quivered as if they were trying to wriggle off into the dark.

"He was never the answer to salvage your adolescence. Stop feeling sorry for yourself. Half of people don't date in high school and half of them not even in college. That's one in four. Now calculate how many actually loved the one they were with. Get over yourself."

The symbols just hung like the statistics I hadn't asked to see.

"This is harder than it's worth," I muttered, jabbing the screen with my finger as if that could shift the sentence into place.

Gary leaned forward and used the mouse to hit an icon, making the mode normal again. His tone moved into something almost tender. "This is only harder, if you make it harder. You see how you can go back and edit? No correction tape needed. You can move things around. Chill."

I finished up the final paragraph. Hamlet finished. I hit save. The screen blinked, the drive groaned. When the directory opened, another file caught my eye. I opened it—an illustrated cover page, bold and neat: *Troilus and Cressida*. A finished paper? A fellow student must work here.

I swallowed. *Troilus*. I'd skimmed the story—lovers swearing fidelity until war and betrayal carved them apart. The one called faithless, the other broken. A romance that turned into ruin, all because promises collapse under pressure. I was no expert, but even in my shallow reading I saw it: desire and illusion stitched together like two sides of the same cloth. This one worked at my temples.

The room was too quiet. Only the radiator ticking, the computer fan sighing. Gary shifted, closer now. I knew what was happening before he touched me. Gary's hand moved to my shoulder, then lower. This was the step he never claimed but always referred to; the one he pretended was inevitable.

Maybe this was just how it worked—you showed up, you said yes, and eventually you felt love. Or maybe you said no to everything that fell short and spent the rest of your life wondering.

I should have said no. But, the storm howled outside, the roads were impassable, and I was so tired of fighting—tired of wanting what I couldn't have, tired of being wrong about everything. And, resisting pleasure took energy I didn't want to waste.

He started rubbing my shoulders, the back of my neck, thumbs pressing into the knots I'd been carrying since September. The storm pushed at the windows. His hands moved lower, slower; I let my eyes close and focused on my body. For a while, I tried to convince myself this was what I wanted, that maybe Gary was right and I just needed to stop overthinking everything. Lighten up and enjoy myself.

So I let it happen—his mouth on me until, despite everything, my body answered. Then, the weight of him shifting into place.

But, then a few minutes later he was on me fully, and I couldn't breathe.

No.

Calvin's voice. I was letting happen what Calvin had refused.

I shoved Gary off.

"Stop," I said. My voice shook. "I can't."

He pulled back, hands up, expression sliding from desire to something paternal.

The shame hit sharp then—not just for what had happened, but for not saving it for someone special. *Calvin would despise me even more for this. Yeah— right! Like he would give a care at all.*

The storm howled outside. My chest clenched. Hamlet's voice rose in my head—to be or not to be. I got up already running. I jumped onto the table and launched myself at the window. Three stories looming below. I had instant regret as my body hit. The glass shuddered but didn't break. I slid back onto the table, gasping. *So glad it held.*

Gary's tone was smooth, oddly clinical. "Who hurt you? Someone must have hurt you in your past to make you act like this."

I stared at him, the screen's glow painting his face an alien blue. The plays had their endings. I didn't know mine yet.

I slept three hours, maybe less. The bench left a ridge in my back, and my dreams were a tangle of ghost voices and broken vows. I lay there thinking: I had crossed the line into gay intimacy. *It wasn't how it was supposed to happen. Still, it was more real than with Jenny. But, nothing like what I knew it could be.*

I'd always kept lust separate from love, as if they were different languages. Love was Calvin playful and calming. Lust was something I dealt with alone with my own reflection, never letting it taint the people I cared about.

I understood, maybe for the first time without recoiling, that desire wasn't a footnote to being gay but part of its grammar. I had treated it as smaller because it was where my shame lived. I tried to see what happened with Gary as a form of masturbation with another person instead of my own hand. But, the crossed milestone loosened something within me.

I wasn't struck by lightning. I just felt a little older. And, I was grateful—deeply grateful—that my clumsy attempt at self-injury hadn't offered a permanent answer to what was, in truth, temporary anguish. I was glad to be alive, even with everything I now had to face. It felt like a fresh start.

And, I knew I couldn't keep circling the same thoughts. I had to turn things around. I had to deal with Gary.

When I got up, the snow outside was blinding—a white sheet pulled over the city. Roads gone. Escape still impossible.

Gary was waiting, bright-eyed, a neat stack of paper in his hands. "Here we are," he said. "*Troilus and Cressida*. All polished. Hot off the press."

My mouth was dry. I'd seen that illustrated title page last night.

"You wrote this?" I asked.

He tilted his head, as if insulted. "Of course. I stayed up while you were napping. Out of care. Out of gratitude for everything you've shared with me. You think I'd let you sink?"

I flipped the top page. The sentences had a clipped, mechanical rhythm about the play I needed.

"You didn't even know the whole question," I said softly.

"I knew enough, and the proof is right there, just read."

"You are really asking me to pass off another student's paper as mine."

"I wrote it for you, couldn't ah done it without ya. It's yours."

"I saw that file before I went to sleep."

His smile tightened. "That? Just a cover page. Girl in the office wanted it fancy. There was no essay along with it." He pushed the stack closer. "What matters is I came through for you. I carried you when you couldn't carry yourself."

The words hit like shackles. Gratitude was the price. Gratitude meant silence. Gratitude meant owing him.

On the monitor, my own *Hamlet* essay still blinked, a little rough but mine. Hamlet was circling death, circling choice, forever putting off the inevitable—but at least those were his words, his mistakes.

I pushed the *Troilus* paper back toward him. "No."

Gary's eyes narrowed. "You're making a mistake. Those are your grades, right there. Safe. Clean. Ready. Do you want the printer code for *Hamle*t at least?"

I stood, gathering my rough draft pages, crumpled but honest. "I'll take my chances."

For a moment the room was silent but for the radiator's hiss. Then, Gary leaned back, chuckled low, as though I were a child refusing medicine.

"You'll see," he murmured. "One day you'll see what I did for you."

As I had suspected, we soon found out all classes were canceled even though I was already at school.

"You've had a reprieve, my friend. A lucky reprieve." Gary said a few different times after we heard it announced over the radio station.

The storm outside had let up, yet the real snowdrift was inside—the weight of his lies, the drift of his control. The plows couldn't arrive quick enough.

I clutched my *Hamlet* draft tighter. It was unlike the counterfeit gift Gary held out like a ransom note.

When the roads cleared, I took my rough draft home, sat at my desk, and began again. Every sentence retyped, many thoughts rebuilt from scraps. The *Hamlet* paper rose out of the wreckage, stronger for the struggle.

For *Troilus and Cressida*, I had time to hatch a desperate bargain. The professor allowed the class one skipped paper, so I slid back to a draft I'd imperfectly finished earlier in the semester, but hadn't passed in. Asked for a kind of time travel—pretending it had been ready on time. Hadn't touched it at all past the due date. Instead of giving into failure, I checked out new possibilities. He agreed. But, added a penalty.

Weeks later the grades came through. An A on *Hamlet*. A C on the salvaged essay.

It should have felt like defeat. But, when I saw those letters side by side, I felt more satisfied than I had in months. The A was earned, the C survived. Both were mine. I could move forward with a real chance to graduate on time.

Gary's paper never touched my hands again. His carrot had rotted on the vine. And, for the first time, I saw him clearly: not mentor, not savior, not even partner-in-crime. Just a man who spun stories, dangled promises, and expected me to kneel in gratitude.

I hadn't broken the glass that night, but I'd broken the spell.

My last final was Educational Psych—multiple choice and short essays, the kind of exam you can do on autopilot. The only drawback was having to drag myself back to campus in mid-December. Snow in the gutters, breath coming out in plumes.

Wouldn't you know it, Gary was right outside the classroom when I walked out. He stood there with his hands in his coat pockets, a crooked grin under the gray sky.

"Wanted to say goodbye personally," he said. "And to apologize. I meant to pay you back that sixty bucks, but I left it at home."

I saw right through him. "What are you going to try and pull now?"

He held up his hands, mock innocent. "Nothing. Just maybe offer you a fast ride to Cambridge. Got my own apartment now. You don't have to come in. I can pay you back, drive you all the way home, or you can take the bus from there—whichever you choose. Honestly, the only risk is what I say on the drive. Words won't move you anymore, right?"

He was trying for lightness, but there was an edge under it.

I shrugged, feeling the last of my finals slide off me. "Sure. Why not? A free ride. Entertain me."

The first half of the drive was small talk, silly talk: traffic, bad holiday music on the radio, some story about his car. It was almost normal.

Then, his voice changed. "You know what?"

Here we go, I thought.

"I was going to tell you to let Calvin go; after he told you to *bag it*," Gary went on. "Because after that it was only a question of paper or plastic. But, you were so sad, I went against the odds with you. You needed to try some more or you'd have been worse. You're just so stubborn."

The car hummed low, the heater blowing dry air that smelled faintly of salt from the road. My jaw ached from clenching.

"You refuse to look at what you have in front of you. I would be blonde and blue-eyed for you if I could."

I stared out the window at the sagging Christmas lights strung between telephone poles, their colors bleeding in the wet night.

Gary laughed softly, almost to himself. "Why couldn't we just relax, have some wine, look at Christmas lights, and yell at the town?"

A snowflake hit the glass and melted in an instant. My reflection looked older.

"I have this tradition—every year I watch that horror flick *Silent Night, Deadly Night*, the one where Santa's the killer. It's hilarious. What do you say?"

His voice was smooth as always, but it skimmed right over me, like a stone skipping water.

I was busy running the numbers in my head. *How long until we reached his new place in Cambridge? How far to the nearest bus stop?* What time the 77 ran, and if I could catch it two blocks over? *If I ran, I might even make the 5:40.*

Gary glanced at me, still grinning, as though his words might yet land. But, I wasn't listening anymore. I was already somewhere else, past his offers, past his apologies. Past the carrot.

My window had closed tight.

Seeing the chance, I said, "I'm getting out at the light."

Gary blinked. "What?"

"I'll get out here. I'll catch the bus."

He inched forward. "Don't be ridiculous, we're almost—"

“Gary!” I looked at him directly for the first time since we started driving. “Stop the car.”

He pulled over, expression halfway between confusion and something harder to read. I got out, closed the door, and didn’t look back. Behind me I heard his window roll down, his voice calling, “You don’t want your money?”

I knew I’d never see that money. He’d never give up his last carrot.

I kept walking.

The 77 bus pulled up two minutes later. I’d caught the 5:20. I sat by the window and pressed my forehead against the cold glass. Not trying to break through this time. Just looking out, watching the city pass, feeling the vibration of the engine carry me somewhere else.

PART IV

Long Lost World

21
Truths Told and Untold

Ron Hanson was home for Christmas break, and it felt like the right time to unburden myself. We sat in his basement den, which had its own Christmas tree—almost as big as the one upstairs. The lights blinked soft colors against the white plaster walls. I just started talking. I told him I was gay. That Calvin had left me spinning for months; that Tommy and Karl had each held their own place in the story, even Bruce. I told him about Gary—the strange detour I hadn't meant to take, the shortcuts that turned into dead ends. He listened without flinching, in a way not typical of Ron in past years. Steady, unhurried, asking thoughtful questions as though he wanted to understand the whole picture.

Then, Ron asked, almost carefully, "Did you ever have a crush on me?"

I laughed, startled by how off base it was. "No, don't worry," I said, shaking my head. "Never happened."

He nodded, seemed to consider whether to continue. Then: "I had a crush on you. Back in middle school."

The room tilted slightly. "You—what?"

"Just a boyish crush," he said, as if that diminished it. "I liked you a lot. Worried about you."

"You sure hid it well," I said quickly to let out some tension.

He smiled.

I stared at him, trying to map this revelation onto the Ron I'd known—my vulgar womanizing friend, my foil, the one I thought I understood completely. The boy who'd been there through everything, who I'd never once considered that way.

"How is that possible?" I said to the universe.

He shrugged. "You were nice. Smart. Different from everyone else. It wasn't—I don't know. It was middle school."

The words meant something. But, they arrived years too late—safe in hindsight, unable to alter what might have changed. My self-image needed that kind of boost.

If I'd known then—if either of us had known we weren't alone—what would have been different? Would I have spent less time convinced I was the only one? Would middle school have felt less like solitary confinement? Even though he was bisexual and I was gay, there could have been some solidarity. There might have been possibilities to explore.

"Thank you for telling me," I said finally.

It was a gift, tender and weightless, and yet heavy with what could never be claimed. Maybe secret crushes were more abundant than it had seemed in Beaumont. Maybe I'd been looking in the wrong direction all along.

It felt right, somehow, that what came next was an act of revision—because that's what the whole evening had been.

Ron helped with a favor I had asked of him. We went about refilming scenes and replacing Calvin with Ron, this time to splice them into flashbacks for a new project—a sequel that honored the first film from start to finish. It was a comic retelling, a parody of everything that I once tried to take seriously. Laughter on screen was the focus, instead of edited out for a blooper reel. Ron and I knew it had greater meaning for me somehow.

Now, I see what I was really doing—not fixing the past but learning how to live beside it. You don't undo regret; you learn how to carry it, lightening it where you can. I couldn't change what happened between Calvin and me, but I could return to those moments, understand them differently, and see who I was inside them. I still needed time to forgive myself, not for loving him, but for abusing the trust and respect that he had given me.

Ron and I filmed what we could over the break, just the two of us working through the flashback scenes. But, the full production would have to wait until summer, when everyone could return. Ron was willing to help me with my healing process as far as he could.

That spring, as I finished my last semester of college, a seven-course load, Seb wrote to me, passing word from his mother that Calvin had turned to her for help—apparently to deal with me. Seb thought the problem was long phone calls. That's what he said in the letter, anyway. There weren't any such calls. So, a glitch in communication. I was at my worst in person. Was it a softened version of the truth? I just admitted my feelings for Calvin were strong, though I didn't give them a name.

Seb was generous about it. He didn't shame me about anything. When he came back from college he carried himself differently—"I'm open to all lines of psychology, except using it on me," he said with a grin. He was more liberal, had more empathy, and included support in his friendship toolbox. He was much improved, but that didn't make him a different person. He threw himself into the new movie with gusto, even if he quit twice before the finish.

Jake returned as well, with no trace of weirdness between us.

Toward the end of filming the sequel I heard that Calvin wanted to help despite the fact that his character had been recast. The offer tugged at me, but I couldn't say yes. It was too soon. I already wanted the request to mean more than it possibly could the moment it left Seb's mouth. And, the scene Calvin would have been shooting had me down to my boxers—too much skin, too much risk. I could handle exposing my body for a laugh, but not if

Calvin was the one behind the lens. The camera would have caught more than slight fabric; it would have caught everything I couldn't admit. Proximity, desire, and ambiguity made me vulnerable, and one slip could spiral everything back to chaos.

As the last hurrah of the summer, Seb and I took a ferry to Martha's Vineyard for a day. We rented bikes, but the ride became a metaphor as soon as we left the shop. He lived for speed, leaning forward, head down, muscles working like pistons. I peddled leisurely, curious about the houses: some grand with white columns, others small with fretwork like frosting. He shouted back for me to hurry, I shouted forward to slow down, and the distance between us grew.

At a picnic stop, after we'd eaten quietly for a while, he put down his sandwich and declared: "There are only two kinds of love. Family and for girls."

I tested him. "What about Thomas and Rob? Do you love them?"

He laughed. "Okay, three kinds of love. The third is love of sports—that's what we three share."

I sat with that for a moment. Family, girls, sports. Those were the permitted categories. Everything else—what I felt for Calvin, what Ron had felt for me, what maybe others felt but never said—didn't make the list. Was he trying to redirect me? To offer me a way to reframe my feelings for his brother as something safer, more acceptable? Or was this just Seb's genuine understanding of the world, the categories he'd been given and never questioned? I didn't ask. I nodded, finished my sandwich, and we got back on the bikes. The ride back was quieter. The bicycle, the ferry, the car ride. Not hostile, just—empty. The kind of silence where you're aware of every gear shift, every breath, the distance measured between lamp posts. I kept wondering: *Was he angry about*

Calvin? About my different priorities on the trip? Or was this just what happened when you couldn't talk about what mattered? A conversation about Calvin would have been the adult thing to do.

When we returned, Calvin was in the kitchen. He'd already spoken with Seb who had entered in front of me, and their mood was casual. I came in bristling, blurting that Seb and I weren't on the same wavelength. That Seb hadn't had a good time. Calvin told me to stop second-guessing everything. His tone carried an authority I hadn't expected, as if he'd slipped into the role of older brother.

At the time, I turned Seb's silences into verdicts, the same way I turned Calvin's laughter into signals. But, the truth was, I didn't know. I only had inklings—shadows on the wall.

What I couldn't admit then, but was starting to realize: I had trouble tolerating uncertainty in love. Romantic or otherwise. So, I tried to engineer outcomes instead of asking directly—danced in ambiguity because it had elements of satisfaction, convincing myself that clear questions only functioned to rip that satisfaction away. I was wrong. Prolonging ambiguity was no way to feel love, and hurried confessions in late stages were destined to fail. Years later, I would learn to disclose and to ask earlier, *before* I even knew how much I could connect with someone—not because I'd become brave, but because carrying all that uncertainty had become heavier than avoiding risk. I got it wrong more than once. But, at least I was trying in real time instead of only in my head.

My practice with longing didn't prepare me for reciprocation—it prepared me to survive its absence. Which turned out to be a very practical skill to have along the way.

Calvin asked again to be involved in a subsequent film—a show of no hard feelings, or possibly just missing the hijinks. He ended up behind the camera for a complicated five-person establishing shot that required perfect timing.

I stood on the set, watching him as I rehearsed my lines. He moved with the same care he'd brought to everything—adjusting the tripod, checking the frame, explaining his plan for the shot to the us with patience I'd forgotten he had.

"Ready?" he called out.

"Ready," I said, though I wasn't sure if I meant the shot or this moment.

He brought his eye to the viewfinder, patient and steady. Called action. We hit our marks. He held the shot, counted silently, panned with the camera, cut leaving plenty of room to edit around.

"Got it," he said, straightening.

"One take? Wow."

I hadn't expected that. I'd worried the shot was too complex, that anyone would struggle with it. But, Calvin had simply done it—no fuss, no drama, just competence.

"Nice work," I said.

He smiled, that easy smile I'd spent years trying to decode. "Thanks for letting me help."

And, that was it. He handed the camera back, rejoined the group watching from the side.

The moment passed like any other, except I knew—though I couldn't have said how—that it was the last time we'd collaborate.

I came away with a reaffirmed lesson and a new insight. I'd spent so long twisting every gesture into a private signal, when maybe the real gift was simpler: steadiness, offered without condition. Calvin wasn't kind to me because I was special; he was kind because that's who he was. Not everyone is.

I recognized in my heart of hearts, I wanted to be the sole focus in his eyes. Not just him, with Ricky, Bruce, and whoever might come next. I now knew that I could at least tolerate the shared focus. I would need to hold my insecurities at bay and accept that the person I loved could connect with others without diminishing me.

I'd needed to see him one more time to understand these things fully.

Gary required a different kind of reckoning. Over the next two years, I made two more films with Mark by my side coming up with comic dialogue. One film was about a charlatan fortune teller, another about a love potion's dangerous allure. I didn't consciously set out to process what Gary had done, but there it was in every scene: the con artist who reads his mark, gains leverage under false pretense, attempts to manufacture feeling where none exists.

He'd known exactly what I wanted to hear, exactly how lovesick I was, exactly how to turn my hunger for connection into his advantage. I remember the small flicker of doubt I felt when his compliments arrived too quickly—and how fast I smothered it. I wanted to believe him more than I wanted the truth.

The films were how I finally wrapped my head around it: not love, not even attraction, but a transaction I'd mistaken for a gateway to intimacy. Sometimes you have to tell the story at an angle before you can face it head-on.

I carried it all forward—Ron's revelation, Seb's half-acceptance, Gary's lesson, and most of all Calvin's blessing. What's gone still echoes. The echo itself is proof love mattered. It shapes how we move through the world, whether it is said or left unsaid.

22
Hymn of the Half-Found

There was a song I used to catch on the radio over the years since high school, scraps of melody and lyrics drifting in and out. I could never quite decipher it, but I felt sure it was relevant to me. The chorus, I thought, was "Long Lost World." The beat was bright but tinged with lament; a promise wrapped in mourning.

There was a line about fearing a lake. A lake of fire? Maybe. I never figured it out. I only knew it sounded like grieving what silence had stolen—and daring, at last, to indulge in something real beyond it.

Long Lost World became my private mythology. A lost gay utopia, perhaps—somewhere sunlit and unashamed. California. Ancient Greece. A world where boys could look at one another directly. A world that might be reclaimed.

A year after college, I found out more about it. My brother had taped the official video from LaserDisc. The images seemed to prove me right: handsome men in a tropical setting, laughing together, bodies unashamed. Women drifted in the background—being splashed, even boiled in caldrons—they weren't the focus. Then, one of the men swung across the screen half-clad, Tarzan-like, his skin flashing in the sun. I felt a rush of happiness. Somewhere, I thought, such a place existed—where people could grow up as their true selves, exploring attraction without regret; where openness was the law, and secrecy never hardened into lies, where no one had to operate in the dark.

But, that wasn't the world I had been given. No instruction, no confirmation, no mirror. Instead, secrecy trained me to believe something was wrong. Fakery became practice; lying became reflex. I was susceptible to good information from questionable people. The Long Lost World I imagined was the adolescence I never got to live—the one where a boy might simply say: "You feel special to me. Let's figure it out?" Without risking social exile. Nothing grander than that. It would have meant everything. Missed opportunities leave a tender spot.

Later, I learned my lyrics were wrong. The song was never about any of this. What I heard was a confabulation born of need, less information than hope. But, hope was all I had, because the truth had been hidden. And, that's the regret that lingers: if I'd been educated—the validation of facts instead of the weight of silence—I might not have spent so many years wandering blind, inventing my own land. I faced a desert; now there is a forest of voices, some clear, some distorted. Information exists—and so do efforts to erase it. Social injustice compounds every private failure. Another generation shouldn't have to invent hope from scraps.

My adolescence was split—inner life without outer expression, false performance before delayed authenticity. Not because of who I was, but because erasure fractures what should be whole.

Epilogue

The new millennium arrived, and life already felt deep into another century when the phone rang. An old name blinked back at me: Jimmy Flannery.

His voice was older now, edged with certainty.

"Johnny," he said, after a pause, too long to be casual. "I wanted you to know. Ricky's in the hospital. Overdosed on heroin. He's in intensive care."

The words landed heavily, like the air itself had thickened. I gripped the receiver, listening for any scrap of hope in the spaces between his sentences.

"He always talked about you, when we were together. Not always—but a lot. He asked what you were up to. Sadly, I didn't have much to tell him."

I swallowed. "I really loved Ricky," I said quietly. "You did too, didn't you?"

The line went still. Then, I asked the question that had hovered between us for decades. "You're gay, right?"

Silence again—even thicker this time. I filled it. "I liked Peach too."

Jimmy's voice dropped. "At the hotel. Something happened between me and Peach. I didn't plan it." Some kind of intimate exchange under the influence.

"I thought I felt something from him."

He exhaled, a sound closer to memory than breath. "I thought about you and me fooling around, that last year we were still hanging out with Mr. Norman."

I was more surprised than I should have been.

"I wasn't ready for that then," I said politely. I had never felt a spark between us, and I never liked calling it fooling around anyway.

There wasn't much left to say.

Jimmy had handed me two truths I hadn't expected—his own secret thoughts about me, and a version of Peach I'd never finished considering. It's easy to imagine now that Jimmy might have been an obvious answer to my isolation. At the time, he hadn't felt like a door; more like an exit ramp. We never really fit. His softness unsettled me, his intrusiveness startled me—and I recognized both in myself.

The potentials I hadn't tested hung there like stray notes, unresolved. I let them be.

Then, the greater weight returned.

When you stop heroin and start again later, the very same dose can become poison.

Ricky didn't make it.

I never told him how special he was to me.

I believe he knew I loved him, and that Ricky loved me too. His love was platonic, but it was still a gift, and I carried it. Ricky was a Big Kid among Little Kids.

For years I'd felt like I was passing through a netherworld—crossing hetero terrain I could never truly claim, moving through a working-class boyhood in a town structured for upper-class ambition. Ricky's friendship, his laugh, his presence even at a distance, had been my compass there. Losing him wasn't just losing a person; it was losing one of the few lights I had in the passage.

Content Note

This memoir includes references to sexual assault, sexual coercion, suicide attempts, accidental death, serious injury, and drug overdose.

www.ingramcontent.com/pod-product-compliance
Lightning Source LLC
LaVergne TN
LVHW100506110826
845146LV00002B/538

* 9 7 9 8 9 9 5 2 6 5 8 1 8 *